Pathways Through to
Space

Pathways through to Space

A Personal Record
of Transformation
in Consciousness

BY

FRANKLIN MERRELL - WOLFF

With an Introduction by
JOHN C. LILLY, M.D.

Julian
Press

Published by The Julian Press, Inc.,
a division of the Crown Publishing Group,
One Park Avenue, New York, New York 10016.
Published simultaneously in Canada by
General Publishing Company, Limited.

Manufactured in the United States of America

Library of Congress Cataloging in Publication Data
Merrell-Wolff, Franklin.
Pathways through to space; a personal record of
transformation in consciousness, by Franklin Merrell-Wolff.
New York, R.R. Smith, 1944.
xii p., 1l., 288 p. 24½'''.

I. Title.

Library of Congress   BF1999.M48   44-36221   133

ISBN 0-517-52777-4 (cloth)
ISBN 0-517-54961-1 (paper)

10   9   8   7   6   5   4   3   2

1983 Edition

DEDICATED

To those who, having found the emptiness of life external, hunger for the Life that is Everlasting

Introduction to Second Edition

BY COINCIDENCE, I was loaned a copy of the first edition of this book by Patricia Olds, the librarian of the Institute of Electronic and Electrical Engineers, at one of my workshops in New York City in the Fall of 1971. She saw the deep basic interlock between this book and my own work. I read it in the one weekend available and became excited enough to start (a) looking for my own copy (found with the help of Samuel Weiser, Inc.); (b) looking for the author; and (c) looking for the publisher and/or the copyright owner. The author wrote of his transformation of consciousness in 1936 at an estimated age of 49; about 35 years had passed; I was not too sure he was still alive and loaned my copy to Arthur Ceppos of The Julian Press, Inc., who had just published my *The Center of the Cyclone*. He shared my enthusiasm and helped initiate the hunt for the author. We both drew a blank.

A year passed. By this time I was back at Esalen Institute, Big Sur, California, giving a workshop. Unexpectedly a couple approached me and said, "We understand you are looking for Merrell-Wolff." A bit surprised, I said, "Yes, that is true." They had heard he was alive and would send his address. A weak later Toni and I received his address, and drove down the East side of California Sierra Nevada mountains to Lone Pine in the shadow of one of the highest of the U.S. mountains, Mt. Whitney. Dr. Wolff was not listed in the phone book. The post-mistress said he had a post box, but she was not allowed to tell us his address. I wrote Dr. Wolff a card and gave it to her to mail to him.

Just then a man came into the post office and the postmistress said, "You know where Dr. Wolff lives, and you can tell Dr. Lilly where to go. I cannot." The man drew us a map.

We drove out of town (3700 ft.) to about 6000 ft. up the flank of Whitney. The road became very narrow and just as we gave up, a house appeared at the end of the road. I went and knocked. A sprightly elderly man with a Van Dyke and a twinkle in his eye opened the door. I said, "Dr. Wolff?" He said, "Yes." I said, "I have read *Pathways Through to Space* and would like to talk with you about it. Can we arrange a time?" He said, 'Come in. Anyone who finds this door finds it open."

In the ensuing discussion of four hours with Dr. Wolff, his wife, Toni and myself, and one of Dr. Wolff's disciples, we covered quite a bit of ground, ranging from the Bodhisatva vow to one's hold on the vehicle and why one bothers to remain on this planet. We discussed the possible republication of *Pathways*.

At one point Dr. Wolff accepted a copy of *The Center of the Cyclone* in exchange for another copy of *Pathways*. He noted that *Center* had been recommended to him by one of his students who promised to bring him a copy. With a twinkle in his eye he said to his wife, "Please tell so-and-so that I now have the book he recommended; the author delivered a copy personally."

Dr. Wolff presented me with his later book, *The Philosophy of Consciousness Without an Object* mimeographed in 1970 for his students.

I very strongly felt that the time for the republication of *Pathways* had arrived. I presented the point of view that literally hundreds of thousands of young adults were now ready for the ideas, experiences, and philosophy expressed therein, and emphasized the fact that there are thousands of people where there were only a few hundred in 1944 who are in need of confirmation of their own experience, and in need of a showing of a pathway basically "jnana," or the head trip route to higher states. Dr. Wolff's own experiences in his transformation and recognition are written simply and have an awesome power to transform those who are ready for his deeply moving help.

In my own reading of this book, I found I was precipitated into states, spaces, universes of very high orders so frequently that the reading of it took several weeks. Each time I read it now, the experiences begin anew, and I have found the same phenomenon when reading his *Philosophy of Consciousness without an Object*. Opening either book practically at random and reading awhile alters my state of consciousness into highly regarded and delightful regions. (Other

viii

than *Center* there are only two other books with this power over me: Olaf Stapledon's *The Starmaker* [Dover] and G. Spencer Brown's *Laws of Form* [Julian Press]).

As I lecture and give workshops, I find increasing numbers of people with mental properties similar to mine and Dr. Wolff's: persons who can be programmed into higher states of consciousness by the right reading material. These are the new, increasingly numerous, audience for these books.

I am grateful that these persons will now be able to share in Dr. Wolff's truly great work and in his profound experiences.

John C. Lilly, M.D.

Los Angeles, California
January, 1973

Preface to Second Edition

IT IS NOW more than thirty-six years since the precipitation of the inner events which led to the writing of this volume. It may be said now that the value of this unfoldment remains as high as it ever was. It is true that I would place this treasure far above anything which may be obtained in the ordinary world field, in whatever domain, such as achievement in government, in business, in science, philosophy, mathematics or the arts. All these stand as values far inferior to these greater values which come from Fundamental Realization.

It remains true to my present state of consciousness that I would say that no accomplishment, in the world field, can be effective in solving the wrongness which is so evident in that field, without the insight and resources which are derived from Fundamental Realization. Therefore, it follows that all the efforts of man to solve his own problems, make life richer, and free it from the manifest evils which we see all about, is ineffective in the sense of achieving an effective resolution. As we look at the report recorded in the pages of history, we see the evils which were there in the past are still here today, and even find that those evils have become, if anything, greater than they were before.

As we advance in our scientific knowledge we not only implement the powers of good that may be in the world but we also implement the powers of evil, with the result that the old difficulties, the old wrongnesses, return again, if anything, in amplified form. Therefore, if we are to resolve in any durable way these difficulties that call for the function of Redemption it is necessary that more and more of this human whole should attain the perspective and the resources that come from Enlightenment.

The traditional solution to the wrongness has been in the form of a retreat from the world field, but it is here suggested that this is not the only possible way. There may be such a thing as transforming the very field of outer action to such an extent that that field itself becomes redeemed and transformed with the result that noble purpose is not distorted into ignoble effects. The task before us is religious in the deepest meaning of that word. But as we look upon the record of traditional religion it must be judged that traditional forms of religion have failed egregiously. This applies to all the religions that we know, less to some than to others, but so far the record of traditionalistic religion is one of essential failure. As it appears to me, that which is needed is a seeking for the ultimate Attainment on the part of as many people as possible—Attainment which is the very Essence of the religious search.

Furthermore, the seeking of this Attainment is not simply for the sake of one's own individual Redemption but for the sake of the Redemption of humanity as a whole and, in addition, of all creatures whatsoever, however humble they may be. He who forgets his own Attainment and his own Redemption in seeking for the Attainment and Redemption of all creatures, is following the Path which is most certain to involve that very Attainment and Redemption for himself. The motive should always be the good of all creatures, not one's own private good.

Franklin Merrell-Wolff

Lone Pine, California
January, 1973

xii

Contents

I

The Light Breaks Forth

August 17, 1936

THE INEFFABLE TRANSITION came, about ten days ago.

We had just returned to our Southern California home after a few weeks' stay in a small town in the Mother Lode country in the northern part of the State, and I was resting from the fatigue induced by the all-night driving of the automobile. At the time, I was engaged in the reading of portions of "The System of the Vedanta" by Paul Deussen, as I had been doing more or less systematically during the preceding three weeks. This work is an interpretation in western philosophic form of the Vedanta as it is developed in the commentaries of Shankara on the Brahmasutras. I had been led to this specific program of reading through the realization that Shankara's words had peculiar power, at least in my own experience. For some time I had spontaneously looked to him as to a Guru * with whom I was in complete sympathetic accord. I had found him always clear and convincing, at least in all matters relative to the analysis of consciousness, while with the other Sages I either found obscurities or emphases with which I could not feel complete sympathy. For some months I had resolved to delve more deeply into the thought of Shankara, in so far as it was available in translated form. It was in pursuance of this purpose that I was slowly reading and meditating upon "The System of the Vedanta."

I had been following this course while completing a cross-cut in a gold-prospect near the small town of Michigan Bluff. Much of this time I was completely alone and was more than usually successful in penetrating the meaning and following the logic of what I

* 'Guru' is a Sanskrit term carrying the meaning of spiritual Teacher.

1

was reading. One day, after the evening meal and while still sitting at the table, I found that, by gradual transition, I had passed into a very delightful state of contemplation. The actual content of the thought of that period is forgotten, but as I made careful note of the state I was in and submitted it to close scrutiny, the quality of the state was well impressed upon my memory. My breath had changed, but not in the sense of stopping or becoming extremely slow or rapid. It was, perhaps, just a little slower than normal. The notable change was in a subtle quality associated with the air breathed. Over and above the physical gases of the air there seemed to be an impalpable substance of indescribable sweetness which, in turn, was associated with a general sense of well-being, embracing even the physical man. It was like happiness or joy, but these words are inadequate. It was of a very gentle quality, yet far transcended the value of any of the more familiar forms of happiness. It was quite independent of the beauty or comfort of the environment. At that time the latter was, to say the least, austere and not in any sense attractive. This quality, associated with the air, I had, in a smaller measure, previously experienced at high altitudes in the mountains, but in the present instance the altitude was only 1800 feet and the air was far from invigorating, due to the period being exceptionally warm. However, introspective analysis revealed the fact that the elixir-like quality was most marked during the exhalation, thus indicating that it was not derived from the surrounding air. Further, the exhaled breath was not simply air expelled into the outer atmosphere, but seemed to penetrate down through the whole organism like a gentle caress, leaving throughout a quiet sense of delight. It seemed to me like a nectar. Since that time I have learned that it is the true Ambrosia.

It is, perhaps, pertinent to note in passing that a few days previously, as a result of thought stimulated by my readings, I had developed an interpretation of the nature of ponderable matter that seemed to me to clear away certain logical difficulties which always have seemed to persist in the efforts to reconcile Transcendent Being with the physical universe. The idea is that ponderable matter—meaning by that term all things sensed whether gross or subtle—is, and Emptiness. *But I Realized It as Absolute Light and Fullness and that I was That.* Of course, I cannot tell what IT was in Its own nature. The relative forms of consciousness inevitably distort non-relative Consciousness. Not only can I not tell this to others, I cannot even contain it within my own relative consciousness, whether of sensation, feeling, or thought. Every metaphysical thinker will see this impossibility at once. I was even prepared not to have the personal consciousness share in this Recognition in any way. But in this I was happily disappointed. Presently I felt the Ambrosia-quality in the breath with the purifying benediction that it casts over the whole personality, even including the physical body. I found myself above the universe, not in the sense of leaving the physical body and being taken out in space, but in the sense of being above space, time, and causality. My karma seemed to drop away from me as an individual responsibility. I felt intangibly, yet wonderfully, free. *I* sustained this universe and was not bound by it. Desires and ambitions grew perceptibly more and more shadowy. All worldly honors were without power to exalt me. Physical life seemed undesirable. Repeatedly, through the days that followed, I was in a state of deep brooding, thinking thoughts that were so abstract that there were no concepts to represent them. I seemed to comprehend a veritable library of Knowledge, all less concrete than the most abstract mathematics. The personality rested in a gentle glow of happiness, but while it was very gentle, yet it was so potent as to dull the keenest sensuous delight. Likewise the sense of world-pain was absorbed. I looked, as it were, over the world, asking: "What is there of interest here? What is there worth doing?" I found but one interest: the desire that other souls should also realize this that I had realized, for in it lay the one effective key for the solving of their problems. The little tragedies of men left me indifferent. I saw one great Tragedy, the cause of all the rest, the failure of man to realize his own Divinity. I saw but one solution, the Realization of this Divinity.

Since that day I have been repeatedly in the Current of Ambrosia. Often I turn to It with the ease of a subtle movement of thought. Sometimes It breaks out spontaneously. Thought and bodily action can be continued in It, provided a subtle kind of inner concentration is not broken. But consciousness focused in action, whether intellectual or physical, stops the Current. The presence of some people affects It adversely, while that of others does not. The effect on the body is interesting. The after-effect of this surprisingly gentle Current, with all Its exquisite delight, is a feeling of intangible tiredness in the body, somewhat like that which would be experienced after a period of protracted pain. Physical effort is difficult. The reason for this seems to be evident. One effect of the Current is clearly purifying, and this action upon the matter of the body is something of an ordeal. There is no emotional nor intellectual discomfort, save that without the Current the world seems barren.

I am studying the effect of the Current upon others. Sherifa is immediately responsive to It and recognizes Its presence, at times even before I do. It will grip an audience, but those who have heretofore given recognition to a consciousness of substantially lower quality do not seem to be aware of the Ambrosia.* Perhaps It is too subtle.

August 20

On the evening of the 17th we attended a musical concert at the Hollywood Bowl. The audience was extremely large. During the early part of the program I had a sense of the crowd as an enormous weight upon consciousness. It was so heavy I could not pierce through it. Later, during the performance of certain Bach selections there was a distinct easing up of the weight and a mild tingling along the spine. Consciousness did rise in some measure, but not to the level of the Current.

On the 19th we returned home. I felt deeply tired and was unable to rise in consciousness. It seems that the inward penetration does make some demand upon the body. Life without the Elixir has become more empty than it was before the Current was first experi-

* At the present date, almost two and one-half years after writing the above, this statement must be strongly modified. After two intervening seasons on the lecture platform combined with several personal contacts, it has been clearly determined that a surprising number of individuals are susceptible to the Current. In some natures it is quite readily induced.

enced. Mere external affairs utterly fail to hold my interest.

The conditions of town life seem definitely adverse to holding consciousness within the Current of Bliss. Driving an automobile in traffic is particularly inimical. The reason seems quite clearly to be that under these conditions it is much more difficult to hold the inner concentration unbroken. To steer a way through the outer confusion requires objective concentration. I, at least, cannot yet move through these conditions with safety by giving only a peripheral attention to them. Perhaps it may be possible to establish the correlation so that it will hold under these adverse conditions, but the demand upon the vital strength is severe.

August 22

Late yesterday afternoon I awakened again to the deeper Consciousness, though not so profoundly as upon the first occasion. The immediate inducing cause was the reading of a portion of Shankara's "Direct Realization." The inciting occasion each time seems to be a new turn in Recognition, combined with a certain creative act of the relative consciousness. The moment of creative discovery is the crucial one. There is then a deepening of consciousness, a sort of retreat of the relative world, in a subtle sense, and then the quality of Bliss flows over the personality. From a profound level thought is stimulated, or, perhaps more correctly, fed.

Throughout this whole period I am engaged in thought of a degree of profundity unprecedented in my previous experience. While, in one sense, the 'I AM' is the uttermost of simplicity, yet there is invoked along with the direct presence of It a new view of the universe that requires to be thought through and the elaborations in this thought are greater than those that I have known heretofore. There is so much to be made clear in thought that there is hardly time to give it expression. There is also a difference in the thought-level. In the past, I seemed, in general, to reach deeper when putting forth the effort to express myself, particularly in writing. Now expression seems more a reaching downward into forms that are inadequate. My inward thought seems clearer in its relative formlessness than when I give it formulation, yet formerly it seemed to me that I could express myself almost beyond my genuine understanding. I have to resist a certain boredom in the effort to give expression. I can understand why the plans of learned men to compose systems sometimes fail to materialize when they break through to Liberation. The objective effort seems too poor in its results. However, the expression is needed, and it is necessary that the work be done.

I find that there is a decided intellectual enrichment, but the outer sensuous life is poorer, at the present time. Does this latter fact constitute a danger to the body? The tide of physical life does run perceptibly lower. How is physical interest, never strong with me, to be cultivated so that the body will take on more virility? Disgust with the external world does help toward Liberation, but it is a barrier to the assertion of the continued will-to-live. Yet this is necessary if one is to carry on among men. I foresee the possibility that will without desire may prove to be an overly severe asceticism.

* * * * *

We have been practicing meditation each evening. I have aimed at the segregation of the subjective factor in consciousness. I have allowed meditation with the eyes closed. S. reported heavy sleepiness and L. nodded in her chair. I think we will have to work with the eyes open. The reason for this is becoming clear. The sensory field of the eye is stronger than that of any of the other senses. With the eyes open, waking consciousness continues stronger than otherwise. Permitting the objective consciousness to continue through its own automatism, the point will be to concentrate on the subjective moment. It would seem that this should correlate Realization more effectively with the personal consciousness. It is not enough to reach the Self in sleep.

* * * * *

I seem to be dreaming more than I have in a long time. Much of this dreaming seems to be a reviewing of events connected with the past, although the scenes and the events are transformed so that they are not photographic reproductions of the physical originals. There also seems to be a continuation of the trains of thought that were started during the waking state. The dreams are quite lacking in sensual intriguery, but are more the nature of a dispassionate reviewing of events, scenes, and ideas.

Night before last the outline of a plan for another book or two developed in my consciousness. The principal one * of these would be on the subject of 'Recognition,' the plan to be a development of the process of knowledge, tied in with the present philosophic thought, and then to have the emphasis placed upon the extraction of the subjective moment in consciousness. The theoretical part would not be new, but along with this there would be a new value afforded by reason of its being written from the perspective of an actual Recognition. It would aim to show that 'Recognition' is the practical end implicit in our own best philosophy. It could be shown that to *Realize* the 'pure apperception' of Kant is to attain Recognition and Liberation.

August 26

The force of physical life is running higher today, but it is far from being really vigorous.

I am exploring a new world. There is so much which requires to be thought into clarity that there seems not to be time enough for the writing, setting aside all more external activities. But it is necessary that a record should be kept as far as the inner events and ideas can be captured. My thought is extraordinarily clear. An increasing amount of it is now within the range of formulation, but my actual thought is in the form of a sort of shorthand which takes much less time than the completed expression on paper or the spoken word. The writing process seems so slow! I shall place down what I can in this record as the material comes to the foreground, leaving systematic formulation to the future.

* Several ideas that are properly a part of such a proposed work subsequently became incorporated in this volume. They are introduced here in the sequence in which they were actually born into formulation.

II

Concerning Meditative Technique

THE FORM OF MEDITATION that I have found effective differs substantially from that generally given in the manuals on meditation.* Repeatedly I have tried stopping thought and closing out the senses, but the artificial state thus effected was barren of results. Heretofore, the rich values have come to me through or while thinking. I finally took this fact as a key and abandoned all effort to stop thought or to interfere with the reports of sensation. In any case, the distraction caused by the latter I have found to be too weak to be of real importance. Through the larger part of my life the thought-world has naturally dominated the sensation-world so that sensation had come to mean little more than do small waves to an ocean liner. The issue thus lay between thought-consciousness and Transcendent-Consciousness while the rest, I found, could be neglected. Now, within a process or manifold, a given phase or aspect may be isolated for special attention without stopping the process or eliminating the balance of the manifold. This is a familiar technique in scientific and philosophic thinking. When I recalled this fact and applied it, I found at once a really effective method of meditation. In fact, I realize, I have done this for many years without regarding it as a meditative technique. It was by applying this method of isolation of the essential element in the midst of a complex, without trying to restrain the other components, that the Transition was effected during the early part of this month.

I think that there is an important principle involved in this method that may be of fundamental importance, especially as it ac-

* Subsequent to the completion of these writings I came into possession of "Tibetan Yoga and Secret Doctrine," edited by Evens-Wentz. In the discussion of meditative practice given in one of the Yoga manuals contained therein, I was surprised and gratified to find that my seemingly independent discovery of a meditative method was actually a re-discovery of a well-established and ancient principle of true meditation.

ena alone and can never reach beyond phenomena. But the phenomenal world rests upon the Real or Noumenal World. Thus it is that the Consciousness of the SELF or 'pure apperceptive consciousness' sustains the whole universe or cosmos. But the latter is an outward projection. Behind the cosmos is the formless or Transcendental World. Within the cosmos is the domain of relative consciousness. From the latter standpoint the SELF appears as formless. Hence the approach—for from the relative point of view it seems like an approach—to the SELF from consciousness posited within the cosmos takes on the form of progressive negation of all identity with form until finally Identity in the Formless breaks forth as Recognition. At this stage Recognition may well take the form of 'I am Formlessness.' But this is really an incomplete Recognition, as Shankara has shown by his acute logic. The final Recognition is "I am not form and I am not formless." This standpoint is neutral with respect to the cosmos and the truly Transcendental or Formless. What this really means is that beyond Nirvana there is a Paranirvana which is a position of metaphysical indifference with respect to the states of manifestation or non-manifestation. At the same time, the individual soul may have a tendency or natural gravitation either toward the manifested or the non-manifested. Thus Buddha, being drawn toward the non-manifested, was tempted not to put forth the effort to establish His Message among men. On the other hand, Jesus, being drawn toward the manifested, faced the temptation in the form of worldly power. Both men conquered the temptation. But the form of the temptation marks what really is the individual bent or tendency of these supremely great Men. Thus we may say that the sublimated Consciousness of Jesus was predominantly 'Cosmic Consciousness,' while that of Buddha was 'Transcendental' or 'Noumenal Consciousness.' The common basis of both is Identity in the SELF.

Dr. Bucke does show a considerable understanding of 'Cosmic Consciousness' but seems to miss completely 'Transcendental' or 'Noumenal Consciousness.' Hence, he very largely fails to understand the significance of Buddha and gives to Walt Whitman a rather too exalted place. But doubtless Dr. Bucke speaks with the natural bent in valuation characteristic of the West, and very likely the form of Recognition proper to the West is more in accord with that of Whitman than that of Buddha. The very genus of the West seems to be foreign to 'Nirvikalpa Samadhi.'

For my own part, I cannot conceive of anyone who has glimpsed the beauty of the Transcendent Formlessness ever preferring cosmic beauty. He may choose to move in the world of form from a consideration of Compassion, but not because of the intriguery of the beauty of form as compared to that other Beauty.

Today, I find that in a deep sense I understand Walt Whitman, for I, too, have Awakened. But heretofore Whitman was not at all clear to me, and his words have not helped me to the Awakening. In contrast, the writings of Shankara have proved of the highest potency, while among Western writers it is Immanuel Kant who did most to prepare the Way for me. This is clearly a matter related to individual temperament. Whitman's Recognition is unquestionably genuine, but for me his words did not clarify but served, rather, to obscure the Way. Of Mohammed's expression this would have been even truer had I tried to make serious use of it. Yet Mohammed did attain some degree of mystical insight. It seems clear that no man can effectively illumine the Way for all men. There is more than one main Road and a great number of sub-roads. On all these, men who can serve as beacons are needed.

IV

The Record Continued

SUNDAY AND MONDAY were spent in Los Angeles. The fatigue induced by the city was considerable and made sleep imperative.

I am practicing the holding of consciousness on the objective or relative side deliberately so as not to drive the physical organism too hard. I find that turning the one way or the other is considerably within my control, but to remain on the objective side requires rather the greater effort. Inclination draws toward the Inward. Without the Current the objective world is like a desert in the invidious sense of the term. How is it possible for humanity to be so attached to this outer life?

Yesterday I deliberately turned Inward and invoked the Current with the accompanying deepening of Consciousness, but in this case in a modified form. Always there is the gentle Joy.

Saturday evening we had the usual meditation. I suggested the technique of not trying to stop thought or the reports of the senses, but to focus upon the Emptiness with the intellectual recognition: "I am this Emptiness." S. entered into a level of peace and joy wherein she found herself one with the stars and all things. There was none of the effect of drowsiness previously experienced. After-wards I called attention to the point that one should aim at the Emptiness as the highest, but that the consequence in relative consciousness is a new richness developing along the lines of the natural bent of the individual consciousness. On the other hand, if one aimed at a conceivable goal he sets that goal as an arbitrary limit. The advantage of aiming beyond all possible limits lies in rendering more nearly realizable the fullest possibilities of the individual. The Emptiness is thus the real Philosopher's Stone which transforms all things to new richnesses; It is the Alkahest that transmutes the base metal of inferior consciousness into the Gold of Higher Consciousness.

*   *   *   *   *

There is a growing compulsion to write. At first I did not care to bother with writing or with any other form of expression. Even the world of thought, hitherto always a rich one with me, became inferior to the Consciousness induced by the Recognition wherein I found Myself sustaining the universe. But I have accepted duty in the relative world and that duty has become, first, thought, and then as complete an exposition of it as its racing current will permit. At first I made myself write but now there is a growing compulsion that sends me to the typewriter.

*   *   *   *   *

Sherifa tells me that I should write of a little incident that I would have let pass as many, many others have already passed. We were at the table partaking of the noonday meal. I had just left my writing and was still active in the current of thought. I happened to glance out of the door where a small yellow kitten was playing on a broad cement platform. It ran across the platform and I felt a thrill of delight. It was as though a tiny melody from out the Cosmic Symphony had trilled joyously into my mind—a little sketch born forth from the Grand Harmony. And from this a wave of Joy was distilled and pulsated through me.

It is not that the physical or photographic fact became different, but surrounding the incident was an enveloping matrix of meaning. It was this matrix that sublimated the ordinary so that it became joyous.

*   *   *   *   *

In glancing over what I have written heretofore I find that I have failed to note the sense of Power that permeates Consciousness when in the Transcendental State. When I was enveloped with the sense that I sustained the universe, there also came a feeling of unlimited Power. It seemed that I could command in whatever direction I might choose and that that which stood below me must obey in accordance with the causal sequences which are My own Self-Imposed forms. At the same time there was no wish to will things to be different from what they are.

V

Evolution and Cosmic Consciousness

"I AM INDEED BRAHMAN, without difference, without change, and of the nature of Reality, Knowledge and Bliss." *

Dr. Bucke in his discussion of Cosmic Consciousness speaks of an evolution of that kind of Consciousness, just as there is a develop-

* Shankara: "Direct Realization"; Sloka 24.

16

ment of 'self-consciousness.' Hence, after the Awakening to the former, while this act involves definite transcendence of 'self-consciousness' in every case, yet there are degrees and levels within the field of Cosmic Consciousness. Consider this statement in connection with the above quotation from Shankara. Clearly there can be no evolution where there can be no difference or change. Yet Dr. Bucke is right, provided we give to 'Cosmic Consciousness' the interpretation given above.* Shankara is speaking of that which is neither formed nor formless and, therefore, that which transcends Cosmic Consciousness. But the Realization of the Brahman, partial or complete, is the basis of Awakening to Cosmic Consciousness. The latter does not, therefore, transcend the relative in the strict sense of the word, though it does transcend consciousness grounded in the subject-object relationship. Thus, in Cosmic Consciousness we are dealing with an intermediate World. In this domain Ignorance (avidya) has been destroyed, yet the Cosmos in a fundamental sense has not been annihilated. Thus unfoldment or evolution remains possible.

In this connection it is interesting to note the statement of a certain Sage who, speaking of unfolded Consciousness above the level of the highest human Adepts, said: "We attain glimpses of Consciousness so Transcendent, rising level upon level, that the senses fairly reel before the awe-inspiring Grandeur."

Here, certainly, is space for evolution far beyond the highest possibility of man as man.

VI

Myself

WHAT GREATER THING is there than this Mystery that is Myself?

All things else I am able to comprehend, if not at this moment, then in time I can do so, and that is why I am able to give them names. And that which I have named is in thralldom to Me. So all

* See section No. III, page 12.

creatures serve Me from the most elemental up to the highest Gods. But the SELF that I AM has no name, for no word that points toward Me comprehends Me. Names mean forms, whether gross or subtle, but I AM without form and, therefore, eternally nameless.

I comprehend all, but am comprehended by none.

I sustain all, yet need no support.

All creatures are but revelations of Me; for in Me abides their very existence, yet though they were not, I AM.

This space I produce that My Glory may be revealed; yet I alone Realize that Revelation.

Upon this space I cast My Shadow in numberless variations, yet ever remain One—apart.

I AM the theme of all melodies and reveal portions of My endless Richness in symphonic elaborations.

I lead all scientists to Me as they seek for the Truth, which is none other than Myself.

The devotee seeks Me through the raiment of My Being, yet *I* abide in that devotee.

He who does violence but seeks Me in ignorance.

I AM the Love of all lovers, and I also am the Lover and the Beloved.

Beside Me there is none other.

Note: In the foregoing a new form of expression broke forth spontaneously. Heretofore, I have never written in a poetic form. In fact, I have been unusually lacking in poetic interest and only regarded expository writing seriously. At the time of beginning this composition I had in mind another exposition but in the midst of the writing a new impulse in expression was born. The shift between the two forms is manifest in a comparison of the first and latter parts. I have left the writing unaltered so that it forms part of the record of the psychological transformation as well as being a vehicle of Meaning in its own right.

18

VII

Jesus and the Way

"NO MAN COMETH unto the Father but by Me." Thus spake Jesus. But many heard, though few understood, and so they sought the Father through belief in a *man* who dwelt for a short time upon this earth. But no *man* is 'I,' since 'man' is an object while *I* AM always the subject. Hence, to translate the above quotation as meaning, 'no man cometh unto the Father but by Jesus,' is completely to change its meaning. The Father is Divinity, God, Brahman, the ultimate Transcendent Reality. Now this Reality is Consciousness wherein subject and object are no longer divided but together form a united Sea of Consciousness. The general tendency of mankind is to seek God as an object, that is, God is worshiped as an object which stands as other than the worshiper. What Jesus meant is that success cannot be attained by this road. It is only through the 'I' that the Father can be reached.

While both the subjective and objective factors are blended in Absolute Consciousness, yet the unitary quality is carried in the subjective moment. There is but one 'I' or subject. Again, this is the most immediate and intimate of all facts. Hence, only through the 'I' is Identity realized. Approached in any other way, God is ever something other than the seeker and, therefore, is at a distance. To come to the Father is to be one with the Father, and this can be achieved only through the pure Subject or the SELF.

With the more current interpretation of the above quotation there is a distinct clash between the teaching of Jesus and that of the other leading spiritual Lights of the world. But with the interpretation here offered nearly, if not quite, complete reconciliation is afforded, not alone with the teachings of the other great Founders of religions, but also with the spontaneous sayings of nearly all spiritually illumined souls. It fits perfectly with the "I AM that I AM" of the Old Testament. It is identical in meaning with the central doctrine of Buddhism and Brahmanism, where we find the

19

clearest and most complete formulation of all. The 'Christ' of St. Paul is a mystic Christ and not a distinct person. It is a level of Consciousness of which Jesus Christ was the symbol for him. This level of Consciousness is identical with that from which Jesus spoke. This agreement can further be noted by reading the works of a number of God-Realized Men, such as Jacob Boehme, Spinoza, Whitman, Hegel, Rama Tirtha, and Inayat Khan. It is unnecessary to elaborate further here.

VIII

The Ineffable Current of Bliss

August 27

AT THIS VERY MOMENT I am again within the Current which, also, is Myself. Speaking from the standpoint of the individual consciousness I shall write of It, as much as I can convey in words.

I had been doing a little manual work and, at the moment, was stooping and looking at some gravel that had been carried from a distant valley. While doing so I sank into a brooding state and seemed to retreat to a distance where there was a profound, palpable, and pregnant Silence. I attended to This as to a Voice and received the value of a Communion. There were no words, no ideas, nor any other form, yet, one might say, It was the very essence of Sound or Meaning. It was utterly satisfactory and filling. It was the very Power that makes all things to become clear. Again there flowed the Current of gentle Joy that penetrates through and through.

I shall attempt an analysis of this Current of Joy as it affects the outer consciousness including the physiological man. To the sensuous consciousness It appears as of the nature of a fluid, 'for there is a sense of 'flowing through.' It penetrates all tensions with the effect of physical release. Spots that are not so well feel both rested and stronger. All over and through and through there is a quality that may well be described as physiological happiness. The organism feels no craving for sensuous distraction in order to find enjoyment. The external life of the individual could appear highly ascetic and austere to others, but all the while it would be profoundly happy. The fact is that the real Sage is anything but ascetic, however much He may appear to be so to the sensual man. For example, from the standpoint of a young animal, a man who sits quietly for two hours listening to a concert given by a virtuoso might well seem to be submitting himself to a rigorous discipline of ascetic self-control. But the man himself, provided he was a real lover of music, would flatly deny that such was the case. He would claim that he was keenly enjoying himself and doing just what he would prefer to do. Likewise, the Sage in his withdrawn life is not imposing hardship upon himself. Actually He faces more hardship moving in public places, administering large affairs, attending the ordinary amusements of men, etc., for in all this there is a distraction that makes the deeper enjoyment difficult and, for many, practically impossible. It is entirely natural for men to prefer gold to base metal, and He who has Realized the Spiritual Gold enjoys more, not less.

I wish, by every means possible, to make the point clear that in the Current lies the highest possible value which, from the relative standpoint, we call enjoyment.* In principle there is no need of denying any phase of external action, save as a temporary discipline, so that the necessary inward concentration may be effected. The Man who has made the Ineffable Transition is Free. Outwardly He lives the life that He chooses, but it is utterly foreign to His innermost Nature to choose evil. Just as the man who is naturally cleanly has to impose no restraint upon himself to prevent himself from jumping into a mud puddle to wallow with the hogs, so the Realized Man is not tempted by evil. Evil is foreign to His real Nature and there is no question of an effort to make Himself good. This places Him

* I am not forgetting what the East Indians have said about the transcendence of enjoyment. They are correct in the sense in which they use the term. But at the present moment I am not speaking to the metaphysician. I am addressing myself to consciousness polarized to the objective.

21

in a position where He can, if necessary, work with the *instruments* of evil and do no evil.

Life in the Current of Joy is not the special prerogative of a small handful of men and women in the world. There are many living who now could Realize themselves as one with this Current, and ultimately all can do so in some Day of Time. Actually the Transition is not so difficult. Yet a lot of hard work has been put forth in the wrong direction through defining the Search in terms of complexity. It is as simple as turning from the object of, to the subject to, all relative consciousness, *plus the spontaneity of the SELF*.

Probably the most important difficulty which has made Recognition a rare event is a characteristic in our type of consciousness. The focus is placed upon the objective content of knowledge. Development in this sense involves an ever greater and greater growth in complexity. Hence, when man learns of a Transcendental Consciousness and he seeks to Realize This, his first effort, rather naturally, is in the direction of a more complex ideology. The greater the intellectual evolution of an individual, the more likely is this to be the case. And this explains why it is so often just the able men who have most difficulty in effecting the Transition. Now, the effective focusing of consciousness is precisely in the diametrically opposite direction. It is toward the subjective moment in the subject-object manifold, and this possesses the simplicity of a point. It is easily overlooked just because of its extreme simplicity. Yet it remains true that if the able man can succeed in finding this, he can reap a richer harvest, both for himself, individually, and for others, than is true in the case of those of inferior ability.

22

IX

Concerning the Spontaneity of the Self

As THE LOWER cannot command the Higher, the individual ego is not lord over the Universal SELF. Hence, from the individual standpoint, the Realization is spontaneous and thus is often called an act of Grace. The SELF, which it must be remembered is Identical with Divinity, does not stand within the causal sequence. Consequently, strictly considered, Realization of the SELF is never an effect of causes set up by the individual man acting in space and time. The latter through his effort prepares the candle, as it were, but the Flame is lighted through a spontaneous act of Spirit. But here is where Love enters in the highest sense, and Love is not constrained by the causal law which governs within space and time. Yet Love never fails the beloved. This Love excludes none, for—

> *I, Spirit, deny none of My children.*
> *Such is not My Nature.*
> *Ever waiting, above forgiveness,*
> *I pour Myself in through the opened doors.*

Practically, the spontaneity of the SELF works through Man to man, though it cannot be said that It manifests in no other way. In the "Gita," Krishna says: "I am in all men, but not all men are in ME." The implied meaning is, 'Some men are in ME,' i.e., Those who attained the Realization. Such Men are the Divine Presence Itself. Thus the Guru, if He is in fact a Guru in the true spiritual sense, is Divinity. Such a Man can light the Flame. The aspirant should seek his Guru in his inner consciousness and turn to Him as to Divinity Itself.

X

Seek Me First

THE JOY IS NOT the end-in-itself to be sought.

Seek Me first, and then My Knowledge and My Joy will also be thine.

Seek Me for My own sake and not for any ulterior motive.

I and I alone am the worthy end of all endeavor.

So lay down all for Me, and My Wealth will be thy wealth, My Power thy power, My Joy thy joy, My Wisdom thy wisdom.

This universe is but a part of My Treasure, and it, with vastly greater Riches, shall be the portion of the Inheritance of all those who come to Me.

Long have ye lingered in the desert of Ignorance.

I desire not thy continued suffering.

Come unto Me. The Way is not so hard.

XI

Expression from Different Levels

WHAT IS WRITTEN HERE is given variously from the standpoint of the Self and from that of the ego—the 'self-consciousness' of Dr. Bucke. It is most important to establish a cross-understanding, in so far as may be possible. Language is the creation and vehicle of egoistic consciousness. It is imbedded in the subject-object relationship. Speech or writing as from the perspective of the SELF involves unavoidable obscurity, analogous to that which would be found in attempting to express abstract thought in the very concrete language of a primitive people, but in the former case the difficulty is very much greater. Only in the Silence can the SELF be Known as It is, and this is not 'knowing' in the subject-object sense. Now, from the egoistic or 'self-conscious' standpoint language can be used correctly. But in this case the expression is *about* the event or reality as seen from the outside; it is not the event or reality itself. Expression as from the SELF, which is expression in the Current, IS the Reality. Necessarily there is a mystical quality in the latter, but not implying irrationality in the sense of anti-rationality. In fact the SELF is REASON, while all external reasoning is but a reflection of that REASON and, in most cases a very poor reflection indeed.

What the SELF, together with Transcendent and Cosmic Consciousness, actually is can be known only through Recognition or 'Knowledge through Identity.' He who Knows can speak and be understood by another who Knows; but others, at best, will feel something or sense a Light which attracts them. They may find induced in them something of the great Joy and Peace. All of this becomes strong evidence that the Kingly Knowledge *is,* and thus builds a presumption of the reality of the Goal to be sought. Then one here and one there and, We hope, many may be stirred to a desire to Know in the Inner sense. And that desire must be planted in the soul before the Awakening can take place.

Strongly developed egoistic consciousness is a barrier, but at the same time it is a power. The barrier can be mastered and the power retained. Highly developed capacity in relative knowledge is not to be scorned. Many genuinely Illumined Men have not seen clearly with respect to this point. The result is that while such Men have made the Crossing for Themselves, They have left poor bridges for others. It is this bridge-building that is the really important work. The Realized Man qua Realized has no need to write either for Himself or for other Realized Men. But he may need notes for himself as egoistic man, and others do require the landmarks such a One can leave. There is also another important point. If the Recognition of the SELF is not to entail permanent immersion in the Silence, but is to be combined with active manifestation, relative powers are necessary. Egoistic consciousness and even the 'simple consciousness' are, in high degree, an eclipse of Real Consciousness. But this eclipse serves a useful purpose for the invoking of relative powers. Otherwise the long journey in the Cycle of Necessity would be a vain travail. Egoistic consciousness does, therefore, forge instruments of value which the truly Wise Man will not discard, although He may very largely transform them. The more perfectly forged instruments of egoistic consciousness have greater potentiality than the less perfect. But the men who have built such instruments naturally have a stronger egoistic force than others, with correspondingly greater barriers to overcome. But having mastered these barriers and having Realized the SELF, They also transcend others in the capacity to make manifest from out the endless Fullness of the Silence. We do not scorn but, on the contrary, desire such men, and will do all that can and may be done to demonstrate the fact of the Inner Reality and clarify the rationale of the Way whereby that Reality may be Realized.

There is a shifting of standpoint in the use of 'I'—the SELF— 'I'—the egoistic or individual man—and the 'We,' employed at times. Metaphysically, I am the One without a second or, more strictly, 'I am not-one and not not-one, and there is no second.' Yet while this remains eternally true, I am, in a reflected sense, the egoistic, one among others. Strictly the egoistic 'I' is "I am I and none other." (It is the 'none other' that makes the barrier noted above.) Now, there is between this and the highest metaphysical level another level or state, in one sense intermediate and yet also beyond, since it involves real Mastery, where I realize Myself as 'I am I and yet also others.' It is in this sense the 'We' is employed, spelled with a capital 'W.'

The rules of literary form will have to be sacrificed when they interfere with the main purpose. At times I write in the midst of the Current, yet at other times more or less out of It. The Current carries Authority, and in the face of this literary rules must be discarded when they act as barriers to Meaning.

XII

The Record Continued

AS ALREADY STATED, I can distinguish three distinct Recognitions that produced lasting effects. As I look back I can discern a progressive quality in the three which, it seems, should be noted. About fourteen years ago an old college friend called upon Sherifa and me and the time was devoted to the discussion of Theosophical subjects. (My friend was an earnest student of the Theosophia.) At one stage in the conversation he outlined the various steps of a very old discriminative technique in which it is shown, progressively, that the Self is not the body nor the various other principles of man, but that it can be only that final principle—which, strictly, is not one principle among others—i.e., the Atman or pure subjectivity. I was familiar with the method, was already convinced of the soundness of the logic and had previously employed it myself. But in this case I suddenly seemed to Realize, with certainty, that, in fact, 'I am Identical with the Atman.' There was a sense of a new Light which made clear much that had been obscure, but this was not a light seen in the form of a subtle sensuous perception. The effect upon the relative consciousness persisted. There was a definite enrichment, but I was not aware of the Current of Joy.

The most significant consequence, within the individual consciousness, was a certain change in the base of thought. As an example, it may be noted that, whereas, prior to that date I had read the "Bhagavadgita" because it was one of the important Theosophic books, I did not like it, and it seemed to inculcate a veritable repression of the life-interest I then cared for; on the other hand, immediately after the Recognition of my Identity with the Atman, I found myself spontaneously thinking, as my own thought, many of the ideas contained in the "Gita." I Realized them as obviously true, and, instead of their carrying a repressive value, they were a source of

27

Light and expansion. I have never forgotten this Recognition and have never felt disposed to question the fact I then saw so clearly. In the intellectual sense that Recognition was, and is, persistent. But other aspects of the personal nature were not included or were not sufficiently included. So, in the intervening years I have often *felt* and *acted* contrary to that Recognition.

The second occasion occurred somewhat less than a year ago. I had been reading with deep interest a book by Paul Brunton in which, among other experiences, he told of his contact with a certain Sage in Southern India. I felt a sympathetic rapport with this Sage and repeatedly read His words with profound attention. Once, while thus engaged, it suddenly dawned upon me that Nirvana is not a field or place where man enters and is enclosed, as in a space which envelops bodies, but I Recognized that "I am Nirvana." In other words, the Real Self is not other than Nirvana, never has been other, and never will be other. All that the individual man achieves is Recognition of this eternal fact. With this Transition in consciousness Joy was realized. Even at that time I sensed It as a Current, though in modified form as compared with the more recent Recognition. I once spent a whole day immersed within It; and, for a period, within certain limits, I could invoke It. At the time, I was engaged in lecturing and class-work concerned with metaphysical subjects. A greater Light came into this work. While previously I had employed a considerable degree of formal organization in lecturing and class-work, I then began to relax the formal aspect so that it stood more in the background as something automatic in its action. I dared to leave a larger room for spontaneity on the platform, and found by repeated experimenting that I could trust that spontaneity, provided I could secure a certain attitude in the audience. Lacking that attitude, I could rebound to the more formal preparation. Since then I have continued to be able to operate between these two modes. I found that a conceptual coordination, produced while one stood or sat before an audience, released, concomitantly, a current-like quality that had, among other features, the effect of holding the audience in a kind of stillness which I would describe as possessed of depth. The attention of the individual member of the audience was held even though he did not understand the ideas developed, as was often found to be the case in subsequent conversation. A simple repetition of the same conceptual coordination did not have the same power in the same degree. I thus found a definite correlation between the Current and creativeness. From the relative standpoint the Current requires a progressive disintegration and reintegration of forms. Once a form becomes relatively fixed, the Current subsides. And yet, in a very curious way, this disintegration and reintegration leaves a certain subtle master-form unaltered. The result is essential consistency between all formal integrations produced in the Current, provided the individual understands the use of language. And, even if he does not understand the art of language, that consistency still remains, though in a deeper sense which is not so easily recognized.

XIII

Nirvanic Bliss

IN THE CURRENT, we stand in the presence of the Ceaseless Motion which, at the same time, can be characterized as Changelessness. In one sense, we may say that the Key to Immortality is to be ceaselessly creative, while remaining eternally Identical. Nirvana is pure creativeness and, consequently, cannot be captured within fixed definition. On the other hand, genuine objects of consciousness can be defined, since they are forms. Nirvana is inconceivable but It is ceaseless Conceiving. Herein is a partial explanation of the Nirvanic Bliss that can fall within the understanding of the more common consciousness. Creative activity, even on the lower levels, such as begetting, does awaken a degree of bliss, though of progressively inferior and grosser quality as we approach the physiological. Usually such minor blisses last but for a moment, or, at best, for brief periods with subsequent depression and exhaustion. Conceive of the intensity of the bliss raised beyond all relative imagination, and far beyond the power of any physiological organism to endure, and then regard it as not lasting merely for a moment or a brief period, but extending with unbroken continuity indefinitely; then something of the Bliss-aspect of Nirvana may be apprehended. Is it so surprising that many become 'God-intoxicated' and fail to go on to the winning of real Mastery?

XIV

The Record Continued

RETURNING TO THE RECORD, it is now to be noted that the second Recognition had produced a change that is persistent, yet, at the same time, certain aspects of my relative nature, principally below the intellectual, were not taken up. There were outer desires that still had strength, although they had become perceptibly weakened. After the period of lectures and class-work there was a sort of partial 'clouding of the sky.' At the time, I could not invoke the Current, though the force of the Knowledge remained unbroken, as far as attained. Subsequently, lectures and class-work were continued in the Middle West. For the first three weeks of this work in Chicago I had what, for me, was a most unusual experience. I felt the consciousness of the city as an almost insupportable weight which enveloped my mind with a sort of lethargy so that I could not really think. Prior to this experience nothing had ever been able so to suffocate the power of thought that I could not, fairly readily, will my way to thought-action. I was on the platform nearly every day throughout this period, although during the greater part of the twenty-four hours of each day my consciousness was so gripped with heaviness that I desired to sleep all the time. I spoke, as it were, with the momentum of past thought, but it seems my state was not realized, at least not generally, by others. After three weeks I broke through with a deep sense of elation and victory. Once again, I

30

found myself moving in a stream of genuine thought and, finally, gave a lecture on the "Crest Jewel" of Shankara which represented the highest point I had attained on the platform up to that time. In subsequent work in the smaller cities I had no further experience of the obscuration.

By the time the work was drawing to a close, I had a feeling as of being emptied, and the desire grew strong to return to the West and live for a time under conditions where I could have complete solitude. This condition was met in July on one of the tributaries of the American River near Michigan Bluff. Two purposes conjoined at this time. It was desirable that some cross-cut work should be done on a gold-prospect for further sampling and, in addition, I found a curious value in underground activity in association with inward penetration toward depth. So, during the latter half of July, I had some days of solitude combined with underground physical work, plus meditative readings in the "System of the Vedanta," as noted previously. Much clarification was achieved in my consciousness during this period, but two facts,* one a correlating idea and the other an experience, stand out above the rest. The experience was a spontaneous development in the Current, but this time in a form that was more sensuously evident than on any prior occasion. Here, for the first time, I submitted It to analysis, in so far as It was reflected in the organism.

The Current is clearly a subtle, fluid-like substance which brings the sense of well-being already described. Along with It, a more than earthly Joy suffuses the whole nature. To myself, I called It a Nectar. Now, I recognize It under several names. It is also the 'Soma,' the 'Ambrosia of the Gods,' the 'Elixir of Life,' the 'Water of Life' of Jesus, and the 'Baptism of the Spirit' of St. Paul. It is more than *related* to Immortality; in fact, It is *Identical* with Immortality.

During the first week of August we returned to San Fernando and, on or about the 7th of the month, the Glorious Transition came. This third Recognition was much profounder than the others.

* Both of these have been recorded in the opening section of this book. The idea will be developed more fully later.

The Recognitions as expressed in the forms, 'I am Atman' and 'I am Nirvana,' were not devoid of an objective element. Each of these forms is a complete judgment or proposition involving, therefore, a subject and a predicate. In the use of relative language such a form is unavoidable, if the statement is to be correct according to the laws of language. But in my own consciousness, in addition to this fact, I also actually retained a degree of the objective element. Hence, the Recognition, in each case, fell short of genuine identification. In the third instance, I isolated the subjective moment from the relative manifold of consciousness, as already stated, and the result was Emptiness, Darkness, and Silence, i.e., Consciousness with no object. It should be borne in mind, however, that relative consciousness by its own momentum continued to function all this time, so that I never for one moment lost sight of my environment or the ceaseless train of thoughts. It was simply a discriminative abstraction of the pure subjective moment and Recognizing myself as That. At this moment, I found Myself above space, time, and causality, and actually sustaining the whole universe by the Light of Consciousness which I AM. Almost at once, there followed the Nectar-like Current and the gentle, yet so powerful Joy. Now, always heretofore with me, as a practical working principle, thought was life, even though theoretically I had for some time recognized that thought itself, no matter how abstract, required a matrix. But with the third Recognition I found myself more than content in a World above thought, since It comprehended thought with all else. I was tempted to abandon thought and draw Inward. All the outer effort and work seemed so useless. But on this point I had been already warned by literature, such as the "Voice of the Silence"; and, further, it did not seem like good sportsmanship to have received an inward aid making possible the Attainment of the most precious Value of all and fail to carry It on to others. So I looked over the world, as it were, to find what value there remained to hold my interest. It seemed to me that I had garnered, at least in seed-form, enough relative knowledge. I had no real interest in the grosser constructions, such as the tangible forms, institutions, societies, governments, and arts. But there was one thing that did remain: a humanity, also part of Myself, that was almost famished for that saving Knowledge and the Divine Nectar that I had found so precious. So, for me, there was a commission to be fulfilled, to 'carry on' in the objective effort so that these others might be brought nearer to the Goal. But then the question arose: How was this to be done? I placed this question before One who has given me much excellent advice and asked for a formula of action. He said, in effect: "None of Us knows such a formula. All other compartments of nature under the sun We can, and have, penetrated and know the laws and, knowing them, We can act with and mold nature according to Our wills. But the human soul is a mystery, and its inner depths lie beyond Our penetrations. We try many ways to reach these human souls, often disappointed where We expect much, and yet surprised at times beyond Our expectations. Find your own way and try."—Well, this book is such an attempt.

XV

The Grand Adventure

I HAVE A SENSE of a Grand Adventure, the most glorious of all.

A veritable World looms before my inner gaze unfolding hour by hour, and day by day, so that I cannot begin to record on paper what is being unfolded within the mind by the shorthand of thought.

Such Joy and Freedom shed their luster about that even this remaining bondage of action is losing, progressively, the sense of restriction.

Within the Grand Abstraction, which is the one Concrete Reality, there is a silent Communion, wordless, thoughtless, utterly formless; yet within it I barely discern, like the dim paling that heralds a new dawn, the silent Voices of Others, separated here by both space and time—even distant time.

There are other Communities beyond this.

There are far more satisfying Companionships than are possible within the veil of gross matter.

The Silence is Full and Pregnant, and out of It flows the Stream of all formations in endless variety: symphonies, philosophies, governments, sciences, arts, societies, and so on and on and on.

XVI

Alternative Roads to Recognition

WHILE THE BOOK "Cosmic Consciousness" is a valuable compilation and analysis of the objectively discernible characteristics which mark Those who have Awakened to the 'Cosmic Sense,' as the author calls it, yet Dr. Bucke has covered only a part of the subject and misses entirely a phase of Recognition that does not possess certain of the signs he has noted. Not all Recognition carries in Its train the profound and, sometimes, intense Joy. There are Recognitions in which the element of Joy is not conspicuous and, though present, may be too hidden to be revealed to the gaze of the observer, unless the latter is unusually acute in his perceptions.

There is a science of Recognition, though in large part it remains esoteric. But some of the science may be uncovered by the uninitiated student if he seeks in the right place. Among the various races, the East Indians form the chief repository of this science, and the language employed, the Sanskrit, involves terms corresponding to concepts for which there are no real equivalents in our current western languages. It will be necessary to turn to a small portion of this science to show how Recognition may be of more than one type.

The ultimate Reality is Nameless, though word-signs have been devised that point toward but do not define It. Among these is the word SAT, designating, but not defining, THAT which is neither Being nor non-Being. This is the One Reality or, rather, THAT which is neither One nor not-One. I, the Atman, am identical with

THAT; hence, the statement, 'The Atman is identical with the Brahman.' This One Reality is Absolute Consciousness and Absolute Motion. Its highest representation is, therefore, a triad and this has been called in Sanskrit 'SAT-CHIT-ANANDA.' CHIT is Consciousness or Knowledge in the highest sense. ANANDA is Bliss or Love, again in the highest sense. But, as already shown, pure Bliss is pure Creativeness, and, as creativeness is motion in the ultimate sense of disintegrating and reintegrating form ceaselessly, we can see how Ananda becomes identical with Ceaseless Motion. Below this highest Triad there is a lower reflection, though still on a metaphysical level. This reflection abides in man as his highest aspect. It is known as Atman-Buddhi-Manas; 'Atman' corresponding to 'SAT,' 'Buddhi' to 'ANANDA,' and 'Manas' to 'CHIT.' Each of these sets of three is often represented as an equilateral triangle with the Atman or SAT at the higher apex, the base being parallel to the surface of the earth—or, rather, tangent—with Buddhi and Manas or ANANDA and CHIT at the other vertices, as follows:

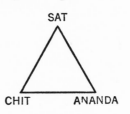

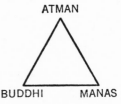

The equilateral form of the triangles indicates a symmetrical relationship while the position at the upper vertex of SAT or Atman signifies that here, with respect to each triangle, is the ultimate. As a consequence it follows that Atman is as accessible through Manas as through Buddhi and, likewise, SAT through CHIT as well as through ANANDA.* All of this is well above the personal man. Now, below the triad, Atman-Buddhi-Manas, there are innumerable roads leading *toward* Recognition; but at the level of Buddhi and Manas there are two contrasting routes, and a third which is a combination of the two. If a man reaches first to Buddhi and then to Atman—the I AM—but has attained little unfoldment of Manas —Intellectual Principle—the Recognition will manifest predominantly through Joy and Love. All such tend to see the Supreme as

* This fact has been strangely neglected by many students, yet the very figures reveal it.

Love and this, apparently, is the more frequent development. But, on the other hand, he who reaches to Atman through Manas, and with but minor development of the Love Principle, will be Illumined in terms of Knowledge, but will know relatively little of the Joy. For such a one the Supreme is seen as Knowledge or Wisdom. The third, or combined Road, is through Manas, thence through Buddhi to full Recognition in the Atman. The Supreme then stands forth equally as Wisdom-Knowledge and Love-Bliss. The latter is, of course, the most completely balanced Road. But if the Atman is reached through Manas, then Buddhi can be Awakened quite readily, or vice versa, if the appropriate effort is put forth. Thus, finally, the culminating completeness is also attained. Buddha is the outstanding example of the balanced Recognition within historic times, and thus He is One equally great in Knowledge and Compassion.

Immanuel Kant is a great example, among western peoples, of a man who attained something of Recognition through Manas. As a result, his philosophy clears the Way in the West in a sense analogous to that achieved by the thought of Shankara in the Orient but, unlike the latter, it is incomplete on the metaphysical side. Hegel partially completed this structure, but the whole of this falls short of the completeness of the pure Advaita Vedanta. Still, within this idealistic structure is to be found the best of genuinely spiritual Knowledge-Wisdom indigenous to the West. Kant's Light is very clarifying but there is lacking in it the Substance which is Joy. This fact is revealed in his features and his writings. Yet there is a very great and clear beauty in Kant. I, for one, am profoundly indebted to him and realize that debt more clearly than ever at the present time. Without him I might have *experienced,* but I could not have understood nearly so well the Meaning unfolded through the Transition, being born, as I am, in a western body and nurtured in a western current of thought. I take this opportunity to make my acknowledgment to this great philosopher who could recognize, and so well name, the pure subjective moment of Consciousness, i.e., Pure Apperception. Is there any greater phrase in all philosophy than this: "The synthetic, transcendental unity of pure apperception?" He who penetrates this phrase and extracts from it its ultimate Meaning will have attained the Recognition.

Among the earmarks of Illumination that Dr. Bucke has noted, Kant does not reveal, at least not conspicuously, the Joy and the 'subjective Light,' but on the other hand the moral elevation is marked. In fact, Kant has made one of the most important contributions, if not the most important, to the theory of ethics of any thinker in our present culture. And his primary ethical principle is one of the most lofty ever formulated by man. The intellectual illumination is stupendous. Few men, if any, in history have ever surpassed the intellectual altitude attained by Immanuel Kant.

XVII

Being Born Again

August 29

NO DOUBT A PRICE is exacted from the personal man. An extraordinary demand is made upon the nervous organism and so a counter activity is helpful, perhaps necessary. But, as even the personal man is much more than the physical body, the price goes deeper than the body. There is here a kind of dying, proceeding in the midst of continued bodily existence. Doubtless it is but natural that the personal nature should dread all this and, in a measure, grieve. For here we have the real meaning of the crucifixion. The personal life is centered upon the world-field; though it is a doomed life in any case, since, inevitably, Death reaps all here. Still, the personality never quite believes this and strives in its feebleness to will its continuance in the outer world, until in ripe old age it craves rest, even though it be at the price of extinction. But when this hour of tiredness has come, it is already too late to achieve the Awakening in that body, for this Awakening calls for a profound, though possibly subtle, virility. To die in the midst of virility—the mystic thirty-three years of age—is not easy. Jesus, now in the sense of the personal man, sweat the drops of blood drawn forth by the agony of Gethsemane. He shrank from the piercing of the crown of thorns and the nails of the cross. But all this is only one side of the shield. Beyond the seemingly forsaken man of this world is the Glory of Exaltation. He who realizes the obverse of the Crucifixion of Jesus forgets the latter in the presence of that Majestic Glory which sheds a Light so potent as to consume all darkness within Its range. The "Eil, Eli, lama sabachthani," seen from one side as "My God, My God, why hast Thou forsaken me" becomes, "My God, My God, how greatly hast Thou exalted me!"

A Fire descends and consumes the personal man. For a time, short or long, this Fire continues. The personal man is the fuel, and the fuel, in greater or less measure, does suffer. But fire does not destroy; it simply transforms. This fact can be realized by an analysis of what takes place through the action of ordinary fire. If a log is burning, the fuel is principally, if not wholly, in the form of carbohydrates, and the fire transforms these into carbon dioxide and water vapor. There remains a small amount of ashes, the persistently earthy portion of the log. The carbohydrate in the log was a fixed form, partaking, for a time, of the earthy solidity of the mineral associates in the log. But as the carbohydrates become carbon dioxide and water vapor, they take on new form in the freer world of the air. So too, does the Fire which descends and consumes the personal man but Transform him. Only the ash of the personal nature is left behind, while the rest, the best of the personality, is taken up to be conscious in airy spaces. The ultimate state is one of a far, far greater Joy.

It is possible for the man passing through the ordeal so to shift his center of self-identity that the pain, instead of being strong, becomes but a shadowy undertone of a Melody that is all Joy. He who identifies himself with the fuel predominantly suffers much and keenly, but if, on the other hand, he unites himself with the Fire, all is changed. The Flame of the Fire is a dance of Joy. There is no pain on this level of Consciousness. The transforming man does not then wait until after the Burning to Know the Joy, but feels It through and through while in the midst of the ordeal, which now has almost completely ceased to be an ordeal at all.

In the days immediately following the Transition, I clearly felt the Fire; and, because I did identify myself mostly with this Fire, those were grand days, despite the fact that there were brief periods of reaction when life seemed low in the physical body and it was difficult to assert the will-to-live. But now, these periods of reaction are growing less, both in that they are shorter in duration and are less intense. Also I do employ more judgment in invoking the Current which is Bliss. There exists a throttle, command of which gives to man the power to control this Current. It is but a due exercise of wisdom so to adjust the flow of the Current that Its action is balanced to meet the strength of the personal man.

In the old days when I read of this Fire, I supposed that It had but a figurative meaning. But while the Fire is figurative, in a sense, yet It is also a quite real and even a sensuously felt and manifested fact. Not only have I felt this Fire, but It has been induced in those who live near me. They report feeling It as genuinely as the heat of the sun and manifest some of the effects of the sun's heat as it acts upon the human body. The Inner Fire does reach down to the outermost of the man. This does imply that, looked at aright, the metaphysical is not utterly divorced from the physical.

XVIII

An Experience with the Fire

A FEW YEARS AGO I experienced the Fire in another form. On that occasion I had been collecting the material for a lecture on the Akasha and the Astral Light. Such knowledge, as is externally available on this subject, is largely descended from the ancients and is expressed in archaic and often deliberately veiled form. I found it peculiarly difficult to grasp the meaning within the medium of our present concepts. I drove into the subject with an especially heavy effort of the will, with the result that some of the facts were forced into organization, but very soon I became aware that Mystery surrounded what we could, at present, comprehend intellectually. But one effect of the intense concentration was a kind of breaking-through the personal mental shell and, briefly, I seemed to possess a veritable universe of Knowledge. It seemed that then I knew all things that were to be known in this world. I simply could not contain this Knowledge within my personal mind. Presently, that Knowledge would have burned up and destroyed this brain and nervous system, had I remained in rapport with It for any appreciable period of time. So, before I could assimilate any of this Knowledge concretely, I had to withdraw the concentration. Still, I retained enough to know that *I* Knew behind the Veil. Now, from that experience there were after-effects to overcome which required some years. One day, soon after this event, I was walking along a street in Los Angeles, and had stopped for a moment at a corner, when a streetcar close by started from a standing position. I was evidently within the range of the electro-magnetic field * connected with the action of the motor. Suddenly something seemed to shift, either in the consciousness or in the brain or both. For a moment I lost orientation with the body. I cannot describe the feeling quite correctly for I know of no other experiences that are analogous. But it seemed to me to be an incipient leaving of the body. I gripped myself and the physical organism intensely with the will and walked slowly up a side street. But I had a bad time of it. The intense effort of will to hold myself tended further to induce the very condition I was trying to master. I had both to hold firmly and relax that hold. It was a kind of tight-rope walking, for either too much relaxation or too much concentration had the same effect of tending to dislodge me from the rope, which in this case represented walking in the body in this world. After a time I succeeded in re-establishing the

* This field must have been the inciting cause as there were later similar, though less intense, experiences of the same sort when electric cars passed near me.

balance sufficiently so that the crisis was past. But it was as though the rope had merely widened to a narrow path which only slowly became a broad plane wherein I was free to move without careful circumspection as formerly. The completion of this correction required years. For a long time I had to be careful in the vicinity of streetcars and also had to abandon reading metaphysical literature. For I found that the reading of the "Secret Doctrine" or the "Crest-Jewel" of Shankara had the same effect.

Now, from the foregoing an important lesson was learned. It is not safe to direct the will with full intensity into the intellect, for here we are dealing with a sort of dynamite. It can be done with safety only when the proper guarding controls are employed, but this is a problem of technique not easily learned. When one concentrates in that way he invokes an Inner Fire and that Fire can easily be too much for the organism. The fact is that the Fire of Knowledge is too intense a Flame for the human organism to endure if it is not sheathed in the Water of Life, the Current which is Bliss. At present I am approaching a level comparable with that earlier moment, but I am fundamentally at ease. The nervous organism is gathering strength. Thought moves more freely than ever before, and while there is present and active a genuinely intense will, it does not manifest as a strong personal effort. I do invoke the will, truly, but I am not this seen man. There is an enormous difference in the action of the will in these two senses. A very high order of will may be exercised while the personal organism remains relaxed and, in that case, there is none of the tension which acts like resistance to an electric current. There is, then, an effect of flowing through with little or no resistance and, as a consequence, the organism is not strained to the point of danger.

XIX

The Drama of the Triune Man

PERSONALITY:

This Space is too large. Where are the comforting bars of my cage? I would like to return to the world that I know so well. I would like to move, inconspicuous, in the domain where I know my way. Release me from the Fire.

INTELLECTUAL MAN:

Be still, thou foolish one. Those pastures and encircling walls thou cravest are barren and small before this Largeness. Be not like the canary bird that refuses the offered freedom, but come on with Me.

REAL MAN:

Be patient, child, thou shalt be guarded and shalt find again all thou dost love. For this small travail, thou, too, shalt drink of the Waters of Immortality, which I AM. The limits of thy strength will not be forgotten.

And as for Thee, MY mediator to the world and all things that stand below, let not Thy restlessness and greater power lead Thee to forget the limited strength of the child. Once, Thou too wert a child and had to be aided over the difficult places. Extend, therefore, Thy aid to those who are weaker than Thou art.

XX

The Meaning of Omniscience

WHAT IS OMNISCIENCE? Those who have familiarized themselves to any extent with mystical or quasi-occult literature will have found it stated that there are levels or states where a man becomes

Omniscient, and yet, at the same time, it will be emphasized that no man is infallible. From the relative standpoint these two statements seem incompatible and the result is mystification, to say the least. But when properly understood both statements can be true. The fact is, no man is omniscient on the relative level; and though the knowledge of such a one may be very great, transcending even the relative knowledge of any figure that has appeared upon the screen of history, yet beyond his attainment, whatever it may be, there lie further mysteries awaiting his resolution. In other words, We find no conceivable end to evolution. But while all this is true, there is another sense in which a man may Awaken to Omniscience, and may do so instantaneously. In fact, such an Awakening cannot be a matter of gradual attainment, for the Infinite is never Realized by progressive additions of finite manifolds. It is all a question of level or state. The SELF is All Knowledge and, as It incloses, but is not inclosed or restrained by, space, time, and causality, there is no question of development on this level, in the sense of progression by finite steps. He who has Realized himself as the SELF is at once Omniscient. But it should be remembered that the SELF is absolute Emptiness, Darkness, and Silence, *from the relative standpoint*. The SELF is the Knowledge whence all proceeds, but this Knowledge is not of the subject-object type nor anything that could be conceived within the cognitive framework of the latter. The Silence *is* All-Knowledge, while knowledge in the field of the subjective-objective *becomes*, and of this it is impossible to predicate infallibility.

There is a way in which we may secure an adumbration of what All-Knowledge or the 'Voice of the Silence' is. Language is composed of words, designating objects in some sense, and sentences. Words or terms, we may say, represent simple apprehensions and are analogous to simple consciousness. The sentences are representations of judgments, which are of the nature of recognition on the level of polarized consciousness, or that which Dr. Bucke has called 'self-consciousness.' Here all is posited in a world where an 'I,' considered as distinct from other selves, is conceived as conscious of an object in some sense. Here, also, we have meaning in a form that is definable, i.e., capable of representation in the form of other terms

43

and propositions and, in the strictest usage, meaning just those terms and propositions. But this is only formal meaning and, by itself, it is barren. Now, over and above this manifold of formal knowledge there is another Meaning, or Significance which, while It may be *aroused* by words and sentences, is not *contained* in words and sentences. This higher Meaning, when Realized, is a veritable food for the soul and, thence, for the whole man. In general, men, by arousing momentary and partial recognitions, proceed to this Meaning from below by the use of formal and empiric knowledge, employed with the appropriate skill. These momentary recognitions are adumbrations, though generally in a very minor degree, of that Higher Knowledge which is identical with Divinity Itself. This is the process when man bases himself in the external, the relative world. But for him who has made the Ineffable Transition there is a radical difference. The man has then found his base in the SELF. The Knowledge from which He now starts is the Silence, and this is Significance devoid of any words or ideas. Here, Communion is on the level of Significance Itself, unfettered by any form. This is exhaustless Refreshment, and there is no waste. Now, from this level there can be a projection outward through ideas and, perchance, ultimately reaching the relatively frozen state on the most objective plane of all, i.e., the field of the visible universe. From this higher standpoint Meaning is the base and not the apex, as It is usually conceived. The universe is the final effect, but it is utterly dependent for its existence upon this base or foundation of Meaning. That is why, from the standpoint of the SELF, the universe is unreal.

Now, on the level of Meaning a man may Know with absolute certainty and yet express himself incorrectly when trying to fit his ideas within the already existing forms of expression. In this case, he shows himself to be quite fallible and yet Knows *what* he is talking about, however incorrect his expression may be. If careful discrimination is not employed, it is easy for the outer man, even though he has Awakened to Realization, to fall into confusion at this point. Knowing the certainty that applies on the level where He really IS, then, as outer man he attaches this certainty to his formal expressions and thus falls into error. Outer correctness, or approximation

44

to correctness, must be acquired by effort, even though the man has attained to a high order of Realization. In formal knowledge, including all knowledge of things, whether gross or subtle, and all knowledge of relationships, processes, etc., technique is essential, including all possible methods of checking and control. Naturally, some men have gained more capacity in this than others and so, in matters falling in their respective fields, have relative authority not possessed by others. Thus, in a matter of formal or empiric knowledge, it may often happen that a man who has not reached beyond the egoistic or 'self-conscious' level can very easily correct another who is genuinely emplanted in the Silence. The latter does have, however, decisive advantages when seeking mastery in any relative field. He can acquire knowledge in the relative sense in but a fraction of the time required by others, for He has the advantage of commanding perspective. But in any case, even for Him, some effort and time are required. Transcendent Knowledge, or Knowledge on the level of Meaning, is acquired instantaneously and with certainty, but the attainment of relative knowledge always demands some time and effort, and never gives certainty.

XXI

The Record Continued

I FIND THAT the Current is consumed, at least apparently so, in the expression of thought. I feel It less after casting It into form. It seems to have gone forth in a kind of new birth. Yet I am happy that this should be so. The Fount is exhaustless, and there remains— enough.

XXII

The Celestial Virgin

TRADITIONAL WOMAN has been the custodian of pleasure, and the dispensing of pleasure has been a large part of her glory and power. Too often, in these later days, womankind has been disposed to discredit her own natural glories and powers by becoming an imitator of man. This is really giving to man-power and man-function a greater tribute than they deserve. That essence the outer embodiment of which is woman in a peculiar sense constitutes a need of this world today that is especially poignant. There is too great an over-balance of harsh wilfulness abroad in the world. Consequently, there is a need for the counter-balancing forces, and these woman, alone, is really competent to exercise. Among these essentially feminine qualities the following stand out: Beauty, Mercy, Tenderness, Charm, Ecstasy, preservation of proven values, etc. It is a grave mistake to regard these powers as inferior to the Creative Will, the Will to Power, the Daring of the Unknown, and the Judgment that peculiarly mark the masculine principle. The latter powers are unquestionably indispensable both in the world-field and for Inward Penetration, but by themselves they are unbalanced and can easily drop from a constructive to a destructive level. The isolated masculine principle cannot check this tendency and, so, right here is where the feminine quality is grievously needed. The feminine powers are just as strong as the masculine, although they function in a more subtle way. We greatly need more women who justly appreciate the ancient and natural feminine powers and arts.

Man is Siva, the formless Light; woman is Shakti, the Current which opposes and embodies the Light. Without embodiment, the Light of Consciousness remains void of self-consciousness. Since self-consciousness is the one great achieved value, it is easy to see how vitally important the Shakti principle is.

In Her highest aspect, Woman is the Celestial Virgin, and this is none other than the Current of Bliss. The Current is a Virgin, because of the quality of ever-becoming-new. Though impregnated by the Fire of Wisdom, yet She remains a Virgin because She is ever-changing within Her own Self-identity. The union of Wisdom and the Virgin gives birth to the Christ, and this is the real Immaculate Conception. This union is the untellable Joy of which all lesser ecstasies are but faint shadows. So, deep and lasting Joy is the true sign of the genuine and noble religiosity. Austere gloom in the name of religion is a sacrilege and sign of failure. Only false religion is dreary. The Holy is Free and Joyful.

XXIII

Beauty

August 31

UPON THE NEUTRAL WORLD of things I cast a sheath of Beauty, which is Myself, and all things whatsoever stand exalted in that Beauty. Plato is right; beyond the beauty that is predicated of various forms and relationships, there is a pure Transcendent Beauty, and this is a mode of the very Being of the SELF. This Beauty is not *something* that is beautiful. It is Self-existent and casts Its luster upon all things for Him who has found Himself identical with that Beauty. When a man reports that he has found beauty in some department of nature, in a combination of sounds, a blending of colors or in the proportions of forms, he has not merely discovered an external existence. He has had, at least, a momentary, penumbral glimpse of Himself, but has interpreted it as something externally apprehended. The failure of many, while in the full possession and exercise of their senses, to see the beauty realized by others, shows that beauty is not something external. A man may gaze upon a drab and somber landscape and, taking merely the photographic record of that view, find no beauty; but let him place over his eyes appropriately chosen light filters and the scene will take on a new quality that is far more pleasing. The light filter acts like a sheath which changes the whole quality of the experience. Somewhat similarly, man projects Beauty upon the phenomenal world and, in most cases, thinks that he simply experiences it. But He who has made the ineffable Transition may say: "I am Beauty and make all things to become beautiful." But the real Beauty is entirely apart from the object, however subtle. Ecstasy is pure Beauty, as well as pure Joy and Knowledge. Beauty is one of the many facets of THAT which is the Fullness appearing as Emptiness. Another facet is Significance, and these two are One.

XXIV

The Record Continued

I FIND IT more difficult to write today. Yesterday we were in the city and, again, I found it acutely painful. Something of the experience may be judged by a familiar phenomenon connected with radio reception and amplification. Sometimes a receiving set is so adjusted by the dial controls that the faint impulses from distant sources may become manifest. At the limits of the receptive power of the set one may just barely discern the impulses coming from a great distance. Now, if without changing the degee of amplification the station dial is turned to a powerful broadcasting station nearby, the resultant effect of violent noise is highly distressing. I find the jazz-like discordance of the city has an analogous effect, intensified to a degree that is positively destructive. Not only does the maze of lights, sounds, and motions have this force, but, in even larger measure, the non-integrated mass of thoughts, feelings, and desires produces the same result. It is, in a measure, dangerous. This makes clear one of the reasons for the call to solitude, characteristically reported by those who are in the midst of the Transition. It is possible to build protecting shields, but this takes time and can hardly

48

be done during the period that the inward rooting is being consolidated, since all the resources that the outer man has are required for this task. It is not easy to bridge the gulf between the worlds.

There are subtle violences and injuries that are very difficult to describe, since their symptoms are of quite different quality from the familiar sensations of the gross body. There is a place of fine-edged balance in the mind that once destroyed the whole structure crashes. There are phases of organization beyond the knowledge of the modern psychologist and the understanding of the psychiatrist. The complete organized being that man is may not be observed by the use of the external senses alone, for man has a metaphysical as well as a physical organization. Essentially, it is only the shell of man that lends itself to observation by methods adapted from the physical laboratory. Behind the shell is another organization where more primary causes operate. As a consequence, in order to trace the causes which manifest as objective effects to their root sources, both subtle senses and something of metaphysical understanding are requisite. As a general principle this rule applies to the whole objective world, but while a fair degree of valid knowledge relative to so-called inorganic nature may be reached through the external senses, this ceases to be true in progressive degree as the field of study advances through the range of life-manifestations from its lowest forms up to its more exalted developments. The real roots of consciousness and mind, together with subtler phases of organization, are beyond the range of external observation. Unquestionably, many effects and secondary causes may be observed by this means, but these do not supply a sufficient ground for unfolding the laws involved and, consequently, do not afford an adequate basis for therapeutic control and correction.

There are domains in the inner constitution of man where the intelligent exercise of a strong will is far more effective than any external agency whatsoever. There is a hidden, as well as an obvious, meaning behind the 'lever of Archimedes.' There is both a lever and a fulcrum, mastery of which gives power to move the world. But these forces act solely at a point of very fine balance, which is attained only with very great difficulty, and which is also not easily

49

maintained after having been achieved. The violent wind of world-consciousness affords a most serious obstacle to the realization of such a balance, and right here lies part of the reason why humanity enjoys so restricted a portion of the benefits that might accrue to it from the great Hidden Powers of Man.

XXV

Both by Thought and Feeling

I HEARD A MAN SAY: "Not by thought but by feeling we enter the Kingdom of Heaven." The evidence is that this is true of the majority, but it is not universally true. It is a mistake for anyone to attempt to measure the limits of the possible by his own limitations and capacities. There are instances of Realization in which thought played a part not inferior to feeling. Gautama Buddha and Shankara are examples and, certainly, in the latter case thought predominated. Further, in the instance of Immanuel Kant we have a genuine, if not complete, Realization, and, if there ever was a man who was a veritable incarnation of cognition, that man was Kant. For my own part, I have always found that cognition, when highly purified, could fly higher than feeling. It is perfectly true that Transcendental Knowledge is beyond thought, but, at the same time, it is equally beyond feeling and sensation. None of these three can be more than accessory instruments, and all of them are left behind at the final Transition. Still, it remains unquestionably true that the preponderant bulk of the instruction pointing out the Way emphasizes the silencing of thought while feeling may still continue. But this is merely a pragmatic rule designed to meet the needs of the greater number. Doubtless, with most men the greater power of soaring is in the principle of feeling, and naturally the greater opportunity for success lies along the course of the most developed power. If, in a given case, the evolution of thought has not reached beyond the lower levels, then this thought may well serve to hobble the freer-roving feeling. In such a case, the shorter road normally will be through an Emancipated Feeling. But all this is only a general rule and should not be universalized into a Law.

This leads us to the practical question as to which sub-path a given individual should follow. It is determined by the quality which actually is most potent in the inner life of the individual. A man may be exceptionally skillful in the exercise of the power of thought and yet, in his inner nature, be genuinely grounded in feeling. Representatives of this class are not rare. Intellectually brilliant men, who genuinely love to attend symbolic religious services, are very apt to be instances. I do not mean men who attend or participate in such services as an example to others—a perfectly valid reason—but those who attend for their own sakes. In this they reveal what they really are, rather than what they seem to be because of an exercised skill. But in the case of the man for whom thought is the really decisive power, it is quite different. He may be more or less brilliant than the former example. The important differentia is that his life is implanted in his thought rather than his feelings. For him, the concept, and not the symbol, is the 'open sesame' that discloses Value.

Thought and feeling constitute the bases of two distinct sub-paths or disciplines, although these two fuse and become One at the end. It is difficult, if not quite impossible, for a man to succeed through a discipline foreign to his essential nature. It is good practice, therefore, for an aspirant, at an early stage, to acquire some familiarity with several disciplines.* He will find himself more in sympathy with one course of self-training than with others, and this will be indicative of what, for him, is the Way.

* These are forms of Yoga, for which, see my book on "Yoga, its Technique and Practice."

XXVI

The Sea of Consciousness

THE GRAND Sea of Consciousness unfolds before me on five levels. At the top is a Sea of Illimitable Depth and utter Calmness. Below This, and fusing into It, is another of mighty sweep, but not so vast in extent. Here there flow great waves in sonorous rhythm. Beneath this is a gulf and then a third sea possessed of boundaries, though its range is expanding. Here there are many sequences of waves flowing in numerous directions. There are harmonies in parts and blendings, but also there are clashings and some upheavals. Now and then, from out of this sea there arises, with a mighty whirling, a column that penetrates through the gulf and, occasionally, reaches the Sea above. Below the third sea, and contiguous to it, there is a fourth sea filled with much agitation. Waves are flowing without harmony or definiteness of direction. There is turmoil everywhere. Finally, at the bottom of all, there is a sluggish sea of no depth with low-powered waves having little meaning or purpose.

At the top is the Grand Sea of Infinite Consciousness, inexhaustible and without bounds. This is the seeming Emptiness that actually is the Fullness of the SELF—Pure Divinity, the Base of all else and the Final Resolution of all things. The next is the plane of Cosmic and Transcendent Consciousness. Here the One is also a Brotherhood. Likewise, permanence stands united with evolution. Below there is a gulf, not easy to cross; a gulf that mankind, in its folly, has widened while the Few, dedicated through Love to that mankind, strive ceaselessly to bridge the chasm. The third sea is the level of egoistic, or subject-object, consciousness in its highest state of development, the genuine upper-class of egoistic humanity. Here is the consciousness of those who move on the higher levels of love and intellect, but still within the limits of subject-object consciousness. These form the real 'Chosen Race.' Without them, the gulf would be impassable for the great human mass, and then, ultimately, all would sink down and out through the sluggish sea of ignorance.

Of the human whole only a handful, relatively, abides in the third sea, yet they are the immediate sustainers of all civilizations, the *real* burden-bearers of this outer life. From among them also come the recruits that, now and then, succeed in crossing the gulf. The fourth sea is of narrow limits, but heavily crowded with a large proportion of humanity. These are the quasi-intellectual, the semi-cultured, the mass that has become conceited with a little knowledge and does not know the saving humility of much knowledge. On this level are the senseless disputations fraught with emotion and passion. This is where the surgings arise that cause the turmoil of nations and classes. Yet there is some Light here, and the energy generated by Desire, the latter, to be sure, untrained and poorly directed, but still affording a force that eventually may be harnessed and guided. There still remains much hope for these despite their great folly. The fifth sea, shallow and very constricted, is densely crowded with the greatest mass of all. These are the sodden ones, drugged from drinking the final dregs of passion, those who bear little of the burden, but who are themselves the great burden. This sea is murky with the stirred-up mud of the depths, so there is only a dim twilight of the self-conscious light here. Yet there is a degree of self-consciousness, and so this lower realm does stand above the animal, even though sinking, in many respects, deep into the animal consciousness, and, by this illicit union, producing something lower than the animal. Often it seems that the passing of the cycles will not give time enough for these to rise again out of the depths into which they have sunk. For nothing is more hopeless than the task of revitalizing the sodden leaf that has sunk to the bottom of the stream. And, with respect to those leaves that have not quite sunk to the bottom, the task is of immense difficulty. It is far easier to transmute active and powerful evil than to arouse consciousness out of the dreamlike trance of soddenness. Yet much may be salvaged, and so long as the Spark is not completely extinguished, it is always possible that the Flame may be awakened anew.

Those of the lowest sea scarcely know that the third sea exists and are utterly ignorant of the realms beyond the gulf. Hence the denizens of this region frequently turn upon their own leaders and, in their ignorance, often destroy the very ones who are their hope. It is better to be the slave of an unkind master, provided the latter is superior, than to be left helplessly alone in the deeps. For a superior man, even though not so great as to have transcended selfishness, when he makes use of an inferior man, however selfish his motive, does raise the latter by the action of an inviolable law. For, inasmuch as it is true, that when a bird consumes a butterfly it raises the latter to its own level, so does the superior man raise the inferior by making use of him. Thoroughgoing and intelligent selfishness would never exploit inferiors. But as selfishness nearly always does so exploit, it is, therefore, made to serve the Great End despite itself, but does not share the Joy of that service. For any attention given by a superior to an inferior tends to raise the latter toward superiority in some measure. The law invoked here is as inevitable in its action as that related one in physics whereby an electric field tends to electrify objects in its vicinity. If ever the effort to remove really superior classes in this world should succeed, then there would soon be left only the lowest or fifth sea, with inevitable extinction as its ultimate doom. Who, then, are the real friends of mankind, the levelers or the exalters?

A simile comes to mind that, quite fairly, represents what the leveling process would really mean if successful. Suppose the lithosphere of the earth were all leveled to a common mean. Then there would be no dry land anywhere, but only an ocean of water, rolling over all. This would mean no sub-aerial life on dry land anywhere. There would be no plateaus—and all continents are plateaus—and no mountain peaks. Now all cultures that we know have developed with dry land as the physical basis of life. So, under our supposition, there could be no development of these. Thus there could be none of the grand procession of the scaled existences we know, leading up to the exalted Consciousness symbolized by the Mountain Top. And without the ascending ladder of Life, there would be no help anywhere to lead on and guide the water-bound existences.

XXVII

I Who Speak

SOMETIMES AS I WRITE, the 'I' becomes 'We' and yet remains 'I.'

There is a Consciousness which, while It remains One, is a symphony of harmoniously blended parts.

I write, and *I* watch myself writing.

I Know, and yet I wonder at the knowing.

I am the student and, at the same time, *I* am the Teacher.

As Teacher, *I* stand in Majesty looking upon the world below.

As student, I look up, humbly and amazed.

I speak and, presently, there blends with my voice the melodious Voices of Others.

One Meaning in many tones is unfolded.

So the tones of the seven-stringed Lyre are all sounded; one here, another there, in groups and, finally, all together.

And before this Melody I sit entranced, filled to the brim and more.

I who Speak none ever will know until, on that final Day he finds Himself, when *I* will appear in all My Glory.

XXVIII

How to Understand Mystic Writings

AS I LOOK BACK upon these writings, I note the curious fact that, at times, there is an impulse to write essentially poetic ideas. In these cases, admittedly, the form is not poetical in the conventional sense, but the essence is. Now, heretofore, throughout my life I have not been a lover of poetry and, much of the time, I had a decided distaste for it. Much less was I ever a writer of poetry. Yet now there comes a thought which requires poetry for its expression!

As I run through the pages of Bucke's "Cosmic Consciousness" I find a notable tendency, in the instances that he gives of what he calls the 'Cosmic Sense,' to give expression in poetry, though generally in the free form. The reason is becoming clear to me. Consciousness, descending from above the field of subject-object knowledge, is distorted just as soon as it is forced into the relative form of expression. In the latter field, discursive formulation has finished its task when it has finally shown what non-relative Knowledge is not. It clears the ground so that no obstruction remains for entering the Darkness and Silence. But when the 'Voice of the Silence' speaks into the relative world, the Meaning lies between the words, as it were, rather than in the direct content of the words themselves. The result is that the external meaning of the words, in a greater or less degree, seems like "foolishness," as St. Paul said. Such writings, read in the ordinary subject-object sense of meaning, are often quite unintelligible and, in cases where they do convey a connected meaning, it is not quite this meaning, but something else, that is the real Meaning intended. We may say that the sequence of words is like the obverse side of an embroidered design. One must turn to the other side of the cloth to see the real figure. But the threads on the obverse side are continuous with those that actually display the design and, thus, there is a correlation. So it is with the words of the poet who is Awakened to the Cosmic or Transcendent. They become threads by which the intuitive consciousness may be stirred to a Recognition of an inexpressible Reality. The obverse may be quite lacking in pattern and, in that case, the writings are wholly unintelligible to the ordinary egoistic consciousness. On the other hand, they may be woven into a secondary pattern that is intelligible, which, therefore, more effectively holds the attention of the subject-object consciousness.

The foregoing indicates how to read poetry or other forms of expression of this type. The reading should be done without strained effort in the intellectual sense. The reader should let a sort of 'current' flow into and through him, and not feel troubled as to whether he has understood anything or not, at the time. He may feel, or deeply cognize, something, though he may be unable to say what it is. If he is responsive, he will presently feel filled in a very curious but satisfying sense. He will return to the same Fount again and again, and presently, from out of Inner Meaning, understanding will begin to blossom in him. Perhaps he will find a degree of Recognition induced. Then, for him, the mystic writers will become progressively less and less obscure. He will enter into Communion on the level of a new kind of Language. On the new Level he will find the Living Presence of Those who have gone before him by the same Route. There is no death There, the possession or non-possession of physical bodies being of no moment.

XXIX

Concerning Opposition Aroused by Sages

WHY DO THE WORDS of a Mystic or a Sage so often arouse such severe antagonism? Take, for instance, poems like the "Leaves of Grass" by Walt Whitman. They have aroused storms of criticism as well as enthusiastic admiration. Yet, on the other hand, readers of all sorts generally are not troubled by the weird meanderings of the written words of an insane mind. This reveals the fact that it is not simply the unconventionality of the form that stirs the antagonism. Now these storms of criticism are really tributes. They indicate, at least, an unconscious recognition of Power in the words of the Mystic or the Sage. The complacency of the forces of Mara—to employ a Buddhist term—has been struck a vital blow, and this arouses resistance. But in all such engagements, Mara is doomed to defeat, for the Power that has burst forth is united with the inexhaustible Fount. The only effective defense for Mara would be complete indifference. For if Mara causes any man to fight the Light, that man, sooner or later, is conquered by the Light and then becomes One with It. St. Paul affords us the classic example. He fought earnestly and sincerely so that quickly the Light conquered him and claimed him for Its own. From the standpoint of Mara there is nothing more dangerous than an effort to slay a Sage or Mystic. The latter, in Their real Natures are invulnerable and, in the end, win to Themselves their would-be slayers.

XXX

The Record Continued

September 1

AGAIN, LAST EVENING, I was in the state of contemplative Joy. In a growing degree, I feel It as something Sacred. Spontaneously, I tend to tread gently in Its Presence. I mean this, principally, in the sense of the treading of thought and feeling, but the physical action must be gentle also. Given a slow and passionless movement with respect to all actions, from thought downward,—the state persists. With rapid shifts, the state tends to break off. Precisely that which is required in the driving of an automobile in traffic is peculiarly unfavorable to this kind of consciousness. Traffic driving requires a rapid noting of impressions and the forming of judgments as to whether those impressions are relevant to action and, if so, then the forming of the appropriate judgment of action. Often a new impression, such as another car entering into an intersection close in front, forces a sudden interruption in the execution of a previously formed judgment. This tends to produce an effect almost, if not quite, like a shock. Clearly there is some danger in this. Steady rhythm in the whole process becomes difficult. Consciousness is forced violently to the surface, and the inner state is broken, also violently.

There is a serious conflict between the requirements of a mechanical age and the conditions essential to inward penetration. I do not refer to the state of consciousness of the mechanical engineer, but to the kind of life the machine forces upon men. Keen alertness on the surface is essential in order to survive in this kind of life. The resultant effect is superficiality, even though an increase of keenness is forced. Profundity is quite compatible with keenness but it is antagonistic to superficiality. It does seem that it is going to be difficult for man to achieve real happiness in the midst of this mechanical age.

This morning I awoke with a feeling of deflation in the physical body, but a little later I entered the contemplative state while tracing out a line of thought. At once there was happiness and comfort in the body, combined with the sense of well-being that penetrates through and through. What a wonderful power lies in a simple turn of thought! I recall the old materialistic outlook wherein we regarded the objects given through the senses as being substantial external existences, subsisting by themselves independently of consciousness. How inexplicable would be all this which I now experience from that standpoint! However, there is naturally in this inward Life a great mystery when It is viewed from the perspective of consciousness grounded in the physical world. We know the enormous energetic effort required to move even a relatively small portion of this world. It seems as though here must be something substantial and massive that is quite too much for anything, seemingly so delicate as a thought or a state of consciousness, to master and transform. Yet such is the case!

XXXI

The Level of Real Equality

IN THE INWARD COMMUNION there is an Equality not known out here. However, it is not equality in the geometrical sense of the agreement of superimposed configurations. Equality does not exist within the space-time manifold. But the basis of the Communion There is not within the complex of space, time, and causality. Evolved degrees or states exist and, in this sense, every man, be he

God-Realized or not, is different from and, therefore, not equal to, any other man. Thus the real Equality is equality with differences, and the range of differences exceeds the range of relative imagination. In the evolved sense, greater and less persist, but in the inmost sense there is Equality.

Within the field of the egoistic consciousness there is no equality, save in the one respect that all on this level are grounded on the egoistic base. To attempt to impose equality upon men in any other sense is to submit them to the torture of the Procrustean bed. There is no other folly more destructive than that. Equality, in this lower sense, if successfully imposed, would require the absolute destruction of all freedom. For freedom implies, among other things, the right to grow differently and to grow rapidly or slowly. Man has a right to choose to become wise, but the inescapable corollary of this is the right to choose the path of folly, but without hope of escaping the price of folly. Now, it is not wise to try to save men from the price of folly, for it is a necessary teacher. However, it is always true Compassion to seek to arouse in men a desire for Wisdom.

XXXII

The Greatness of Man

THERE IS A GREATNESS within every human soul.

I sense this greatness in growing degree.

Something there is in every man to which I offer the gesture of respect.

As men become truly sane they reveal to Me new facets of Myself, and I feel a kind of wonder before these.

These Brothers enrich Me by revealing Myself to Myself and myself.

XXXIII

The Moral Problem

THE PREPONDERANT PORTION of the literature outlining the conditions favorable to the Awakening lays heavy stress upon the cultivation of the moral qualities. The central emphasis is placed upon the elimination of a selfish point of view, i.e., a base of action, thought, motivation, valuation, etc., grounded in a self regarded as distinct from other selves. Now the Awakened Consciousness tends to manifest on the ethical level outlined in the above literature. It does this, not as a matter of forcing upon the individual an externally formulated and imposed code, but as a spontaneous expression growing out of the very Consciousness Itself. The egoistic perspective is completely submerged in fully Awakened Consciousness and, in progressive degree, this is so as the Consciousness unfolds from the Twilight stage to full Glory. For the Awakened Man, the moral problem ceases to exist in the usual sense. There may remain the technical problem of what in action is the wisest course, but there no longer exists for Him the task of mastering egoistic consciousness. There are higher fields of moral choice within the Awakened Consciousness, but they lie beyond the range of apprehension of purely egoistic consciousness.

Now the rationale behind the ethical discipline is clear. He who causes himself to act, think, feel, etc., in a form that is, in fact, the natural expression of the Awakened Consciousness, sets up a condition that tends to induce that consciousness. It is simply another illustration of the familiar relationship manifested between electricity and magnetism. An electric current always produces a magnetic field, but, likewise through the appropriate employment of a magnetic field, we can induce an electric current.

In spite of the practical importance of the moral discipline, however, it remains true that the Awakening can, and has, taken place in the midst of a life even less moral, in the *objective sense,* than the average. To be sure, the Awakening, in such cases, effects at once a moral revolution and a radical change of character. This simply shows that the preliminary moral discipline, while of the highest desirability, is not a *sine qua non* of Recognition of, at least a minor order. Some other contributory external circumstance or, perhaps, pure and unaided spontaneity may effect the Transition.

The moral discipline may be regarded as an approach toward the Goal through emphasis of the negation of evil. But that, which from one standpoint appears as evil, in other aspects, appears as ignorance, hate, and ugliness. We may call that which appears in such multiform negative aspects by the name 'Mara.' Now Mara may be destroyed through any of its facets and the destruction of the other facets follows sooner or later. There are thus disciplines of Beauty, Love, and Knowledge which effect the same consummation as the moral discipline. He who becomes identical with Beauty is incapable of producing ugliness, including moral ugliness. During the intermediate stages of aesthetic consciousness there may be a considerable association with immorality, but in the end the devotion to Beauty must destroy the latter, because of its essential ugliness. The man whose nature is Beauty cannot help but be a good man, once he has become identical with that Beauty. Love achieves the same end by another road. The negation of Love is hate. He who identifies himself with Love drowns the capacity to hate and, therefore, does not act along the lines that are the normal expression of hate. Thus spontaneously he tends to act, feel, think, etc., in accordance with the code of selflessness. Love, too, in its intermediate stages may violate the code, but if the devotion to Love remains unabated, gradually or rapidly it becomes purified. Then unlovely conduct becomes impossible.

There remains the Path of Knowledge. From the perspective of the highest Knowledge all evil is ignorance. My own conviction accords with the teaching of Shankara, in holding that there is no such thing as an essentially evil will. Definitely I take exception to St. Paul on this point, and challenge all of that phase of so-called Christian orthodoxy that is built upon the doctrine of the existence of an autonomously evil will. In fact, Will is neither good nor evil but an entirely neutral power. The Will directed by ignorance becomes evil in its manifestation, but if directed by Knowledge it either becomes good or manifests on a level where the duality of good and evil is not relevant. Thus, from the standpoint of the Path of Knowledge, the only problem is the destruction of Ignorance. With the destruction of Ignorance, Mara is destroyed automatically with all Its works. But this Knowledge is not to be confused with information. A man may have Realized his identity with Knowledge and yet be poorly informed; likewise, a well informed man may be quite blind to this Knowledge. Now, let us say, that through Knowledge a given man has attained Recognition of his identity with the SELF. At that moment he has placed himself knowingly outside the reach of all powers inferior to the SELF, and that means he is beyond all relative powers, including evil. For him the selfless code becomes spontaneously his mode of expression, and then progressively the personal nature becomes freed from old habits. It has been my personal conviction that Knowledge is the greatest Power of all and in this I seem to be in accord with the preponderant judgment of the Indian Sages. But if the Path of Knowledge is the one of greatest Power, it is also one that is least available. Thus practically other disciplines have the greater pragmatic availability.

We are not here concerned with the problem of the origin of evil, but only with that practical one of its destruction. Evil causes suffering; Knowledge destroys evil; seek, therefore, for that Knowledge and, having attained It, all evil and all suffering will vanish as has the forgotten dream of long ago.

XXXIV

Solar and Planetary Recognition

THE MAN who has awakened to Cosmic Consciousness may become a Planet, but likewise, He may become a Sun. I do not mean that, at once, He becomes enrobed in those great bodies known to astronomers as planets and stars. But I do mean something that, in the essential sense, is the same thing, although there is a wide range of difference in degree. The point is that whereas the earmark of the common consciousness of humanity is egoism, the Cosmic Consciousness is planetary or stellar in the *primary* sense. He who becomes a Sun is grounded directly in the SUPREME and thus is in high degree a Self-luminous and independent body. A planet is a body of minor luminosity which moves in an orbit around some sun. Thus a man may attain Recognition, but be so drawn by sympathetic attraction to another Liberated Soul as to revolve in the orbit of the latter. As one reads through the record of Those who have awakened Cosmic Consciousness, it is not difficult to recognize these two tendencies. Many place themselves in very humble relationship to a transcendent Greatness that has burst out within them; and, while they may say, "I am this Greatness," in practice they identify themselves with the outer man and bow humbly before a transcendent Otherness. Or, again, there may be an attitude of subservience to another God-Realized Man who may have been the inspiration that aroused the Awakening. Here is revealed the planetary tendency. Shankara has warned that no man should regard any Realization as greater than his own. Each Realized Man should hold this thought, if he can, "There can be nothing greater than the Supreme Realization which I have." If this attitude is held unshaken, then that Man becomes a Sun. The following point should be borne clearly in consciousness: 'However true it may be that there are greater Suns and greater evolutionary unfoldments, my own Inner Realization is the highest.' Any other view involves duality and, hence, a planetary state in the Cosmic Life. But if a man cannot become a Sun, let him, by all means, become a Planet and play his part in the Grand Symphony—the Communion of Free Souls.

64

XXXV

Recognition and the Physical Body

IT IS NECESSARY that the Current be attuned to the resources of the body and particularly to the nervous system. While in the Current, I feel exaltation and a sense of well-being that reaches well down into the outer organism, yet this does not change the fact that the Current is a powerful energy and does tax certain powers of endurance. In the deflated state there is a feeling of fatigue, not unlike that which accompanies a conflict with illness. At such times it is necessary to resist a psychological depression. The physical body is clearly the weakest link, and there is a temptation to retreat from this in the periods of deflation. I can suggest the feeling, if the body is thought of as something like a ten ampere fuse, while from the transformer, just beyond, there is being delivered a current on the order of one hundred amperes at a high potential. One is constantly under a pressure to use more than ten amperes and thus strain the fuse close to the point of burning out. Yet, if that fuse is burned out, correlation with this plane is broken and the expression here will remain unfinished.

Ecstatic states, experienced after placing the body in complete trance, do not involve the same problem. But in that case very little of the Inner Consciousness is likely to be carried down through the physical brain and the nervous organism, thus resulting in a corresponding limitation of outer expression. So from the standpoint of expression in this world, the physical brain and nervous system are the critical links.

From the standpoint of Recognition, the gross body is valuable only as an instrument, primarily for the reaching of other embodied consciousnesses. It is no longer of vital importance for its own sake or as a means of experience, since, for him who has once reached the Source of Joy and Knowledge, all of the delights and information which may be derived from experience become mere shadows for which he tends to feel a certain disgust. But the gross body still remains valuable as an instrument of action and requires the attention which a good artisan would give a useful tool, but no more. Here we come face to face with one of the higher temptations, i.e., the neglecting or letting go of an instrument which is a brake upon the play of the Higher Consciousness, whether in the sense of Knowledge or Ecstasy. An instance which illustrates this point is found in the case of a certain Oriental who, in the early part of his life, had become a college professor. He attained Illumination, and then naturally his center of interest shifted to the Higher World. He did not forget this physical world, however, and did leave it considerable benefit from his new insight. According to his own account, he finally planned a systematic philosophic statement, but the inward attraction had now become so strong that the desire to give expression to his Recognition withered. He moved more and more into the life of meditation, and finally, when bathing in a stream, was drowned, owing to his having entered an inward state while in the water. The world lost something this man could have left, for he had the power of expression in high degree. From His own standpoint, to be sure, He had merely dropped a fetter, but the present is not a time when, in general, such men may rightly feel themselves free to disregard the needs of others while satisfying Their own inner convenience.

It is difficult for the average individual, caught in the hypnotic glamour of embodied consciousness, to understand the attitude toward physical embodiment which Recognition, at least above a certain level, induces in the Realized Man. Let me assure the reader that this position is not artificial, nor forced, nor due to pessimism. It is just as natural as the distaste the normal man would feel for life in a front-line trench during a modern war. Cheerfully he may choose to accept his tour of duty in the front lines because he feels that his country needs his service there, but wholeheartedly he abominates the life. He will not feel it a hardship when circumstances so change that he will not be needed at the front. Well, let me assure anyone who doubts, that the Inward Life is so immeasurably richer than outer life that the keenest sensual enjoyment is relatively pain. Hence, a tour of duty in gross physical embodiment is relatively like a period of life at the front during warfare. In addition to the inmost and grandest State of all, there are other Worlds, more subtle than this outer field of life, where Consciousness is also embodied, and the Life There is immeasurably richer than all life here below. Therefore, why cling to the false glamour of life cast in the dregs?

Upon the stagnant water of a swamp, filled with rotting vegetation and sewage, there is often seen an oily film, reflecting iridescent colors. In this there is a small measure of beauty, but so poor when compared with other and greater beauties. This oil-film is a fit symbol of the keener delights of the unillumined sensuous life. Is it other than natural that a man who has found greater and richer beauties should wish to turn his back upon the oil-film of the swamp?

XXXVI

Concerning Occult Powers

IN THE BROAD SENSE, the 'occult' means all that is hidden to the given level of consciousness which is taken as the base of reference. Thus, to the simple consciousness of the animal, the egoistic consciousness which underlies our familiar culture and civilization is occult. A few of the higher animals, such as some dogs, do show signs indicating adumbrations of values characteristic of egoistic consciousness, and thus they are reaching to the morning twilight of the latter level. But this happens because these few individuals have come close to man, who plays for them an analogous part to that of the Guru to the Chela at a still higher level. Relative to the consciousness of the vast majority of animals, these few favored individuals occupy a position similar to that of a partial initiation into an occult domain. In these cases we have simply instances of devoted aspiration, on the part of the individuals with the less evolved consciousness, and induction from him of the superior consciousness.

Within the egoistic field, there is a relatively wide range from those individuals who have just sufficiently established their base here to be called men—such as the Bushmen of Australia—, up to the highest evolved consciousness which yet falls short of the higher Awakened Consciousness. In a secondary sense, we may say that the higher cultures are occult for primitive man. But, in time, evolution will cross this range without an act of radical transcendence. For this is development within the field of a given type of consciousness, in this case, egoistic or subject-object consciousness. When the term 'occult' is applied in this connection, it is not employed in the strict sense, for the latter implies a radical shift of base.

With reference to the preponderant portion of humanity, the 'Occult' means that Consciousness which is realized when the Awakening has come. None of the Knowledge which is the common possession of this Higher Level can be understood by the purely egoistic man. Efforts at cross-translation do enrich the egoistic consciousness and tend to arouse the Awakening in those who are still sleeping, but whatever is understood within the egoistic range is essentially different from the Awakened Consciousness, as such. There is an irreducible incommensurability which forever makes correct cross-translation impossible. Even though a man is functioning on both levels, he cannot effect the really correct cross-translation in his own consciousness. He is, in a sense, both the circle and the square. He has, or is, Knowledge in both senses simultaneously, yet the essential nature of the higher type remains inexpressible in terms of the lower. Still there is such a thing as approximation to cross-translation in much the sense that a mathematician can give an approximate rational evaluation of an irrational number, such as $\sqrt{2}$. But though this approximation may be carried to any number of decimal places —the greater number of decimal places corresponding to the greater skill in cross-translation—and a value be attained which serves all the practical requirements of applied mathematics, yet, from the standpoint of the values absolutely essential to pure mathematics,* the effort has been a complete failure. For the Man who has Awakened in the higher sense and who still continues to function within the egoistic level, neither domain is any longer occult in the strict sense, however much remains occult in the sense of not having yet been mastered. So, to Awake is to Know the Occult or, rather, to become identical with Occult Knowledge.

In certain respects it is perfectly proper to attempt a cross-translation of the higher Occultism into the egoistic level, by as skillful means as may be devised. This applies to the more highly spiritual phase of the Occult, and that phase actually is the most important, for it affords the Key which ultimately renders possible the unlocking of the rest. This is the Occultism of Self-Recognition. He who has become well rooted in the SELF is superior to all the lesser powers, and thus stands, in principle, in a position where it is safe for Him to acquire the technique requisite for their manipulation. But even in this cross-translation there is such a thing as 'spiritual dynamite.' However, in general, the individual not qualified for use of this is protected by a lack of interest, or a deficiency of understanding, so that such literature seems either uninteresting or meaningless to him.

There are, however, other domains of the Occult where enough of real power could be conveyed in cross-translation so that a dangerous misuse would become possible. There are powers, sufficiently within the range of egoistic control that, if they are viciously employed or, through inadequate understanding or control, misapplied, would effect far worse results than the simple destruction of physical life. It is clear that such powers must be artificially veiled and guarded, if the human race is not to suffer incalculable injury. Naturally, only men of proved character and capacity can be safely admitted into the knowledge of such arcana.

It by no means follows that because a man has Awakened and therefore crossed the Gulf, thus becoming essentially a citizen of the

* The relationship between the two levels of consciousness is represented, in the form of analogy, very beautifully by just the difference which separates pure from applied mathematics.

Inner World, He consequently enters into possession at once of all Powers subject to that level of Consciousness. Some Powers He has, by reason of the simple fact of Awakening, and these are reflected automatically in his life, his writings, etc. He does influence others in certain respects quite beyond the range of other men who, however skillful and able they may be, yet remain centered within the egoistic consciousness. But there are innumerable specific Powers affecting all departments of nature, both in the sense of knowledge-penetration and of capacity for active manipulation, that can be aroused and mastered. Probably few, if any, Proficients in this field actually have unfolded all possible Powers that fall within the range or level of evolution on which They stand. We have here a natural analogue with a familiar fact that obtains among men on the egoistic level. Some have capacities in one direction, others in still other directions, and no one man in one embodiment is equally proficient in all. Specific powers are awakened by the appropriate effort and evolution. The Inner World is not poorer, but richer, in the range of variety It unfolds; and, save in the very highest sense, there is in this Domain that which corresponds to 'time' on the objective levels. It is another kind of 'time,' to be sure, but, at least, there is that which is analogous to that which is called 'progress,' in this inferior world. So there is much to be done, and while Proficients move within a totally different base of reference, still They are Men and not strange Beings wholly beyond the limits of all relativity. The Awakening is one fact, the most important of all, the list of developed powers quite another; and the forms of development are distinctly variable from individual to individual.

The primary principle whereby these Higher Powers are possible is simple, once the essential nature of Reality is apprehended. If the primary assumptions of the naturalists or the materialistic realists were correct, these Powers would be quite unthinkable. But the Real is Consciousness, and the development of the universe is a projection from pure subjectivity outward. At least it is so, when conceived from the relative standpoint. I produce, therefore, this world through My Power of Ideation, Will, etc. Hence, within the limits of the Law, which is also Myself, I can mold and transform that world by the same Power which produced it. The Adept Man is identical with the Divinity, which I AM, hence through Him I act in the manipulation of My universe. This, of course, does not give the technical details, which can be learned more or less quickly, but it does give the principle whereby the whole idea of Occult Powers can be apprehended as rational, and not involving the supernatural, however much the Powers may be super-normal so far as the common experience of humanity is concerned.

The question is often asked: "Why, if there are Men who have such Powers, is the manifestation of them so rare?" It has, in fact, seemed to many that the demonstration of Powers would go far in convincing men of their own erroneous ideas in such matters, and thus serve to stimulate research in the right direction. In answer, it may be pointed out first, that there have been a few, well-attested demonstrations; and, second, ancient traditions are full of reference to them. Signs are not wanting, though admittedly they are not numerous and generally have to be searched out. But there are reasons why care is always exercised in the demonstration of Powers. The most important of these is based upon a consideration of the effect the manifestation of Powers has upon men whose understanding is not sufficiently prepared. The average man regards such Powers as supernatural or miraculous. Note, for example, the predominant attitude that has obtained throughout Christendom during the last 1900 years with respect to the works of Jesus. Now, if men regard a Power as supernatural, the result is growth of superstitions, instead of progress toward the essentially rational outlook which is so vitally important to real Mastery. In such cases, the demonstration of Powers produces just the reverse effect of that desired. Superstition is a fatal barrier to God-Realization. Divinity, for the superstitious, is either an object on which to place irrational confidence, or one to be feared. The result is a widening, not a closing, of the gap between man and his God. Few effects could be worse than that. So it remains a rule that before a man may witness a demonstration he must first become well familiarized with the philosophy that will enable him to comprehend it within a rational outlook. He must come to see the Power, as in principle, at least, within the range of his own latent capacities, once they are unfolded. When this is the case, demonstrations may be helpful.

We do not tamper with the growth of men in such a way that they cease to be self-determined. No man is endowed with Powers as a free gift. They must all be acquired, and while We may exercise a directing hand, the impulse to effort must spring up spontaneously from within the consciousness of each individual. A Power, once achieved, is a possession of the man who has mastered It and can be lost only through his own unwise action, although temporarily We may suppress It when its premature exercise would do injury to larger issues, either within the individual himself, or to the larger whole.

XXXVII

The Underlying Force in Religion

IN A FUNDAMENTAL SENSE, sometimes in a highly exalted form, but often not so exalted, the underlying force in religion is the same one that draws men and women together. When there is genuine religious ecstasy, some phase of the creative principle is manifesting, occasionally on an exceedingly lofty level, but more often on levels of progressive inferiority until, in the depths, we find the Voodoo and similar practices. A study of religious history shows a recurring tendency for religious practice to assume a phallic form, sometimes quite gross, at other times more or less hidden.

In the higher sense, the Creative Principle is sacred and is properly a part of pure religiosity. In the Christian religion it is veiled under the word 'Holy Ghost.' This should make clear why the sin against the Holy Ghost is regarded as so serious. Now the sin consists in dragging the Creative Principle into a gross and impure consciousness. Here is a realm where only the Pure in Heart may enter with safety. Let others beware!

The physiological aspect of this Principle is only one of its more inferior modes. Real creativeness is conscious. Now, while there is no sin in the normal manifestation of the physiological aspect, as such, the quality of consciousness associated therewith does determine whether the effects shall be good or evil. Impure human consciousness has its most serious effect when it is brought into correlation with the action of the Creative Principle on any level, but the higher the level the worse the effect. This is one way in which evil can be inoculated into Life. This is a very serious matter, for right here is where humanity has produced its own worst curse.

The higher aspects of the Creative Principle, of which there are several levels, become progressively more potent and more sacred until, at the top, we come into Recognition of the Celestial Virgin. He who fuses his consciousness with this Virgin no longer simply believes in or seeks Immortality, but Knows himself to be Immortal, nay more, He is Immortality. This should help to make clear what Supreme Value is veiled in the words 'Holy Ghost.'

But, however great the benediction of the Current of Bliss may be, he who would be Master must not abandon himself even to this Glory. There is such a thing as Divine Intoxication, and while many look upon the implied abandonment as a kind of virtue, they are only partly right. The true Priest must never permit himself to lose command, even in the presence of the highest exaltation, else for him the Supreme Enlightenment will remain unknown.

XXXVIII

Knowledge Through Identity

September 3

IT IS BECOMING CLEAR that there is a radical difference between formal and empirical knowledge on the one hand and Knowledge from the standpoint of the Awakened Consciousness. Unless this difference is understood, the speech and writings of the Sages and

Mystics will remain fundamentally incomprehensible for all those who remain confined within the egoistic consciousness. Formal and empirical knowledge—and here I mean all knowledge for which language is an adequate vehicle—is a knowledge of relationships. Thus, a word stands for an object which is, in some sense, other than the word. The objects, in this case, are not simply those represented by substantives, but also objects in the sense of actions, relations, qualities, etc. These objects may be gross or subtle, but, in any case, an otherness is implied. 'Truth' becomes defined as some sort of relation between the verbal ideas and the objects for which they stand. All of this knowledge is thus essentially external and stands out as something other than, or counter to, the egoistic self.* But Knowledge in this sense is of instrumental value only. Hence, through this knowledge, the 'Thing-in-itself' is never realized, for it imposes upon consciousness the seeming of distance. The result is that intellectuality, *if not consciously or unconsciously united to Real Knowledge,* has the effect of emptiness or 'thinness' which so impressed William James. Here we have the reason for the failure of the attempts to prove, formally, the existence of God. Formal demonstration cannot rise above its fount, but can make explicit all that is contained in the latter. Thus, a demonstration which starts from a fount that is less than Divinity can never prove the existence of Divinity. *God is either Known directly through Identity, or He is not known at all.*

In contrast to formal and empirical knowledge, Real Knowledge is essentially wordless, for It does not deal with objects. This is Knowledge through Identity. Hence, It does not *represent* Substance, but *is* Substance Itself. So, it is true that 'I'—the self or Atman— am not different from that Knowledge. The speech and writings of the God-Realized Men are not representations of external existences, but are the actual embodiments of the SELF. The Sage and the Mystic live in the words that They utter as truly as in Their fleshly encasements, and sometimes even more fully. Hence, to the reader or hearer these Words carry the very Presence Itself. Such Words, therefore,

* It is the external quality of this knowledge that makes the development of materialism possible.

74

have magical power to transform the man who attends to Them. Real Knowledge is not instrumental but is an End-in-Itself. It may be clothed in highly organized intellectual form and, in that case, we have true Philosophy, which also is an end-in-itself.

The way to reconcile William James and Hegel now becomes clear. Both men had a high degree of insight; and, if for them the Sun had not risen to shine with the clearest brilliance, then It was either near the horizon and about to rise, or had done so already and was merely obscured. If it had been shining clearly for James he could hardly have failed to recognize Hegel. Now with Hegel, the individual man, the principal development was in the intellect, while in the case of James it was in sensation and feeling, and this remains true in spite of the high development of intellectual skill which he possessed. With him intellect was foreign to the essential man, but not so with Hegel. Now Real Knowledge is most successfully expressed through and to a man in the phases most highly developed in his personal and individual nature. Not all Embodiments of the Word are equally accessible to all men. Even a God-Realized Man who lacked a given faculty could not Realize a manifestation of Real Knowledge through that faculty in an effective sense. On the levels of only partial Realization, a greater or less degree of Recognition may be given through the most highly developed doors, and yet fail through other avenues which are less developed. Hegel's philosophy is genuine and is grounded in Real Knowledge, however much, as a matter of logic, he may have failed to prove his Knowledge so that all rational men must agree.* Hegel's intellectuality does incarnate Substantiality and carries the Light, although James was unable to see It in that embodiment. Yet James did see the Light, else he could not have had so much sympathy with the essence of religion and responded so enthusiastically as he did to mystical writings, such as those of Gustav Theodor Fechner. But he was so constituted that he could not see that Light through the Door that Hegel opened.

* The logically perfect formulation of Real Knowledge has not yet been written. Not even Shankara was wholly successful, for in the light of our, at present, greater understanding of logic, it is possible to show inadequacy in Shankara, so far as formal demonstration is concerned.

It follows, that from the standpoint of James' vision, he was quite correct in regarding the intellect as only instrumental. He was wrong in universalizing his own standpoint. Intellectuality may be an embodiment of Substantiality, no less completely than may be the sensations and the affections; and, in that case, it enrobes Ends, and not merely means. As will be shown more fully later, all three modes of relative consciousness, cognition, affection and sensation, taken by themselves, equally fail to give substantial actuality. It is only when they are united to Knowledge through Identity that they actually embody Substantiality.

In the case we have just discussed, we come face to face with an example of a very common error among men who have at least a degree of genuine insight and may, in fact, have had their Suns rise to a considerable height. Such an individual often sees his way as the only Way and says, in effect, "By this road alone may you enter." It is not so. Any route which egoistic man may devise, in principle, can become a Way. It is a mistake to take one's own individual limitations and predicate them of Spirit. Always He who has Arrived may say: "This Way that I have traveled is a possible Way, for I have proven It; come and try It, for It may be a Way for you also." But for a given human soul that particular Route may be impractical, while some other Route may be the 'Open Sesame.'

The understanding of the place of logic is also becoming clear. There is no doubt that logic wields the final authority within the kind of knowledge that belongs to the subject-object manifold, in so far as logic has applicability. The law of contradiction is absolute in this domain. Every logical dichotomy divides the whole of the relative universe into two parts, so that of that universe we may always say: "It is either X or not-X." ('X' in this case standing for any concept whatsoever.) But from the standpoint of Real Knowledge such a dichotomy is neither true nor false, but simply irrelevant. It involves even more fundamental irrelevance than that contained in questions such as the following: "Is a lion organized according to the principles of a fugue or a symphony?" Likewise, from the perspective of Knowledge through Identity, there is no meaning in applying the logical criterion of contradiction. Here, within this subject-object, time-space manifold, there is no principle more fundamental than that 'A cannot be both A and not-A at the same time and in the same sense.' But what bearing could that possibly have upon a Consciousness which transcends both space and time, as well as the subject-object field? For all possible spaces and all possible times and every sense in which an idea may be employed are at once comprehended in the pure apperception of the SELF.

Still, it remains true that every expression within the subject-object manifold may be tried very properly by the canons of logic and, if found wanting, that expression must be judged incorrect. And this remains true of expressions cross-translated from Real Knowledge as well as others. But, despite all this and however incorrect the expression may be, if it is a cross-translation from Real Knowledge, it is True in the fundamental sense, for it carries Meaning. It is merely the vehicle that is inadequate. None the less, I am convinced that the Way is made clearer as the vehicle of expression is made more highly perfect, and that He who speaks from out the Fount should try to make himself as clear as possible.

XXXIX

The Meaning of Substance

FOR THE FIRST TIME, the word 'substance' has become really intelligible to me. I turn again to Spinoza's "Ethics" and read the third definition of the first part: "I understand SUBSTANCE to be that which is in itself and is conceived through itself." Many times I have struggled to give this definition an intelligible meaning, but never quite successfully. But now it stands out clearly and I know just exactly what it means. Heretofore, I tried to relate the notion of 'substance' to objects, even though in a subtle sense. But this is an error. No object, whatsoever, is 'in itself and conceived through itself.' I am that SELF and Recognize that I am that SELF, and now I

Realize what Substance is. Substance is not other than Myself.* But this Substance is just precisely that which cannot be predicated of ponderable matter, or of objects of the senses or of thought.

Spinoza's thought takes on a new clarity. There is difficulty in his mode of expression, for he uses words in a different way from that current now, but the real thought becomes clear without much effort. And why is this? It is simply that I now cognize his thought from the same standpoint from which he wrote. Take, for example, a chance sentence to which I turn in his "Short Treatise." It happens to be a sentence from Albert Schwegler's introductory summary of Spinoza's philosophy, but it very clearly carries Spinoza's meaning. "Felicity, then, is not the reward of virtue—it is virtue itself." In other words, real Happiness is virtue, and not merely an effect of virtuous living. This is quite clear. Happiness is the only praise or glorification of God. Happiness is the only worthy prayer. Happiness is virtue and gloom is sin. Now I arbitrarily shift myself back into the old egoistic consciousness, and all this sounds like nonsense. This is all due to the difference in the kind of knowledge, the Real Knowledge standing in incommensurable relationship to egoistic knowledge. But the Real Knowledge saves man, while the egoistic kind, by itself, cannot.

Which of these two kinds of knowledge is rational and which irrational? I should certainly say that the Real Knowledge is rational and commensurable—the latter term being interpreted in the sense of 'intelligible' rather than of measurable. But the subject-object standpoint would reverse this view. It is all a question of level or standpoint. But in the profounder sense my view is right.

* It is a very interesting fact, that in the experiencing of the Current which is Bliss on the 7th of last month, spontaneously I thought of It as Substance.

XLIII
The Record Continued

Now I PERCEIVE the progress of effects upon the physiological level. There is a perceptible increase of vigor in the gross body. Also there is a changing preference with respect to food. The desire and taste for meat is declining. Meat is not yet distasteful, but with continuation along this line, it will soon become so. I am becoming rather indifferent to concentrated sweets and, in general, I care less for the prepared foods. There is a mild increase of desire for fruits. But the predominant attitude toward food is one that is rather well filled with indifference and some distaste. However, on the other hand, I feel rather less need for gross nourishment.

Some years ago I had become completely disgusted with the doctrinaire dietetics, and have since taken a purely pragmatic view toward this subject. The latter course I have found practically the most satisfactory, and am continuing it at the present time. The changes of inclination, noted above, are quite free from pressure due to theoretical considerations.

XLIV
The Relation of Karma to Recognition

THE GREAT authoritative sources on Recognition, such as the Teachings of Buddha, the Writings of Shankara, the "Bhagavadgita," and the "Voice of the Silence" all state that the Realized Man is freed from the karma of past actions, save the karma that has already 'sprouted' and is the causal power which maintains the continuance of the current gross body. I have already testified to the sense

83

of feeling free from the action of karma at the time of the Transition. Further, it is a very common testimony found in the records of those who have attained Recognition; only, in many instances, the report is in the form of a statement affirming a feeling of freedom from sin. There is a very important principle involved here that should be made clear.

In its broadest sense, 'karma' means the concatenation of cause and effect that produces and sustains the existence of the universe, as a whole, as well as every unit within it. Everything in the universe exists in its present state or form as the result of past causes and, in its turn, is the cause of future states of the universe. Because of the interdependence of parts, it is impossible to know completely the karma of any part without knowing all that is to be known of the universe. But within the whole there are integrations about centers which have become individualized and thus are transformed into microcosms within the macrocosm. Whenever such a microcosm is integrated, it comes within a karmic stream that is its own in a peculiar sense, in addition to the general karma that involves all. Most generally the term 'karma' is employed as restricted to the narrower meaning, but there is no sharp demarcation between the two kinds of karma, and the lesser aspect can never be satisfactorily understood if it is taken in complete abstraction from the larger.

Necessarily, karma is limited to the field of space, time, and causality. Accordingly, the Man who has Recognized His Identity with the Supreme SELF, which abides beyond space, time and causality, and then completely withdraws within that SELF, will have destroyed all karma related to him as an individual. The objective elements, gross or subtle, that have been associated with his various embodiments, continue in the karmic stream in the Cosmic sense, but the microcosmic field of that individual is dissolved.

Since the dissolution of the microcosm is the negative equivalent of Liberation, the idea has been suggested by some that by the complete balancing of karma, thus effecting microcosmic dissolution, Liberation could be won without prior Recognition of the SELF. Shankara has pointed out the fallacy of this view and answered it at length. While such a course may not be strictly a theoretical impossibility, it is quite impractical for several reasons. We may regard the microcosm as something like a vortex in the universal plenum. It is produced by an impulse that tends to disturb the universal balance. But as the most primary law is Equilibrium—the noumenon of all other laws—karma is at once invoked as a counter-action. Further self-induced reactions to this opposed-action complicate the sequence until finally the microcosm is involved in a very elaborate bondage. Every action brings its fruits, and the experiencing of these fruits is what is technically called 'enjoyment,' whether pleasant, painful, or indifferent. A cause must be exhausted as effect or *balanced by just the right amount of appropriate counter-action*. Thus, an evil action can be exhausted by experiencing the corresponding suffering or by a good action which would balance it. But a surplus of good actions brings its effects, which must likewise be exhausted, and so on. It would require a superhuman wisdom to achieve just the perfect balance requisite, and all the while the individual would have to live a life so perfect that no shade of additional action was initiated that, in its turn, would require further balancing. Further, it would be rare indeed that all the seeds of past karma would sprout in any one life, since other conditions than those afforded by that given life may be required for their germination. So not one, but a series of perfect lives, without one flaw in the balancing of counter causes, would be required. All this must be done by a man who, by hypothesis, is not Illumined and therefore is bound within the subject-object manifold—a condition which makes superhuman wisdom impossible. So, it seems the unavoidable conclusion that there is no hope of 'breaking-through' in this way.

But by Recognition man destroys his identification with the microcosm and Realizes himself as identical with the SELF of all. This destroys the microcosm so far as he, himself, is concerned. This microcosm continues, for a time, as an appearance in the space-time world, because of the karma that has already sprouted, but the Real Man is no longer incarnated there, in the usual sense, and sooner or later dissolution will finally liquidate the apparent embodiment. This temporary continuation is like the continued revolving of the fly-wheel of an engine from which the power has been shut off. The engine is stopped in the essential sense, and will become fully stopped shortly.

One of the consequences of the nature of the Law is that good works bind men as much as evil works. Thus, unfinished 'good' karma is as truly a source of bondage as unfinished 'bad' karma. Also, in principle, Recognition frees a man whose residual karma is predominantly 'bad' as truly as in the case of the man where the residue is mostly 'good.' But the former condition is the more un-favorable one, and so the practice of positive virtue is of distinct importance. The really vital point to note is that it is not action, whether 'good' or 'bad,' that frees, but an attitude of detachment with respect to all action. Thus, a self-righteous man, by which is meant one who is attached to his good works and is overly self-conscious of them, is further from the Recognition than the man who, while doing much evil, has really freed himself from interest in and attachment to his evil works.

In the case of the Man for whom the Sun of Recognition has risen sufficiently so that during life in the body He has entered the fringe of Nirvana, it is possible, after the dissolution of the physi-cal organism, to enter Nirvana, or the Kingdom of Heaven, com-pletely. He has now fully severed himself from his former micro-cosmic karma. In choosing such a course, in general, He invokes a higher Law which has Its effects upon another level, but that may be ages hence so far as relative time is concerned. The question now arises: What becomes of his former karmic seeds that had not yet sprouted when He became fully one with Nirvana? The answer to this question introduces a principle of the Higher Knowledge which is considerably at variance with an important working hypothesis of physical science. Accordingly this point will require some discussion.

The term 'universe,' as employed in this discussion, is restricted to manifested existences, whether in a gross or subtle sense. Behind the universe is the unmanifested actuality, called here 'Transcen-dental Consciousness' or 'Absolute Consciousness.' To enter the Nir-vanic state is to leave the universe in this respect, that is, the whole field of space, time, and causality, in the usual sense. But this Higher World is to the lower as the Infinite is to a finite manifold, and the whole universe depends upon the former as its sustaining principle. What becomes energy and ultimately matter here is derived from the Substance of that higher level. The interplay between these two domains, speaking now from the relative standpoint, is not an event which took place once for all in the historic past, but one which continues, either intermittently or continuously, throughout the present. Thus there is such a thing as the total supply of energy and matter in the universe increasing at times and, at others, decreasing. This does imply the ultimate falseness of the hypothesis of physical science to the effect that the total supply of matter-energy in the universe remains constant. It is true that such matter and energy do not come from nothing and do not, in turn, become nothing, but these modes do come into and leave the universe. This fact, among other things, affords a totally new statement of the problem of perpetual motion. Another important consequence is that we will have to forego the hope of setting up an energetic equation between the universe as it is at any given time and that universe at some other time. In fact, the recognition of this principle would in time utterly change the form of science, including even sociology and economics. For, if an infinite resource, covering all departments of life, actually is and may be tapped, then the human problem in all these departments takes on quite a different form from that where a finite or limited supply is assumed.

Now when a man enters Nirvana, He closes His karmic accounts, as it were, not by becoming inaccessible to his creditors, but, on the contrary, by paying all His debts in another and immeasurably better coin. It is as though a man had contracted debts in terms of the various base metals and then finally paid those debts in an equal or greater weight of pure gold. Thus none of the creditors are cheated, but quite otherwise they are enriched as never before. The method involved in this process is, in one sense, simple, yet at the same time quite mysterious. When, through Recognition, a Man pierces into the Nirvanic Level, He becomes consciously One with an Infinite Sea of Consciousness and Energy. From this inexhaustible supply, at once and automatically, He pours forth values to all those with whom He has karmic obligations, and this act leads all such forward, in some degree, toward their own Recognition. There is no debt that such a service would not repay abundantly. Thus no Man enters Nirvana without in some measure blessing the world in that very achievement.

The difference between the Man who enters fully and finally into Nirvana and the Man who refuses this Bliss consists in part in the fact that the blessing left by the former is restricted to those with whom He, as an individual, has karmic obligations, while in the case of the latter, in addition to this service, He also volunteers to continue to lift, as far as may be, the general load of the human whole. The latter, having squared His accounts, is free to choose future Bliss, but He reveals a Heart of Compassion in refusing to do so while other creatures are still suffering. These Men really occupy a station in the Gulf between the Higher and lower worlds, and are in a position to employ the resources of Wisdom and Power of that Higher World to lead on the weaker and more ignorant human beings.

Those who have made the choice of the Compassionate heart are often pictured as making the Great Renunciation, but this is only one side of the picture. They have entered an evolution toward a superior Greatness and some Day will stand on a Cosmic or Transcendental Level far beyond Those who accepted Bliss at the earliest opportunity. Essentially They dwell in a domain intermediate between Nirvanic and egoistic consciousness. Thus within Themselves They unite the two worlds. Furthermore the primary reason for making this choice is a great Love or Compassion, and sacrifice made for Love ceases to mean sacrifice to the individual making it. For, in large measure, such an One lives in and for the Beloved. In this case, however, the Beloved, instead of being the Transcendent Divinity, is that Divinity as manifested in the Child, Humanity.

The Man who has made this higher choice does have a subtle kind of embodiment which, since the Law acts without exception on all levels, does imply a kind of karma. But this is karma under quite a different aspect from that which operates upon the crystallized, egoistic level. He may *choose* to take objective embodiment in the subject-object domain for a definite purpose, but in this case the incarnation is distinctly different from the ordinary type. In the first place, it is voluntary, whereas the ordinary individual is reborn whether he will or no, because of the causes he, himself, has invoked, usually quite blindly. In the second place, inasmuch as His former microcosmic vortex has been dissipated, and as He has mastered the glamor of matter, He incarnates in quite a different way. In fact, it is not properly an incarnation at all, if we are to understand the term in the strict sense. It is simply a mode of correlation with this plane so that something of His Consciousness may be united with this lower level. In all this there is considerable mystery for those who have not yet understood the fundamental unity underlying the apparently multiple and diverse forms of outer life.

I cannot too strongly emphasize the fact that Liberation is no more the end of life than is a college commencement the end of the young man or woman who graduates. It is simply the end of one stage and the beginning of another. The really worth-while Life begins after Liberation. When this new Freedom is attained, a Man may return Home, as it were, and spend a long period enjoying the warmth and comfort of that Home. On the other hand, He may return and continue with his chosen profession in a larger field. Some, who have been highly exhausted by their labors at college, may need a long rest, but obviously Those who are strong should occupy Themselves with the activities of Real Life.

XLV

The "Awakening," the End of All Religion

THE REAL END of all the higher religion and philosophy is the attainment of the Awakened Consciousness. Call It what you will, Cosmic Consciousness, Specialism, Liberation, Nirvana, Enlightenment, the Kingdom of Heaven, Moksha, Transcendentalism, Christ Consciousness, Seraphita, Beatrice, or any other name, these all point to one and the same fact, be it well or poorly understood. From one point of view It may be regarded as the Awakening of a new Sense but, if so, the difference is at least as radical as the shift from sensation to conceptual thought. The change is so great as to form an entirely new Man within the frame of the old. He may apparently still live here, yet in the essential sense He is not here. For Him the great and baffling questions of reflective consciousness are solved; the problems that underlie the great antinomies are resolved. His deep soul-yearning is satisfied, and the tragedy which dogs the steps of this life here below is gone forever. With the Awakening the end of religion is attained. The man, at last, is born again, and a new 'Twice-born' steps into a New World.

The Awakening is a Death and a Birth. Then Real Life for the tired man begins. And what is that Life like? No words can really convey It as It is. Art in language, or in other forms, conveys adumbrations, but these are easily misunderstood and have often been grossly misinterpreted. There is but one way to Know and that is by Awakening. We report the Glory, the Joy, the Freedom, and some of the wonderful possibilities. We demonstrate, from time to time, the Powers beyond the command of the merely egoistic consciousness. All These are signs of the Beyond. We give testimony as to what We have found and move for seasons among men, awakening foretastes here and there, both when the latter are in ordinary waking consciousness and when asleep. But We cannot carry to the egoistic consciousness this other Reality. Man must Awake to Know and thus to solve his really great problems. Without Awakening there is no solution of these problems. Brother fights brother for the crumbs that have fallen from the Feast, seeing not enough for all. Yet, if but for a single moment man would look up, he would see on the Table an endless supply, a limitless abundance for all. So We are not much concerned with vain social plans and programs, with the changes of governments and economic reforms, for We Know that all organizations, all institutions, all systems are sterile if they do not incarnate the Light. We use all possible means to bring that Light nearer and to arouse in men the desire for It. But We cannot do that part which each individual man must do. We urge him to turn his back upon the trivial pleasures, combined with real bondage, so that he may Know a real and enduring Joy and may live a Life that is full. The Crossing to the Promised Land has its difficulties but these are small beside the new Values that There will be Realized. Arise, men, and come into your ancient Inheritance! All old pleasures and activities have their higher correspondences in that Beyond, but with an inconceivably greater richness of Value.

XLVI

The Conditions that Favor Recognition

September 5

WHAT ARE THE CONDITIONS, both essential and favorable, for a man to Realize the Glorious Transition? Now we are face to face with the practical question, it being granted that the Illumined Consciousness carries the Supreme Value. In spite of the fact that the record of the western cases of Illumination shows a preponderance of apparently spontaneous Awakening, there are conditions, both essential and contributory, that prepare the way for the Awakening. These we will now consider.

First of all, the individual must desire the Liberation. This desire may not be intelligently formulated, it may not be well understood, and it may take any one of a number of forms, but it must exist. If the desires are centered in the external world and there is a strong resistance to the inward development, a definite, if not insurmountable, barrier exists so long as that attitude persists. Yet it must be noted that superficially a man may seem, even to himself to care most for external things while deep within him he has the inward desire, and this latter may ultimately prove to be the triumphant one. This may be the case where the Illumination breaks forth suddenly and spontaneously, without the personal consciousness being prepared for It. The moment of Transition, in that case, effects a radical revolution in the visible outer life. The man may be utterly 'floored' and personally have no idea of what has happened to him, perhaps even imagining that he has become mentally unbalanced, as some have testified. But if the outer personal desire cooperates with the deeper inner desire, a much more favorable condition is produced and the Illumination will tend to come with less of a shock and will be more quickly recognized for what It is. St. Paul is the classical example of Illumination involving great shock. The personal man, in this case, was even actively persecuting the followers of a great God-Realized Man and trying to destroy His influence, and it was while in the very midst of this activity that he suddenly received the Light in the most dramatically intense form of which we have record. It is said he was even physically blinded. But he was transformed, at once, from Saul of Tarsus to St. Paul, a God-Realized Man in His own right, and became from that time on the greatest single power in the Christian Current since Jesus.

The desire for Illumination, even though weak, does produce favorable effects, but these are much slower in their action and less far-reaching than when the desire is strong. When the desire becomes the dominant force in the man, and finally consumes his whole being, other factors being equal, the Illumination is not far away. There is an East Indian story that is illustrative of this point. One day, so the story goes, a Guru with his Chela or disciple was in a boat on a body of water, when the Chela asked, "How greatly must a man desire God to Realize Him?" The Guru then threw the Chela out of the boat into the water and held him, head and all, beneath the surface until the latter was close to the point of inhaling water. Then, drawing the Chela into the boat, the Guru asked him, "What was it that you desired while under the water?" The Chela answered, "Air, air, air." Then said the Guru, "When you desire God as intensely as you just now desired air, then you will find Him." This simply illustrates the importance that attaches to desire, the other conditions being satisfied.

Now, before a thing or goal can be desired it must be known, felt, or sensed as desirable, either clearly or dimly. The example of

Those who already have attained the Recognition, together with Their testimony as to what They have found, supplies the basis whereby the man who still is engulfed in the subject-object consciousness—Sangsara—may see or feel that there is something Beyond, the Realizing of which will mean for him the possession of the Value beyond all other values. So We raise visibly before men, not one, but many Witnesses of the Truth that makes man Free, that they may know that Others, who once were men like themselves, have found the Way and Know that the Value attained is beyond price, and also may know that the Awakening is a latent possibility in every man.

The second requirement is a spiritual Guru. The Guru performs the part which is beyond the power of the as yet unawakened individual man. The highest authority has always promised that when the pupil is ready the Teacher will appear. So it is not a question of the students seeking far and wide in distant lands for some one to take him under direction. The Guru can, and does, appear in an inward sense, often without the personal consciousness of the pupil being aware of the fact. Sometimes He appears outwardly and, again, may or may not be recognized. But let all aspirants remember that effort put forth in the right direction will draw the attention of Those who watch, and, when the time is ripe, They will do Their part. Thus, while the student cannot command the Guru, yet all may trust Him, for His is a service of Love. So, in effect, the student by doing his part does invoke the aid he needs.

The importance of the Guru lies in the fact that the Recognition is not the effect of any causes set up in the space-time or subject-object manifold. This must be so, for THAT which transcends causality cannot be Itself an effect of something else. Recognition actually is a spontaneous induction out of Spirit Itself. Man's personal effort merely removes barriers in his nature that inhibit this spontaneous induction. So there is a real, though greatly misunderstood, truth in the statement that man is saved through the Love of God. But this Love manifests to men through the Sons of God, i.e., through Those who have attained God-Realization. The Guru is the embodiment of Divinity to the disciple and, through Him in general, the spontaneous 'act' of Spirit manifests in the individual disciple.

So long as the pupil has not established a personal relationship with his Guru such that direct outer instruction is possible, then the Guru-current may be entered by the personal man through attending the words and works of the God-Realized Men who either are now living in physical bodies or have lived in the past and have left Their visible signs. Remember that the Illumined Man is actually present in His works, in His speech and His writings. Walt Whitman truly said, when speaking of his "Leaves of Grass," "Who touches this book touches a man." Such writings are not merely symbols or concepts. They are the embodiments of a living Presence which is actually God as manifested through the particular God-Realized Man who wrote them. Jesus is the best known instance in Christendom, but He is not the only one. It is well to become familiar with the writings and sayings of as many Such as possible. For not all Aspects of the Divine Manifestation are equally accessible to all men. The 'Open Sesame' for one is not necessarily the 'Open Sesame' for another. When the student has found One with Whose Words and Consciousness he stands in particularly close rapport, he should then delve deeply into that One's writings and sayings. In such cases there is a magnetic harmony that is most favorable to success. Further, Realization manifests in a vast range of forms, some *seemingly* the opposite of others, and so for all men there is somewhere the easiest and most direct Way.

In connection with the foregoing, it may be well to remark that the writer, for a definite reason, does not lay especial stress upon the Illumined Men who are best known within the Christian world. These Men are best known to the West and do not, therefore, need to be introduced. Further, the real meaning of these Men is obscured by the over-growth of theological teaching, produced by men who have not understood the Higher Consciousness. In addition, these Illumined Men tend to be so largely taken for granted and placed in grooves, even in the consciousness of childhood, that They have become practically hidden and inaccessible for vast numbers of human beings. The result is that the man who is trained within the

94

Christian complex from childhood is actually more apt to find his genuine guiding Light in other God-Realized Men whom he finds free from theological preconception. The unintelligent and more or less automatic repetition of phrases, even though they may be correct formulations of the Truth, often serves to hide Meaning instead of making it clear. For it is the active cooperation of intelligence, rather than the mere sound of words, that is the vital power for awakening Recognition of Significance in the Consciousness of the individual. Thus the fresh discovery of the same Truth in another form where the intelligence of the individual is active is far more likely to be effective in arousing this Recognition.

An illustration of this point is afforded in the case of Mahatma Gandhi. Jesus, according to Gandhi's testimony, played a very vital part in bringing the Light to him. Yet Gandhi came from India, the very Fount of Spiritual Wisdom, so far as It is embodied more in one race than another. But Jesus could come to him as a fresh discovery, for there was no background of merely taking Jesus for granted, nor in this discovery was there any need of clearing away theological rubbish or overlying superstition.

The present writer can also testify that, although he was born in the very sphere of one of the evangelical branches of the Christian Church and in his early youth was trained in that current of thought and imagined that he had accepted it, yet he actually found and appreciated the real Jesus only after passing through a period of atheism and, later, discovering Buddha. Only then, and in the Light of the Wisdom of the Tathagata, did he realize that Jesus carried the same Light. It was only by reaching beneath the imposed crust of Christian Theology, and then, by taking Jesus out of the peculiar Hebraic stream and seeing Him as more truly one with the Buddhist spirit, did it become possible for him to see Jesus directly for what He was and is. Since that time he has had far greater love for Him than ever before, for now Jesus is, for him, a symbol of Freedom, whereas Christian theology had made Him a symbol of bondage. It is the old, old, story of the followers of a Great Light mutilating and obscuring that Light through misunderstanding. It is, indeed, a question whether the great corporate religious organizations have not been more of a curse than a blessing with respect to the mission of the very Saviours in whose Names they are formed. There is no great religion that has not effected such damage in greater or less degree. So there is an ever-recurrent need for new Lights and new Saviours to arise who reaffirm the ancient and unchanging Truth, but who, first, must needs tear down the extraneous and weedy growth which chokes the real Message of earlier Saviours and Sages. Then the Message must be dressed in a new Garment and sent forth to leaven the hearts of men until, in time, It also suffers the old fate and is obscured in Its turn.

If the student has found a Guru, it is essential that devoted attention should be given to the sayings of the latter. If he has not found such a Teacher—and the greater number have not—then the same devotion should be given to the sayings of the Incarnations of Spiritual Light that he has found somewhere in history. It is not merely the conceptual value of the words of such Men that is important. The formulations may well be not the best possible. But surrounding and within the words is the real Message which has the transforming power. It is this more or less veiled Message that should be accepted without resistance. But while such fundamental acceptance is of high importance, it does not follow that the concepts which clothe the Message are to be taken blindly. It is the Meaning that is vital, and it often happens the true Meaning is clothed in incorrect concepts. So the requisite attitude of mind on the part of the student is a combination of discrimination with a profound pliability in an inward sense.

Besides the foregoing there are other subsidiary aids which, however, vary in their form in the different types of training. Some systems of training are intensely ascetic, while others are not. All of this meets the variable needs and possibilities of differing individualities. For that which helps to open the Way for one may not be appropriate for another. If the individual is so fortunate as to have a personal Guru, then the appropriate help can be given most effectively in directing the specific personal practices.

There is one factor that is always highly helpful that has been variously called 'leavening,' 'contagion,' and 'induction.' To be in

96

called the 'unlearning of that which has been learned.' I have found this to be the severest of all genuinely necessary austerities, but not everyone finds it so. Still, in every case it is unavoidable, and this is so for reasons that are not difficult to understand. A mind that is filled with ideas based upon an inadequate or false point of view must first be emptied of those ideas before it can be filled with others that are more correct. This principle applies, not alone in the Transition from subject-object to the Awakened Consciousness, but, as well, frequently within the subject-object field itself. Thus, part of the training involved in becoming a competent physical scientist consists of the development of the capacity to be so detached with respect to pre-conceptions that they may be readily abandoned when proved to be no longer adequate. The development in physics during the last forty years has required in unusual degree the replacement of old by new conceptions. If physicists, as a class, had been incapable of unlearning the older physical notions when the facts proved the inadequacy of the latter, we never would have acquired our present knowledge of the radiant and subatomic state of matter. Now when we come to the Transition to Transcendent or Cosmic Consciousness, the necessity for this unlearning is far greater and the method is applied in a far more sweeping sense. A too rigid holding of preconceptions is a barrier to Recognition. By such holding, the mind is bound in a vise that prevents its turning about to a new base. So it is necessary that ideas of the subject-object type should be held in a detached way.

However, the intelligent use of the process of unlearning does not imply that the aspirant should begin systematically to discard all knowledge that he has, in every sense. It means, rather, entertaining that knowledge in such a way that it is free to fly away just as soon as a greater insight proves its inadequacy. In other words, we may say that the principle is to remove all chains from the Bird of Truth and let sympathetic attraction be the only bond. Truth naturally makes Its nest within the receptive mind and does not have to be held. Further, Truth is invulnerable and therefore needs no defense. It requires only demonstration so that It may become clear. Thus it is always proper to seek the Truth and to be receptive to It, but not to try to bind It by a fixed preconception of what It is. Earlier conceptions serve a valuable function in preparing the way for more adequate understanding, but, having served their function, should, like scaffolding that has facilitated the construction of a building, be torn away.

The Transition to the Awakened Consciousness is a Copernican change which not only transforms the essential level of the individual involved, but alters his whole relationship to the subject-object world as well. When Copernicus demonstrated the superior power unfolded by regarding the sun, rather than the earth, as the center of the solar system, the world was not destroyed as an empiric fact, but its relationship and significance within the whole was radically changed. This transformation, while affecting astronomy most immediately, produced secondary effects with ramifications reaching far into different phases of social life. This change has brought enormous clarification with respect to many vitally important problems that had formerly been quite obscure. The Awakening involves such a change, only in a much more radical sense. When It has come, the whole life of the individual is affected, and part of the effect is a profound clarification and simplification of a vast number of obscurities. So much is this the case that if the Awakened Man chooses to direct His force within the subject-object field, then in whatever compartment He may focus His attention He has superior capacity as compared to others who have not the advantage of His perspective. He now looks down on things in their relationships, rather than being involved in those relationships. The highest excellence in government, business, engineering, science, religion, art, etc., are at His command, restricted only by the limitations of his personal vehicle. But before a man can operate upon relationships from Above, he must first break his bondage within those relationships, and in part this is represented by unlearning what has been previously learned.

It does not follow that all previously acquired knowledge will be found false. To a greater or lesser extent, the Realized Man may still be able to judge it correct. Its Significance, however, will be radically changed, and He will be enabled to tie together parts that formerly had seemed irreconcilable. He stands outside and above the 'game,' as it were, and so is enabled to play with a master's hand.

Even though from the highest standpoint relative or subject-object knowledge has been completely Transcended and no longer affords a field of function, it does not therefore follow that it has not served a useful purpose in its time. Man builds a certain integration while in the subject-object field without which Recognition, as a self-conscious achievement, is impossible. The training in subject-object knowledge serves something of the function of a scaffold in the construction of a building. When the building is ready, the scaffolding may be and should be abandoned, for it ceases to be, in general, any longer valuable. The man may now enter the building which, in this case, represents the Transcendent or Cosmic Consciousness. However, a scaffolding should not be wrecked while workmen are still standing upon it. So the Compassionate Man who has found the Building to be ready and then enters into It will also leave the scaffold standing until all others have likewise left it and Entered In.

XLVIII

The Record Continued

September 8

A RADICAL CHANGE in the whole relationship toward life is developing within me as time goes on. Throughout the larger portion of my life my focus of consciousness was centered in inward-penetration, with the primary emphasis placed upon understanding. I entered college, having a general idea of preparation for a professional life in the legal field, but planning to take a cultural course for the first four years. I chose pure mathematics as my major subject, for in this field lay my greatest intellectual love. Now prior to and during all this period the search for the adequate religious value was continuing *pari passu*. I had been through the orthodox church and found it utterly barren, so far as cognitive values were concerned, and puny in what it offered for feeling. As I later realized, I somehow chose a course of study that was very nearly ideal for my individual purposes. It consisted of mathematics as a central interest, supplemented by philosophy and psychology. Here I found the values the church was wholly incapable of supplying. I discovered in mathematics what religion usually gives to men. I realized in this the presence of reality in a form of extraordinary purity, and the point of inward penetration that I reached in those days, though I lacked adequate understanding and appreciation of what it was at that time, was not surpassed at any time since, prior to the 7th of last month. I soon lost interest in the legal profession, while the natural sciences held my attention in only a subsidiary sense, but I drove on, choosing, if need be, to sacrifice financial and professional interests. Time after time I abandoned an effort just as I reached a point where I was nearly arriving at a position of outer recognition which would have given me employment. Actually, I abandoned an effort in a given direction when I had extracted the essential value from it and something else was needed to 'carry on' to the main goal. When this happened, there seemed to be no energy or ambition left to finish the structure of previous partial accomplishments. By the end of five years of mathematical concentration the center of interest had shifted to philosophy. What I had attained through mathematics in terms of symbols—and it was a rare level of consciousness—had to be supplemented by philosophy so that it could become clear to the understanding. Philosophy added reflecting and focusing power to the pure light of mathematics. By the end of seven years I found myself in sight of the limits to which our present egoistic consciousness has reached, and also had found adumbrations of another kind of Consciousness where alone, it seemed, solution of the antinomies of the subject-object consciousness could be found. This made necessary a new kind of search. My focus was withdrawn from the academic world and I renounced a profession, not fully understanding that I was doing so. This new search required, or

104

seemed to require, descent from a point well up on a noble mountain range and a long passage through valleys, including some minor and briefly experienced mountain peaks. But after many years I reached the foot of a far more majestic range, the heights of which were ever hidden above enveloping clouds. Here I climbed anew, finally mounting close to the clouds and glimpsing through their rifts now and then something of the Beyond. Then, no longer painfully climbing, but as though lifted instantaneously by a power of inward levitation, I pierced through the clouds to an unmeasurable height and found their seeming darkness transformed into a new kind of Light. THE SEARCH WAS ENDED.

But now, from the standpoint of the new perspective, the clouds again intervened between the World above and the world below, causing the lower field to take on obscurity. A new problem presented itself in the form—"How may those clouds be pierced again, this time from Above?" It is not enough to be There, and then again here, with a blind spot in between. Individually, I am quite satisfied to be wholly There, but a work remains to be done in the clearing away or making thinner the intervening obscuration between the Above and the below. For so long as I am only There individually, I am not wholly There, since these other parts of Me— the rest of sentient life—still move in consciousness below the clouds.

This view is not merely altruism in the usual meaning of the word, for in the latter sense altruism involves a difference between one's own self and others. In contrast, that view implies that in striving for the Realization of others I but complete my own Recognition. I attain more in every man's attainment. I Recognize more in every man's Recognition. I am delayed by every man's failure. Every new facet opened by another individual man breaking through is a new facet awakened in My understanding. Thus, from this standpoint the duality of selfishness and altruism is destroyed. In serving others I but serve Myself, and in serving Myself I serve others. So, I am beyond all sacrifices and choose only My greatest pleasure. Personally, I only fail in my duty when I fall short of choosing perfectly My own supreme delight. If any one would help

Me, let him progress toward his own highest Glory. That is the only aid from out of the world that can reach Me.

The thing that requires the greatest amount of courage on the personal level I find is the employing of a form of expression which seems, superficially, to be a sort of monstrous egotism. It is not such in fact, but simply a positive reflection within the egoistic or subject-object manifold of the genuinely Selfless Consciousness; and this unavoidably takes on a form that seems egotistical. The same expression, if grounded wholly within the subject-object consciousness, would be thoroughly egotistical and indefensible. But *I* who speak am not different from the 'I' in every self-conscious creature.* The form in which, and the facet through which, the words come are individual and personal, but the Meaning is universal. Use this facet if it helps you; use some other facet if it opens the Door; but use *some* facet until you have found that One which is indigenous to yourself.

* * * * *

I have need of the other facets of Myself, both Those already Awakened and those who have not yet Awakened. Until all have arrived the Communion is incomplete.

* * * * *

Such a wonderful inward delight do I feel at this moment! I apperceive clearly. But what is it *I* apperceive? Part of It, I, the personal man, know and express, Much more, I, the intellectual man, apprehend. But beyond this, *I*, the REAL SELF, Know all and AM all. And of this All-Knowledge the glow descends to me, the personal man, and even here I know that *I* Know and AM beyond all doubt.

---

* Let the reader repeat My words given in the last sentence as coming from Himself, and he will find a key to their real significance.

XLIX

Sleep and Death

IT IS A COMMON EXPERIENCE among Those who have attained the Realization to find that the fear of death passes. In my own case for some time death has possessed more the value of an interesting adventure than of something to be feared, save in the sense of dreading physical pain that might be connected with the process. In fact, heretofore I have had to put forth an effort to resist a desire for death in the physical sense, not because of a great personal pain in this life, but for the reason that I sensed very clearly that physical embodiment acts like a brake on Consciousness, so that death is in some measure a kind of liberation for all men, save in the case of some very low types. But Recognition has brought to me a reconciliation with life in the world-field; or, in other words, It has brought me to a point where I can willingly accept a brake, since I see that it serves a useful purpose. In addition, I know that release will come in its own time when the particular work here is finished, and thus all that is required is to be faithful to a duty which will not be of unreasonable duration. So actually I am more concerned now with the well-being of the physical personality than at any time previously. But my concern for it is like the artisan's care for a useful tool, plus a certain feeling that it is meet to do justice to the child— the personality. But so far as death itself is concerned I find it quite devoid of grave dramatic significance. For I realize clearly that what we commonly call death is but a shifting in the modes of life or consciousness, and most emphatically not a terminus. I cannot say that I feel any personal yearning for immortality, as I am attracted rather by the Bliss of pure impersonal Consciousness. However, I do accept the responsibilities of indefinitely continued individuality, as I realize that there are very important reasons for doing so. Thus, today, I stand in this position: I know that, in the real sense, there is no death or birth; that, in the individual sense, I can maintain continuation indefinitely; and, finally, that physical death is merely a passing incident which effects but a transformation in the mode under which Consciousness manifests. In all this there is no room for any real fear.

In a profound sense, I have already died, though the body still persists, and I did not have a hard time in the essential dying. The organism very soon acquired more from the Transition than it lost, and it is now clearly becoming stronger. But it is a fact that I cannot too strongly emphasize that the essence of dying is not the dissolution of the physical body. Fundamentally, it is a change of level of percipience and appercipience. Now, we come to a point of the very highest practical importance. If a man, while embodied, has not learned to integrate consciously the embodied with the disembodied levels of percipience, then so far as the personal consciousness is concerned, death involves entering a state like dreamless sleep. In the higher sense it is not an unconscious state, but it is unconscious for the personal man, except that he may experience a sort of dreaming consciousness apparently constructed along the formal lines of his embodied experience. Let the reader keep it well in mind that this is not a matter of an arbitrary or imaginative eschatology but, rather, of a necessity that must be clear from purely epistemological considerations. The point is simply this: If a conscious being has integrated self-consciousness in a given kind of complex mode, such as the 'five-sense' perceptive consciousness of man, and if it is familiar with no other mode of consciousness, then if it is suddenly severed from that mode and thrust into one utterly different, no matter how bright the Light of the latter may be, it will seem to this being as unconsciousness. After a time self-consciousness may awaken to function in the new mode, but there will be no basis for recognizing the new entity as being the same individual who experienced in terms of the former mode. This is radical interruption of the continuity of self-consciousness, and, while in the Higher or Spiritual sense Consciousness *per se* has not ceased, yet the individual, as individual, has proved to be no more than a mortal being. Actually nature guarantees man no more than this. But he may by his own self-induced effort and by the aid of Awakened Men achieve continuity of self-conscious or individualized consciousness. This is acquired or conditional immortality and constitutes an important part of the significance of Cosmic Consciousness.

The crux of the whole problem in achieving individualized immortality is the learning to integrate while still embodied the outer and inner levels of percipience. This is, in fact, the mystic process symbolized by the squaring of the circle. The relationship between the square and the circle is incommensurable, and this means that 'circular' relationships or values are not comprehensible in 'square' terms. Embodied man is a square while the Inner Man is a circle. The mass of human beings shift from level to level through unconsciousness, and thus in these cases the one level is to the other like dreamless sleep. The two states are discrete instead of continuous, and, therefore, we are faced with a condition where we have, as it were, two distinct men instead of one self-conscious Being. The circle is birthless and deathless and consequently immortal, but the square is generated in time and in the course of time subject to dissolution. But by 'squaring' the circle, or more correctly by 'circularizing' the square, the latter kind of consciousness is taken up and blended with the immortal Consciousness of the circle. This gives to the individual consciousness immortality. It should be clear that the cross-transference in sleep or during the trance state is not enough. Man must win the power to be awake here and There at the same time. Once he has done this, even though the cross-correlation were achieved for but one moment in a given lifetime, he has mastered death and is immortal in the acquired sense. Now, when a man has succeeded in 'circularizing' the square, he has shifted his center of self-identity to the circle and thus has really died while remaining in the physical body. Consequently, while moving *in* the world he has become One who is not *of* the world.

There is a field of tensions, or a 'gulf,' between the domain of the circle and the square. This is sometimes spoken of as a zone of clouds or an intervening sea. Some in crossing this field of tensions with a partial holding of self-consciousness report a sense of whirling which may produce an effect like dizziness. It is possible to hold the correlation steady without the whirling effect, but for my part I do find a tension that tends toward something like dizziness, which however may be controlled. But this does require the effort of a close, though subtle, concentration. I would say, that the effort required of the individual parallels very closely certain demands made upon the imagination in higher mathematics. In fact, the man who has been able to comprehend 'rational,' 'irrational,' and 'imaginary' numbers as one integrated and real manifold, and not merely as an arbitrary creation of pragmatic value alone, has mastered the knack of conscious cross-correlation between the domain of the circle and that of the square. However, this is not the only way but simply the one with which I, personally, am most familiar. As previously noted, the Transition may be greatly facilitated by the process of induction.

Those men who have not mastered cross-correlation while still embodied go into a state of essential sleep after death. Sooner or later they have a kind of experience in a dream-like consciousness, and these states constitute the ordinary heaven worlds, when they are of the better sort. The dream is a continuation of consciousness in the subject-object sense, but in the heavenly worlds the quality is entirely blissful. There is practically no opportunity for the exercise of discrimination in such states. It is the contrast of pain and joy, united with their appropriate causes, that tends to shock the dreaming consciousness into wakefulness. This contrasting condition is found in ordinary earth-life, and thus constitutes an important part of the reason why the vital or determinative steps can be taken only here. Dreaminess is the great barrier. But most of human consciousness even in this world is in a sort of waking-dreaming or somnambulistic state. However, we have here the instruments that can shock to wakefulness, while such is not the case in the after-death states of the ordinary individual. Unquestionably, pain is one of the very greatest of these instruments, and thus is much less an evil than a beneficent agent. The more I have studied the problem, the more I have become convinced that it has been a great mistake to concentrate so much attention upon evil. The real difficulty is the almost universal somnambulism in which men pass the bulk of their lives, some spending many lives without leaving that state at all. It is, in effect, an hypnotic sleep, and the real problem of religion is not the saving of human souls from evil but a dehypnotising of the mind.

An excellent opportunity for studying the fundamental nature of ordinary death is afforded in the phenomena of familiar waking and sleeping states. A man goes to sleep to be active in dreams, or occasionally to enter the dreamless state. Ordinarily, while dreaming the man does not know that he has gone to sleep. That means that he has not mastered the cross-correlation self-consciously, and in this case he has a foretaste of what happens in ordinary death. But it is possible to dream and know that one is dreaming at the same time, holding in the mind a memory of the waking state. In this case self-consciousness has made the cross-correlation. Now to have done this once in a lifetime is sufficient to supply a means whereby the after-death state of dream can be broken by the man who has departed from his physical body. It is most certainly a definite step toward Recognition. So the student would do well to study carefully all of the phenomena connected with sleeping and waking.

It is even possible to go to sleep and later wake up without there having been a break in the continuity of self-consciousness. In such an instance the body does go to sleep and consciousness ceases to function on the physical plane, but it remains active on other levels with the continuity of self-consciousness remaining unbroken. It is, in addition, possible to correlate at least some measure of the inner state with the brain-mind so that the outer memory will retain something. But this memory is not the essential mark of the continuity of the self-consciousness.

The dream-state is so important that something more should be said concerning its nature. Just as it is true that man can be essentially dreaming while active in the physical body—and most life here is in this state—it is likewise true that some of the states entered while the body sleeps are far more truly waking-states than any which are possible while in the physical body. The experiencing of these states with most men is very rare, but they do occur more or less frequently with some individuals. They have certain noble earmarks. The most important of these is the effect they have on the waking life. They may enrich, deepen, or give new direction to the outer life. They tend toward an increase of genuine rationality. These are adumbrations of the Real Life.

In contrast, the dream-state casts a glamour, which may be painful or pleasant, but in any case tends to produce a drug-like effect both upon the will and the reason. In addition to drugs, the light of the moon often produces a somewhat similar effect. The hypnotic state is a dream-state par excellence. This consciousness has the property of possessing a man, instead of the individual possessing and commanding it. It tends to lead him away from the decisions made in the light of clear and discriminating judgment. It is very characteristic of the consciousness found in psychological crowds and affords the reason why the control of crowd-consciousness is effected most successfully by psychological devices rather than by appeal to rational judgment.*

Dream-consciousness, characteristically, has a quality which may be called 'blurred' or 'smudged.' It is quite lacking in crystalline sharpness or the quality of precision. The logical capacity is weak in the dreaming states. There is also a lack of firmness of will. The dreamer floats along in his consciousness, instead of being an achiever in it. He may dream in terms of ideality and beauty and be highly freed from the gross and the sensual, but the dreamer, as such, lacks character and strength. On the whole, his equipment is peculiarly poor for breaking from bondage to subject-object consciousness. He may be a good man and earn long periods of dream-like bliss, but all this is less than the Liberated State. So, all in all, it should be quite obvious that for him who would attain the Higher Consciousness one of the first necessities is the mastering of dreaming tendencies. To effect this mastery there are several useful disciplines that can be devised, all of which cultivate the qualities that are the opposite of the dream-like consciousness. Thus, all activities that require a strong, positive, and incisive use of the mind, and all will-directed efforts, particularly if in directions that are more or less distasteful, are highly helpful.

* Incidentally this affords an explanation of the fatal defect in all popular governments. Democracy can succeed in an effective sense when, and only when, the mass of the electorate have become awakened in the real sense. Otherwise, folly has the advantage with respect to wisdom in casting the glamour that appeals to mass-consciousness.

Strong intellectuality affords one of the best resistances to the dream-like state. Its danger is that it may develop egoism to such a degree that it becomes a serious barrier. But my judgment would be that it is easier to master an overly developed egoism—for here we have strength to work with—than it is to build the necessary strength in the too dreamy consciousness. So I should place somnambulism, rather than egoism and evil, as the first among the problems that must be mastered in this humanity if it is to progress toward Liberation.

L

The Well of Ignorance

I DIP INTO THE WELL of Ignorance and pull forth toads, slugs, and blind fish.

I offer them Light, and quickly they slither back into the slimy darkness.

I pour acid into the pool and hold tempting baits above its rim.

Goaded, they come forth and glimpse the bait.

I lead them to a cleaner pool and a darkness not quite so dense;

And then on to a greater cleanliness and a clearer Light.

In time, slowly they build the strength to endure the Light and a desire for cleaner waters.

Finally, one here and one there ventures out of the pool into the Brilliance.

It is a long and slow labor, but in the end I will win.

LI

Beyond Genius

THE POWER OF GENIUS is a partial Ray descending out of the grand Sun of Cosmic Wisdom, and It drives the men It engulfs like passive instruments. But the Man who has penetrated to the core of Recognition moves consciously and in command, where mere genius is moved helplessly. I do not pretend to measure to what Deeps in the inmost core of the SELF I may have penetrated. Other witnesses may measure; I admit to Myself no limit. I permit Myself no bounds There and acknowledge no inferiority. From out the Deeps, which are the Heights, I descend immeasurable distances and find the thought of abstraction so vast that I barely discern Its Presence. I think Thoughts, the 'sentences' of which are volumes here, and the Volumes whole libraries of formation. Yet below This there is a Consciousness of more distinct, and yet far from distinct, delineation; and here, too, is the ineffable Communion, the Grand Love. Still, I descend and I grasp in half-forms values that are thinkable but not yet writable. And, below this, a level where I form slowly and painfully in the words of this outer consciousness a small fraction of a fraction of a fraction of a Grand Formless Thought. And that Grand Formless Thought: How may I suggest it? Pure Significance packed tight. Stripped protons and neutrons in close consolidation. (A thimble-full of neutrons is a million tons.) So there are DEEPS beyond Deeps beyond deeps, and, on the surface, this little culture of egoistic man to which he clings like a beggar to a crust.

LII

*The High Indifference**

HOW SHALL I EVER DESCRIBE what transpired last night? It is utterly baffling to language as such. At best, what I say may suggest something, but can never communicate the Reality. It was neither an experience, in the proper sense of the word, nor a logical penetration, for both cognition and perception are hopelessly inadequate either to represent or contain it. As the Infinite is to the finite, so was that Consciousness of last night to the relative consciousness of the subject-object manifold. I penetrated a State wholly beyond the relative field, and also well beyond that Realized by me heretofore. Truly, within the Infinite there are Mysteries within Mysteries, Deeps beyond Deeps, Grandeurs beyond Grandeurs. Just as in mathematics there are infinitudes of higher orders infinitely transcending lower infinities, so is it in the Transcendent World. Is there no end to possible Awakening? Is there no end to the progression of infinities? It may be so. I Know that I have found an Infinite World, and then another Infinite consuming the first. I can say these Worlds are, but I can place no limits upon the Beyond. Mystery of Mysteries, reaching inward and outward, but ever Beyond! And from that Beyond ever there come new whisperings of other imponderable Glories. Ah! How little is this world at the beginning of the Trail, barely a point in a Space of unlimited dimensions!

Let us try and see what may be said. After retiring last night I lay awake for some time. My mind, instead of being calm, as has been its dominant quality during the last month, was rather agitated. In general, outer calmness of the mind is one of the prerequisites of inward penetration; but last night the mode of Consciousness which was unfolded, or was superimposed, or burst forth—none of these expressions is quite right—was so strong that the state of the

* On The High Indifference see also the Appendix, p. 446.

mind was seemingly quite irrelevant. The agitation of the mind meant no more than the dance of the atoms in a bar of steel that quickly align themselves in regular and steady form when introduced into a strong magnetic field. Last night I was taken up into such an all-encompassing and potent Field. Enveloped with this greater Power, the activities of the outer mind were but puny, insignificant, and irrelevant. They were utterly devoid of any power to interfere. In fact, it may well be that the mind needed its strength in active and positive form to be enabled to stand by throughout the stages of the deepening Transcendent Consciousness. Otherwise, it is likely that all I could report would be a sort of inchoate Thatness. This Consciousness had no marked quality that I would call Joy in a differentiated sense, but, rather, It was a Higher Integration wherein the Joy was but an incidental moment.

I first became aware of being enveloped in an extraordinary State of Consciousness when I found myself seemingly surrounded by, and interpenetrated through and through with, a quality for which there is no adequate word but which is most nearly represented by calling it "Satisfaction." I do not simply mean that the State was satisfactory. It was Satisfaction. The difference in the significance of these two modes of expression is of fundamental importance. To say that a state is satisfactory implies the idea of relationship or qualification. All this is quite valid in the field of relative experience, but it radically falsifies the essential nature of these inward States of Recognition. The mark of these inward States is 'Identification' and not 'relationship.' Despite the fact that my personal prejudice, fortified by academic training, would naturally lead me to employ the relative and qualifying form of expression, yet I am absolutely forced by the actuality of the Consciousness invoked by inward Recognition to employ the language expressing Identity. Further, when I employ the term 'Satisfaction,' I do not mean merely an abstraction, such as a state of being satisfied, but, rather, a substantial Actuality. It is not satisfaction considered as a state derived from a concrete and external experience or object. It must on the contrary be regarded as a pure self-existence, a somewhat which could be bestowed like a blessing upon objective and concrete experi-

116

ences but that is not a derivative from the latter. He who is enveloped in this Satisfaction is in need of nothing whatsoever to satisfy him. The Satisfaction I realized is a real and substantial Existence prior to all experiencing. I experimented with this Satisfaction and found that I could even effect the equivalent of swallowing It, and then felt, specifically as in the stomach, the state of satisfaction something like a nutritive value without the use of a material food. I have never experienced any gross or material food that could even approximate the sense of nutritive well-being that this pure essence of Satisfaction actually did give me. But this nutritive phase was only one minor aspect of the full Satisfaction. It was the essence of aesthetic, emotional, moral, and intellectual satisfaction at the same time. There was nothing more required, so far as desire for myself was concerned, for at that time I had the full value of everything that could possibly be desired. It might be called the culminating point, the highest to which desire, individually centered, could reach. Only in one sense did I find a desire that could take me away from that State, and that was the desire to convey this new value to others. The memory of the others, as yet left out, was the one unsatisfactory element. This factor was enough to awaken the will to withdraw and to remain, as long as necessary, outside the immediate Realization of the State. I must confess that I know of no other consideration adequate to awaken the will to forego it, once an individual has Known the immediate Presence of the High Satisfaction.

Throughout this whole experience and the following more profound state, the egoistic or subject-object consciousness was actively present. It was present, however, as a witness on the sidelines, while all about and through and through there was an immeasurably vaster Consciousness. Could I have asserted the egoistic will and withdrawn from the State? I cannot give this question any certain answer. I certainly had no wish to try to do so. The greater Consciousness was more powerful than the egoistic energy, but on the other hand I had no feeling of a will in It that would have been asserted against my individual will to retreat from the State. It was as though, all the time, the Higher Consciousness dominated the individual energy, with my individual permission. Of course, I was more than glad to give that permission, but I believe I could have withdrawn if I had so chosen. There is one sense in which it may be said that I, individually, made use of this Higher Consciousness but could have, had I so chosen, abandoned myself to It completely and forever. Not so to abandon myself was an act of sheer austerity.

Through the continued presence of the egoistic consciousness and its activity in recording in the form of thought as much as could be comprehended from the State, it has been possible to carry much of Its value into my ordinary reflective consciousness. Among other effects, this had made possible the expression that is now being written down. Through the presence of this value in the reflective consciousness I am enabled to recognize in the expression of some others a reflection of a comparable form of Recognition. Also, I am enabled to understand the Meaning behind the expression of such writers. Further, I retain at all times in my personal consciousness a memory and understanding relative to the Higher State that is substantially more than a sense of a mere inchoate Thatness. One who entered the Higher State with the relative consciousness completely paralyzed either would be unable to return, or, if he did so, could carry into his outer consciousness only a dim adumbration of a something Other.

How long the state of complete Satisfaction continued I do not know, save that it was for a protracted interval as measured in terms of objective consciousness. But as time went on there was a gradual dimming, or fusing, or being enveloped, on the part of the Satisfaction, by another and considerably more profound State. The only expression that reasonably well represents this higher State is the term 'High Indifference.' Along with this was a sense of simply tremendous Authority. It was an Authority of such stupendous Majesty as to reduce the power of all Caesars relatively to the level of insects. The Caesars may destroy cultures and whole peoples, but they are utterly powerless with respect to the Inner Springs of Consciousness, and in the domains beyond the river Styx they are as impotent as most other men. But the Authority of the High Indifference has supreme dominion over all this, as well as being the Power which permits the Caesars to play their little games for brief seasons. The Caesars, as well as many who are greater than they, are capable of reaching only to some goal well within the limits of Satisfaction. They certainly do not know the Powers lying beyond the utmost sweep of individual desire. But there is such a region of Authority, supreme over all below It, and this is the High Indifference.

In this State I was not enveloped with satisfaction, but there was no feeling, in connection with that fact, of something having been lost. Literally, I now had no need of Satisfaction. This state or quality rested, as it were, below Me, and I could have invoked it if I had so chosen. But the important point is that on the level of the High Indifference there is no need of comfort or of Bliss, in the sense of an active Joy or Happiness. If one were to predicate Bliss in connection with the High Indifference, it would be correct only in the sense that there was an absence of misery or pain. But relative to this State even pleasurable enjoyment is misery. I am well aware that in this we have a State of Consciousness which falls quite outside the range of ordinary human imagination. Heretofore I have for my own part never been able really to imagine a state of so superior an excellence that it was actually more than desirable. And here I mean 'more' in the best possible sense. Within the limits of my old motivation there was nothing that craved anything like this, and I do not find anything in man as man that would make such a craving possible. Yet now, deep within me, I feel that I am centered in a Level from which I look down upon all objects of all possible human desire, even the most lofty. It is a strange, almost a weird, Consciousness when viewed from the perspective of relative levels. Yet, on Its own Level, It is the one State that is really complete or adequate. What there may be still Beyond, I do not Know, but this State I do know consumes all others of which I have had any glimpse whatsoever.

The word 'Indifference' is not altogether satisfactory, but I know of no other that serves as well. It is not at all indifference in the negative or *tamasic* sense. The latter is a dull, passive, and inert quality, close to the soddenness of real Death. The High Indifference is to be taken in the sense of an utter Fullness that is even more than

119

a bare Infinity. To borrow a figure from mathematics, It is an Infinity of some higher order, that is, an INFINITY which comprehends lesser Infinities.

What is it that leads one on into this Level? As already shown, it is clearly not desire. Further, the State certainly seems to be beyond the limits of human imagination. Here we are in the presence of real Mystery. Is it Nirvana? There are excellent reasons for believing that It is something more than Nirvana in the simplest sense. Let us consider this.

Nirvana, in the simplest and most customary sense, is not so far beyond imagination as generally supposed. To be sure, Nirvanic Consciousness cannot be expressed in subject-object terms and thus must be approached largely through negative definition. But It does have some marks that are partly understandable. It is a State somewhat qualified by the terms 'blown out,' 'Bliss,' and 'Rest.' Most certainly It is a desirable Goal for him who is weary from the burden of egoism and the misery of world-consciousness. There is a stage in spiritual progress such that the step of entering Nirvanic Consciousness finally appears as a sort of temptation. I do not say that every man who has reached the point where he may enter this State in a relatively final sense necessarily fails of his best in so entering. With some the state of soul-fatigue is so great that no other course is reasonably possible. So no blame attaches to those who do so enter. But there are some Men who reach this point with such a reserve of strength that They can choose another course, and there are alternative courses of superior dignity. But even for Them, Nirvanic Consciousness is naturally highly attractive. But if They do enter Nirvana, They may no longer aid suffering mankind, whereas by following a certain alternative course They may be of the very greatest assistance, and thus it follows that for Them Nirvana appears as a temptation. All of this implies that here we are still within the field of conceivable desire. Whatever course may be chosen, desire in some sense is active, even though it is that lofty kind of desire that is born out of pure Compassion.

This choice, induced by consideration of pure Compassion, is everywhere in literature, so far as I know, designated as utter Renunciation, and there is nothing said relative to any alleviating compensation. I have for some time suspected a blind here, for the Law of Equilibrium is universal in Its scope. Thus there can be no exception in the matter of Compensation even on the higher Levels where still, in some sense, differentiation remains. And there certainly is differentiation so long as it is possible to speak of Nirmanakayas * in the plural number. What, then, is this superior Compensation?

The answer to the foregoing question is at last clear. Nirvana is complete Satisfaction and the highest possible object of desire, except that purely selfless Desire aroused by Compassion. Because the characteristically human thought is of such a nature that desire, in some sense, is absolutely essential to define an object for it, it is impossible to place before mankind any Goal of aspiration higher than that of selfless Compassion. Further, it is only the very best among men, in the moral or spiritual sense, who are capable of being aroused to emulation of the Compassionate Ones. Hence, the few words written on this subject are dedicated to the Few. Compassion is the absolutely final word of human goodness; in fact, It is a sort of God-like goodness. There is nothing beyond that mere man can imagine as either desirable or worthy of emulation. Beyond this the Sages have been silent.

But now We will speak further.†

He, who can turn his back upon the utmost limit of individual desire, comes within the sweep of a Current of Consciousness wholly beyond the action or lead of Desire. Human vocabularies afford no terms for representing what governs or leads to movement or transformation Here. But beyond the Great Renunciation is a Compensation that places Man where He is Lord, even over the first Nirvana. It emplants Him on a Level that is beyond Rest as well as beyond action; beyond Formlessness as well as beyond Form; and this is the High Indifference. He who abides on the Plane of the High Indiffer-

* The embodiments of Those who have made the Great Renunciation.

† Note these words. They came with that strange Authority of which I have spoken. With them there was the cool, tingling and electric thrill up the spine. At such moments I dare to speak far beyond myself, in the personal sense, with a deep Knowing that it is authorized. Right here is one of the Mysteries of the Inner Consciousness.

121

ence may enter Rest or Action at will, but He remains essentially superior to both, since from that Level both these are derived. There is a Completeness, superior to that of Satisfaction, from which Satisfaction may be employed as an instrument and not merely stand as a final Goal. So Rest can be blended with action and the Balance remain unbroken. But the High Indifference unites much more, for in It are blended, at once, all qualities, all dualities. It is the End and the Beginning and all between. It is the physical as well as that beyond the physical; It is Form as well as the Formless; It spreads over and through all, not excluding time and space. It is the Desire and the desire fulfilled, at this moment and forever. It transcends all Renunciation, even the highest. Thus, the balancing Compensation is fulfilled. Here, Knowing and Being are at once the same. Literally, Here is the utter Fullness, beyond the highest reach of the imagination.

*   *   *   *   *

How long I continued in the state of the High Indifference I do not know. I was long awake that night—well beyond the midnight hour—and the state continued to deepen. Throughout the whole period the relative consciousness remained present as a witness. The personality, with the physical form, seemed to shrink toward a point-like insignificance. The 'I' spread out indefinitely like space, enveloping and piercing through all form, so far as my personal consciousness took note. So far as my thought could reach, there were no limits. I was quite indifferent whether the body passed into the state commonly called death or continued to live. Either outcome was equally unimportant. The evils, strifes, tragedies, and problems of this world shrank to an insignificance that was actually amusing. I saw that human catastrophes, even the most terrific, were relatively all less than 'tempests in a teapot.' There did not seem to be any need sufficiently important to require the service of Compassion. But, on the other hand, there was absolutely no reason why one should not choose to be active among and for men. From the standpoint of that State it seemed utterly impossible to choose any course that was a mistake, or one that was better than another. There was no reason for choosing to continue to live in the physical sense, but likewise there was no good reason for choosing to abandon the body. The State was too completely non-relative and too utterly absolute for any kind of particular choice to have any significance. So, in the subject-object sense, I was quite free to choose as I saw fit. I chose to continue with the job, but from the standpoint of High Indifference there was neither merit nor demerit in this. For There, both wrongness and rightness, as well as all other dualities, are completely absorbed in the non-relative.

I moved about in a kind of Space that was not other than Myself, and found Myself surrounded by pure Divinity, even on the physical level when I moved there. There is a sense in which God is physical Presence as well as metaphysical. But this Presence is everywhere and everything, and, at the same time, the negation of all this. Again, neither I nor God were There; only BEING remained. I vanished and the object of consciousness vanished, in the highest, as well as inferior, senses. I was no more and God was no more, but only the ETERNAL which sustains all Gods and all Selves.

Is it any wonder that SILENCE is the usual answer to the question: What is the High Indifference?

LIII

The Evidence for the Higher Consciousness

September 10

FOR MANY YEARS I have worked with the hope that more than a presumption favoring the actuality of the Higher Consciousness could be found, such that every rationally alert mind within the subject-object manifold would be satisfied in the same way that mathematical demonstration convinces. I must admit that so far, at any rate, no such conclusive demonstration has been produced. For instance, there is no question about the breadth of information or the intellectual keenness of a mind such as that of Bertrand Russell. Russell is a master logician, and yet as revealed in his philosophical writings he is not convinced of the actuality of the Higher Consciousness. The fact that this is true of him and of many others, who are in this respect similar to him, is very nearly conclusive evidence that coercive demonstration of the actuality of the Higher Consciousness has not been formulated, at least not within the range of available literature. I must confess that with all his elaborate carefulness and unquestionably great intellectual power even Shankara failed to produce proof in this sense. In places he even falls into what we would now regard as rather obvious logical errors, such as the undistributed middle. Even more clearly, Plato failed in his effort at demonstration. In our present culture we have witnessed the greatest systematic effort of all, i.e., the development that commenced with Immanuel Kant, attained its crown in Hegel, and was given detailed finishing by the hands of Hegel's disciples. Yet again I must say, though I do this regretfully, that this effort has failed in the logical sense no less truly than the others. There are two considerations that seem to be conclusive evidence of this failure. In the first place, the Hegelians sought to demonstrate the essential unreality of the subject-object consciousness by showing that it necessarily involved self-contradiction. But since the time of Hegel there has been an enormous growth in the understanding of logic through an analysis of the foundations of mathematics and the isolation of the logical principles involved. It was soon found that the principles of rigorous deduction could not be reduced to Aristotle's logic of identity. There are other principles employed in the logic of relatives that are equally conclusive in their results. So today under the general title of symbolic logic we have a more powerful logical instrument than ever before. In the light of this greater power it seems clear that the apparent contradictions which both Kant and Hegel thought they had found can be resolved. This fact, by itself, destroys much of the coercive power of Hegel's philosophy, though by no means challenging the validity of his fundamental insight. The second consideration is brought to light in the development through Karl Marx.

Marx took the dialectic logic of Hegel and employed it to develop a philosophy which actually contradicts the central core of the Hegelian insight. This reveals, again, that as a matter of pure logic alone, Hegel failed in his fundamental objective.

But is this failure in all existent efforts to produce a coercive demonstration merely due to insufficient skill? Or does it reveal a fundamental inadequacy in formal logic, taken by itself? Almost up to the present day I have held the former view, but now I see no way out save to admit that the task is beyond the power of logic, taken in the purely formal sense. Now, unquestionably, pure mathematics does afford a genuine road to Recognition, but it is not the kind of mathematics that remains after men like Bertrand Russell are through defining it. Mathematics in that sense becomes merely a formal definition of possibility, but it is stripped of all spiritual actuality. Mathematics is a spiritual power just because of that element in it that is stripped away in Russell's "Principles of Mathematics." Thinkers of this type do not see it because, however great their intellectual powers may be, yet in one dimension of themselves they are blind. They see the skeleton but do not Realize the soul of mathematics. And right here is the key to the failure of the coercive method. Without the Recognition of the Soul, in some sense, such as the soul of mathematics or of logic or in some other form, formal demonstration proves merely possibility or the hypothetical imperative but never arrives at a categorical imperative. The only Knowledge that can possibly Liberate man is categorical, i.e., certain knowledge of actuality and not merely of possibility alone. Recognition transforms the hypothetical into the categorical and is the only power that can do so. Experience cannot accomplish this, for experience can give only the material filling of subject-object knowledge, and never by itself can it lift the individual out of that field. Further, It never gives categorical certainty, for all too obviously growth in skill in observation changes the determination of what is experienced. Recognition is neither experience nor demonstration in the formal sense. The result is that the Key to the Higher Knowledge inheres in a kind of Knowing that does not fall within the subject-object field. Thus demonstration of the Higher Knowledge, in terms that are coercive strictly within the limits of the subject-object field, is impossible. Consequently, the final word relative to these higher concerns must remain absolute agnosticism for pure subject-object consciousness, as David Hume showed so clearly long ago.

The ultimate word of *pure* subject-object consciousness to those who yearn or are soul-sick is: "There is no hope. If a man would ease the deeper pain, let him play backgammon, as Hume did, and thus through concentration upon the detail of activity forget the pain." And there are many now who are doing just this, though the 'game of backgammon' takes many forms. It may be a concentration upon business, upon profession, upon sports, politics, the army, the various arts and sciences, etc., etc. Some commit suicide, and they are probably the most logically consistent of all, though frightfully unwise. For the fact is that *pure* subject-object consciousness is absolutely barren of any real or soul-sustaining Value, and in the end it is as useless and purposeless as running a treadmill that does no work. It is a life of pure misery without any real hope whatsoever. The average materialistic physician or psychiatrist regards this kind of life as the measure of sanity. We regard it as the acme of insanity.

It is perfectly true that Kant did reveal the Way to escape the agnosticism of Hume and opened the door so that the soul might at least hope and not despair. But buried deep in Kant's thought lies the Recognition; so here, as ever, That remains the magic Touchstone.

For him who penetrates deeply into the roots of logic itself, the Recognition can be aroused. It lies in those very logical constants upon which the validity of all logic depends but which can never be themselves demonstrated by logic. There seem to be but a small number of such constants, perhaps ten or twelve, yet upon their recognition all the compulsive power of logic depends. Nearly all men who have understood what these constants are find it impossible not to believe them, but no man can prove them since they form the ground on which all proof rests. Now whence comes the compelling assurance that these constants are necessarily true? Experience gives probable knowledge at best, but never compelling assurance; so the source is not in pure experience. The answer for me is perfectly clear. The power of these constants is due to the fact that they constitute a veiled Recognition that the race has never completely lost, and they are probably the principal agent that has kept this humanity from becoming wholly insane. Let a man unveil this Recognition and make It immediately and consciously his own, and then he will find in logic a power which, if followed with a single eye, will take him through to the Higher Consciousness. Once given that original Recognition, logic does supply unanswerable demonstration, and thus breaks through the closed vortex of subject-object consciousness.

So finally I must conclude that the only hope for man, taken individually or as a whole, rests upon a process of Awakening which I, together with some others, have called 'Recognition.' This is neither pure experience nor pure formal demonstration but a totally different kind of Knowledge. I have called It 'Knowledge through Identity.' It is Intuition, in the highest sense, but the word 'intuition' covers other meanings; so the former term is less ambiguous. Genuine Knowledge through Identity is infallible and absolute. It is substantial and not relative. It does not merely *mean* something other than Itself but is absolutely Its own Meaning. Knowledge through Identity is not possessed by any self but IS the SELF. It is not 'knowledge about,' not even in the sense of 'about God,' but is Divinity Itself. Thus we have these six primary propositions which, when exalted to Recognition, reclaim man unequivocally:

1. "I am not other than God."
2. "God is not other than I."
3. "I am not other than Knowledge."
4. "Knowledge is not other than I."
5. "God is not other than Knowledge."
6. "Knowledge is not other than God."

Let a man repeat these affirmations, but not as mere propositions. Let him add to those repetitions some measure of that indefinable quality We call 'Recognition,' and they will at once become magical agents with some measure of potency, ranging from a faint stirring of a bare sense of a Beyondness up to a Power so great that the whole universe is, as it were, dislodged from its commanding position. I Know this to be true, but how can I transfer this certainty?

* * * * *

But if conclusive demonstration of the Beyond is impossible save for one who has in some measure, however small, glimpsed It, yet it remains true that much evidence exists which builds a presumption that there is an Otherness quite outside the comprehension of mere subject-object knowledge. This presumption can be made stronger, and We will not cease in Our endeavor to make it so. But We do ask, nay demand, in the name of that spirit of open-mindedness and willingness to let evidence outweigh prejudice (which has been the secret of the greatness of science), that the evidence which builds a presumption that the Beyond is actual should be given the fair valuation and consideration it deserves. We ask no more than that man should dare, upon the showing of a probability that is certainly much greater than that which led men to gamble upon far less worthy enterprises. Now let us examine the case for the presumption that there is a Beyond.

First of all, there is the evidence growing out of the lives and works of all the genuine Mystics or God-Realized Men. At the core of every great and enduring religion such Men are to be found. Thus there are Buddha, Krishna, Shankara, Lao-tzu, Moses, Christ, St. Paul, Mohammed, among others. Judge these Men by Their enormous influence with hundreds of millions of human beings, extending over periods of the order of many centuries and even millennia, and bear in mind that this influence strikes at the very core of human motivation, and then the conclusion seems unavoidable that before these Men we stand in the Presence of a mysterious and tremendous Power. Then penetrating surface differences, go to the core of these Men's Teachings and Their general relationship to Life, and a fundamental similarity is to be found. In every case They place the Source of Their Messages and Power in something that cannot be reached when standing solely within the subject-object manifold. They, with Others of Their own kind, are indubitably the greatest moral force in the world. But They are not solely a moral

128

force. Some of Those named, together with some others, stand on the highest level of intellectual influence. There are, to be sure, men of great intellectual power who have not attained Recognition, but the more powerful and the more lasting any intellectual current, the greater the probability that at its fount are to be found Men of Recognition. This is a notable fact in Hindu philosophy, but it is also an outstanding fact in Greek philosophy and science. The earmarks of Recognition are very strong among the pre-Socratics. Of the great triumvirate of Greece, Socrates, Plato, and Aristotle, two have It. At the fountainhead of our own science and philosophy stand men like Francis Bacon, Descartes, and Spinoza. The lives or writings of two of these, Bacon and Spinoza, reveal unmistakable evidences of Recognition of, if not the highest, at least a high, order. And as for Descartes: What were the words with which he began his constructive reflection and at the same time ushered in the modern period of thought? They were the famous "Cogito ergo sum," "I think, therefore I am." These words are but a new turn upon the essential mystic Recognition. Descartes did not apparently enter fully, but in him a mystic phrase starts the current of modern thought. Newton, himself, clearly had a mystical side, much to the disgust of some scientists who imagine themselves to be tough. It is said that his original inspiration came from hints in the obscure writings of Jacob Boehme, a genuine Man of Recognition. And there is no greater sun in all our science than just this Sir Isaac Newton. What of Paracelsus, who occupies an important place in the history of chemistry? Clearly, He is a Man whose Fount is in the Beyond and One who possesses true Wisdom, even though He obscured It under the barbarisms of alchemical expression. What of Kepler? And what of Gustav Theodor Fechner, a man great in the science of physics and regarded by many as the founder of experimental psychology? This man has many of the marks of the real mystic, as revealed in certain of his less well-known writings, yet at the same time he was simply a tremendous force in science. But we must go on. We cannot pretend to complete the list. So let us turn to literature.

Consider men like Plato, Dante, the author of "Shakespeare,"

129

Balzac, Emerson. Every one of these Men carries the marks of Recognition in at least some degree. And what do They mean in literature? The best of all are in this list. Fortunately, in one of them we can trace the difference between the man before Recognition and the Man afterward. This one is Balzac. Before Realization he produced voluminously a very inferior literature that has never lived at all, but afterward he rose to a literary height, comparable to that of the author of "Shakespeare." This same phenomenon can be seen in another man, this time in our own country, and while he does not occupy as high a place in literature as the others named, he is none the less gaining recognition as one of the great poets of all time, and he lived among us a life of nobility and enduring influence. I refer to Walt Whitman. Before his Recognition he, too, wrote inferior stuff that would not live, yet afterward he was able to infill with living richness a peculiarly obscure prosody.

I wish, finally, to call attention to an event almost of our present day. Consider the "Secret Doctrine" of H. P. Blavatsky, simply as a phenomenon, if not in a profounder sense. Let the reader examine this book, disregarding, if he can, the force of the thought contained therein, and regard simply the phenomenon of its erudition. The references alone might well require half a lifetime of research, yet the life of the writer, though fairly well known, reveals nothing like adequate scholarly labors. Competent testimony states that when she wrote her library resources were very meager. In addition, she was practically a sick woman throughout the productive part of her life. In her work, alone, we have a peculiarly compelling witness of some Power beyond the field of pure subject-object consciousness.

I might continue listing several cases. A volume could be written. But the reader, if he desires, can complete this for himself. The important point to note is that these Men all carry a somewhat which comes from Beyond. Many of Them have claimed that Beyondness as Their Source, but all carry the familiar earmarks in one form or another. Further, They all wield Powers in the moral, intellectual, or artistic fields of the very highest order. Education and breeding do not make Them. They can flame forth out of poor educational backgrounds as well as out of the best that education can offer. Their children, if They have any, do not show the same type of capacity, and thus it is clear that Their peculiar capacities are not due to special modifications of the genes. In some of Them, because of sufficiently complete biographical records, we can see the radical revolution between the man before and the Man after Recognition. Altogether, we have a strong case showing that Here is something from outside the range of understanding and control of the pure subject-object consciousness. Now, consider what a debt those within the subject-object field owe these Men. Just imagine this world as it would be without their influence, direct or indirect. Of religion there would be little, if anything, more than animism left. Philosophy and science would lose their greatest classics. And how greatly impoverished would literature and art be! It is a very strong case, if fairly considered.

Let us now turn to other lines of evidence, admittedly of a distinctly inferior sort but yet much more common. The cases considered have revealed the highest excellence in moral, intellectual, and artistic values. But there is a large number of other instances of weaker manifestation where the Sun of Recognition has not quite risen, and hence there has been but a Twilight of the Great Consciousness, or, if the Sun has risen, It has appeared but briefly or has been obscured as by a cloudy sky. Here we would have to include the lesser mystics, and at least much of genius. In these cases again we have that which neither education nor breeding explains. Here is a lesser Well of Mystery out of which choice values come to enrich the lives of men.

But below all this are other domains of progressively inferior character where some of the values are excellent and even exalted while others do reach to profound depths of ugliness in some sort of inferior world. But all of these are important to us as revealing one characteristic in common, i.e., a kind of consciousness that does not fit into the common framework of the subject-object manifold. Thus they all have a kind of mystic quality or consciousness-mode utterly alien to the dominant and common form of consciousness which we teach in our schools and which is the only form under the command of our pedagogical methods. All of these instances, from the lowest infernal ones up to those of the Christs or Buddhas, have in common the fact that a certain shell must be broken before a new domain of consciousness can be realized. No amount of development within the shell can attain this. Observation within the shell may be able to note certain phenomena that attend the 'breaking through' and may be able to detect certain similarities that mark all such 'breaking out,' as well as some divergencies. Observers may very correctly find that such phenomena are contrary to the norm of usual behavior. But the observer, confined within the shell, is wholly incapable of evaluating the actuality beyond the shell. He may be able, in some degree, to evaluate the fruits from the Beyond as reflected back within the shell, but he does not and can not know their immediate content. He has no logical justification in concluding that that which is contrary to the norm is inferior. Some of it is inferior, to be sure, but also much of it is infinitely superior. But before one can be really competent in this differentiation he, himself, must have broken out of the shell. The one important fact that all this body of testimony does concur in, be it on the one hand noble, able, and beautiful, or, descending from that level progressively through inferior forms until we reach at the bottom something anything but admirable, is this: that there is another kind of consciousness or kinds of consciousness which do not fit within the forms governing the familiar subject-object consciousness.

Briefly, I would call attention to the very extensive but inferior field of evidence. Several volumes exist for the reference of those who are interested and qualified. There is a mass of testimony coming from the effects of various toxic substances, such as the common anaesthetics, alcohol, and the narcotic and hypnotic drugs. A few of these temporary unfoldings are of a high order, but most are distinctly inferior, and some very inferior. This sort of 'breaking through' gives no voluntary command of the new level entered, and the capacity for cross-translation into the objective mind is very defective. But the reports show the presence of a consciousness of a nature quite different from that which is typical within the shell. Here we have, clearly, a kind of externally imposed violence that effects a sort of 'breaking out.' Most emphatically, this technique is not to be recommended, as it is very apt to prove a fatal barrier to the real Awakening, for the latter involves self-conscious Power. But since the drug-technique does exist in point of fact, and does produce a kind of result, it is of value as evidence.

Certain phenomena in connection with sickness supply further evidence. The wasting away caused by certain sicknesses and the process of dying, when it has been arrested before quite complete and the life-current is re-established, afford a number of instances of 'breaking through' of variable value. Here there exists a considerable body of testimony revealing a consciousness or consciousness-mode quite alien to the form of common consciousness. There is also the large field of mediumship and the negative yoga-practices, but to these I shall only refer in passing, as there is an abundant literature covering them. In addition, within the more common and normal domain there are minor adumbrations of otherness that still are significant, if less striking. I refer to the effects often produced by strong emotions. In this class there is frequent partial 'breaking through' to other values that do, in fact, point to a beyond.

If, now, we take the whole field of evidence, briefly summed above, there is built a presumption of tremendous strength to the effect that beyond the shell of the familiar subject-object consciousness there is another kind or are other kinds of consciousness. Further, the testimony is clear that in this other domain, or in some of these other domains, there are levels of Intelligence and Joy far transcending any that men have been able to find within the shell. The question of fact concerning this other domain or domains, regardless of what the values may be, is in any case one of scientific or epistemological interest of the very highest importance. For, so long as this other kind or kinds of knowledge are not understood, we can never justly evaluate the more familiar forms of knowledge. If there is a Domain where enduring Joy can be found and a kind of Knowledge which solves all problems that here distress the soul of man, then what is of greater importance than that men should find the Way to reach this Domain? Those who have witnessed to the actuality of such a Region have built an exceedingly strong presumption. Under these circumstances is it not the duty as well as the privilege of every man, whose courage is not too weak, to reduce that presumption to actual personal demonstration?

*   *   *   *   *

Much that I have written in this book is in the form of an intimate personal testimony. Other portions are in the form of reflective discussions, or more or less mystical compositions that are, in large measure at least, the fruit from a shift in consciousness level which I, individually, have experienced. My purpose in this was not merely the satisfying of a demand for self-expression—in fact I do not feel such a demand—but to report and reveal, as far as may be, a fact that I know to be of the very highest importance to myself, and a fact that is potentially capable of having that same value for others. From previous training I know something of the importance and technique of introspective observation. I have not neglected watching the personal transformation, while in process, with a view to keeping a record of as large an objective value as I could achieve. It has been my purpose not to neglect the recording of unpleasant or negative features if they should arise. In point of fact, I have found the unpleasant features to be of remarkably minor importance and only of temporary duration. Thus any ordinary athletic achievement in the fields of sport involves more bodily and emotional discomfort than I have experienced at any time since the 7th of last month, while on the other hand I have known the Joy of finding a World far greater and far more significant than all that which came out of the discoveries of Columbus. I simply wish that others may find the World, or have the Way made clearer to them because of what I have already accomplished.

There is one point that I wish to have understood very clearly. The initial Transformation did not just happen to me as something coming unexpectedly out of the blue. We have several records of such spontaneous Awakenings, and while there exists a rationale explaining such cases which shows that they are not quite so spontaneous as they seem, I shall not enter into that question at the present time. In point of fact, I have sought this Awakening for several years. I was finally convinced that, at least in all probability, there was such a thing or event, while I was in the midst of the discussions of a metaphysical seminary held at Harvard during the academic year of 1912–1913. I saw, at once, that if such Knowledge were an actuality it was of far greater importance than even the greatest intellectual achievement within the limits of the subject-object field. At that time I had a very imperfect idea of the Goal, but I knew that among the East Indians was to be found the greatest development of knowledge relative to It. I resolved to make the search and pay what price might be demanded. In the years since, I have been more than once discouraged and have permitted lateral desires to lead me into side-excursions. But I always returned to the search. I tested various different routes, finding values and defects in all, and then at last by combining the best that India has to offer in the field of metaphysics with the best of western science and philosophy, and then adding thereto some modifications of my own,* I found a road that has proved successful. While during the interim there have been partial Transformations and Recognitions, it has taken twenty-four years of search to attain a culminating point which I can recognize as definitely culminating. All of the steps within the subject-object field were conscious, and therefore I can formulate and evaluate them. Also, I am aware of the Transcendent Factor and know the Significance of the part It plays. If I had known in the beginning all that is here for the first time collected together between the covers of one book, many years of time would have been saved. Perhaps, also, for some others this book may have a similar value. But from the standpoint of evidence for a Beyond-

* At the present time, some two and one-half years since writing the above, I have a further contribution to offer on the creative effort supplied by the individual himself. I have made many experiments with the meditative and yogic techniques given by the various authorities. In no case have I had any results that were worth the effort so long as I did not supply at least a self-devised modification of my own. Apparently the modification is suggested intuitively. Often I got results by a method diametrically opposite to that suggested by a given authority. At least, so far as my private experience is concerned, the successful method always had to be in some measure an original creation. I suspect the presence of a general principle here, but I am not at present able to deduce a conclusion of universal applicability.

ness, the point I wish to make is that in the present case an individual was finally convinced of the validity of a search from the discussions that formed a part of the classwork in one of the leading western universities. He tried to find the Way, at times following others, but in the end carving his own course, and did that without renouncing the western form of intellectuality. What one can do others also may do.

My final word on this particular subject is: I sought a Goal the existence of which I had become convinced was highly probable. I succeeded in finding this Goal, and now I KNOW, and can also say to all others: "IT IS ABSOLUTELY WORTH ANYTHING THAT IT MAY COST, AND IMMEASURABLY MORE."

LIV

A Poetic Interlude

September 11

Am I a man? Yet also am I a god,
For I am that which comprehends both gods and men.
I move among men in the form of a man,
Fallible, more or less good, like the rest.
Yet, also, I shine with the gods in Glory.
I compress Myself in the mineral,
Inert and long-enduring.
Ceaselessly I grow as a plant,
And am driven by desire as animal.
I am in all, yet ever Beyond all.
A Flame am I that nowhere remains;
I consume all.

*   *   *   *   *

As I write I am sitting on a pavement of cement.
A tree grows near, its roots, soft and brittle, beneath
 that pavement.
Ceaselessly, slowly, but inevitably, those roots expand.
The cement gives way, its resistance impotent.
So, too, I expand, inevitably, remorselessly, in this
 world.
Before Me no crystallization can stand.
In the end, all other powers fail;
My own, once more, return to Me.

* * * * *

What matters health, sickness or death;
Passing modes in the endless Stream of Life?
In health I go forth, perchance to forget;
In sickness I look within and remember.
Which is the greater blessing?
I know not.
Men seek health. I seek not at all.
I give health and accept the blessing of sickness.
Yet, beyond all these, AM *I*—Unbound.

* * * * *

Do I look for faults in men?
Then surely I will find them;
Dishonesty, lust, greed, hatred, and all the rest.
All these come with immense fecundity.
Do I look beyond to the good?
Then what a glorious paragon is man!
Generous, kind, and fair-dealing.
Which of these is the real?
Neither and both. Man reflects just what I seek.

LV

The Real and the Unreal

WE ARE IN A POSITION at this point to arrive at a clearer understanding of what is meant by the "Sangsara" of the Buddhists, the "Maya" of the Vedantists, and the "illusive nature of the phenomenal world" of the Hegelians. The State of the High Indifference is absolutely Real, and most emphatically not an airy abstraction. However, It may seem to be such an abstraction from the standpoint of relative consciousness. It is incorrect to imagine that when a man has Awakened to Real Consciousness then the objective universe vanishes in the photographic sense. In the Higher Consciousness the Inward and the outward blend, as do all other dualities, and are at once an eternal fact. So it is incorrect to regard the outward as unreal while, at the same time, predicating reality of the inward. No branch of any duality is real by itself. It is the separation of one or the other phase of inter-knit dualities that results in the vicious kind of abstraction, i.e., the kind that produces an illusion or Maya. It is because subject-object consciousness has characteristically produced such a disjunction of inseparables that it has been the great creative cause of unreality. When Shankara speaks of the universe, or the Buddhist of Sangsara, each means the subject-object manifold. And it is just because of the false abstraction in this manifold that life here below is essentially one of misery. Awakening is re-integration for the individual consciousness of the inseparable parts that have been, apparently, divided. Thus, this Awakening does genuinely destroy the universe, in the sense of Its being a power over the Awakened Man. The latter, after the Awakening, may focus attention upon and act within the relative universe at will, but the significance of his doing so is precisely that of entering a dream and consciously playing a part in it.

For the fully Realized Man, Sangsara or the illusive universe is without value. This is very difficult for the egoistic man to understand, and so the latter may be led to question the value of the

138

Awakening. The Realized Man largely ignores those values which still seem important to the unawakened. The latter sees the apparent lack of ambition and desire in the former, and thus finds Him an utter mystery. Thus, for example, the man of the world makes a god of what he calls progress and laborious accomplishment; yet he sees these things, if not despised by the Illumined Men, at least looked upon with a certain detached aloofness. Quite naturally he resents this, though he may be forced to give respect when he finds that the Awakened Man, when acting within the relative manifold, wields an extraordinary and unconquerable skill. But, on the other hand, the Realized Man may choose not to act, in an apparent sense, and His life then is often judged as a wasted one both for Himself and for society. But the egoistic man is quite wrong here. In fact he is just as wrong in this attitude as would be the judgment of an animal, if it were capable of judgment, in viewing the scorn of the cultured man toward the essentially animal field of interest. The cultured man knows the superiority of his field of interests, when compared to anything possible to the strictly animal consciousness. Far more clearly, the Awakened Man Knows the superiority of the Infinite when contrasted to anything within the finite universe. This superiority is not measurable in finite terms, but is in fact infinitely superior. Life in the infinite is one with everything, and so the finite cannot possibly add anything to it. The last possible value of the finite, or subject-object domain, is realized once the Awakening has culminated within it. The Awakened One, who returns, does so not to learn more but to be of aid to those who are still sleeping. The best possible growth in this lower world is growth *toward* the Awakening in the Infinite. For Him who has Awakened in the Infinite, all Real Life is Life *in* the Infinite.

Too much emphasis cannot be placed upon the fact of the Reality and substantiality of the State of the High Indifference. Nothing here below is felt so immediately, so fully, and with such utter completeness. Nothing here is so completely *solid* or dependable in the essential sense. The Higher Reality merely *seems* abstract to the relative consciousness. Actually, what we call concrete here is abstract in the real and invidious sense. The higher we rise in what we com-

139

monly call abstraction, the nearer we approach substantial actuality. It thus follows, that he who can arouse in himself the sense that the apparent abstractions of our language in fact mean real and substantial actualities, will be preparing himself for the Awakening.*

LVI

Integration

September 13

MOST OF YESTERDAY was spent in the city. I found that I had better control of the problem of driving in traffic than had been the case for some weeks, and, in addition, I maintained my own center in the midst of the crowds more successfully than at any other time since the Transition. However, I found that this required quite a strong effort of will, and fatigue developed rather rapidly. Toward the end of the day my control was not so strong, and at the same time I was thrown downward into the more barren levels of the personal consciousness in a larger degree than has been the case since the 7th of last month. Clearly, the whole problem is one of winning a new kind of control. Quite evidently this can be accomplished, but a price is exacted. In this, experience confirms theory with respect to the principle that there can be no avoidance of the Law of Compensation on this outer plane of life. This leads to the following practical question: In what field, at a given time and under given circumstances, is one's functioning most useful, due consideration being given to the Law of Compensation? It is not merely a question of what one can do. In addition, consideration must be given to the probable value of an effort in comparison to its cost.

* It should not be concluded that this is the only way of preparing for the Awakening. There is no one method that is exclusively valid. The process that proves effective for one psychological type may fail completely for a very different type. It is possible to outline an effective Route, but it is impossible to say that *only* by this means may anyone Attain.

140

What is required in achieving the control necessary for meeting modern city-conditions is becoming clearer. Through the will one must surround himself with a strong shield of integration. To accomplish this, the aid of a certain kind of rhythm is required. I find it necessary to move, both mentally and physically, in a rather slow and stately rhythm, and refuse to accept impressions that I do not choose. Acting as a contrary force, the rush of traffic always threatens to break this rhythm, although yesterday it seemed as though circumstances were combining to favor me. Toward the end of the day the integration weakened to a degree, and then the interrupting cross-currents began to break through into my own consciousness. I find that when this happens, it begins to be dangerous and I have to struggle in order to secure simple physical safety. It appears that the action of subject-object consciousness is more certain, keener, and more powerful when supplemented by the Higher Consciousness, but when this correlation is interrupted, the personal control is less effective than it was in former days.

The meaning I am trying to convey by the word 'integration' at this time may be illustrated by a familiar phenomenon in magnetism. When a bar of steel is made into a magnet, it is said that a certain force in the molecules or atoms is polarized in some measure, with the result that one end of the magnet is positive and the other negative. In a non-magnetized bar this force exists but acts in all directions among the molecules so that there is little or no residual magnetic energy that acts beyond the bar itself. The result is that such a non-magnetized bar is a sort of neutral or closed field, although there is just as much force in it as in the magnetized bar. Now, subject-object consciousness may be thought of as a non-magnetized bar which forms a closed field within itself. In this way the Beyond is shut off. But the man who is magnetized is in a position to pierce beyond the shell or closed field of relative consciousness, and so long as he maintains that magnetization he stands correlated with the Beyond. Similarly, to the extent that that magnetism is lost, he tends to drop back into the field of mere subject-object consciousness. A magnetized steel bar can lose its magnetism very easily as it is brought into contact with non-magnetized pieces of iron, as in ordinary usage. The same phenomenon occurs when an individual with a magnetized consciousness moves in the field of ordinary consciousness. There is a dissipation of the integrated force, and the chaotic condition of the environing consciousness begins to invade the former. This leads to something analogous to demagnetization. But this demagnetized condition can be corrected subsequently by the action of the Current, just as a current of electricity may be employed in the re-magnetizing of a weak magnet. But all this takes effort, time, and the right conditions. It is true that so long as the Current is active, the magnetized man can dominate the demagnetizing influence of the environment, and in addition he will tend to magnetize the latter. However, it is not easy to maintain the Current under the conditions imposed by a modern city.

The magnetized condition is that which is meant by "Isolation." Physical solitude in the midst of wild nature, and particularly at high altitudes, affords an especially favorable condition, though this is not essential. This should make clear something of the rationale of the hermit-life of so many Sages, and also why the Illumined States are so sporadic and temporary in the cases of most of those who move in the midst of general society, particularly in the West. It also makes clear the rationale of the monastic or ashrama life. For in this, when it is genuine, we have a community formed of those who have attained some degree of Recognition, together with others who aspire to this State. Life in such a community is a great help to the latter and is not too severe a load for the former. Below the ashrama the next most favorable life is in communities where the population is not greatly concentrated and primitive nature dominates the environment. In contrast, the most unfavorable condition of all is afforded by the modern megalopolis, for in this we have the rushing and 'jazzed' consciousness, heavily concentrated on the surface of things.

As a counterpoint to the foregoing fact is the other fact that it is precisely in the megalopolis that the human need of the God-Realized Man is greatest. The average city dweller faces the greatest soul-starvation and maiming of all. The city life supplies the greater bulk of suicides, insanity cases, and pathological radical movements, as well as a strong tendency toward sterility. All of these are symptoms of a very abnormal and unwholesome life. So the need in the city is the greatest of all, but likewise it is just in the city that the danger of suffocation of the Realized Consciousness is greatest. How can this problem be solved? It certainly calls for the highest kind of generalship.

LVII

The Gold Mine

September 14

THESE DAYS I am facing the problem of embarrassment of riches. It seems I have a very peculiar gold mine. As the mine-car comes forth each morning it brings a load of Gold Nuggets—Ideas, rich in the power of clarification and coordination. Always, I am unable to gather them all and store them in this vault of expression before the day closes. The remainder goes on the mine-dump of the hidden recesses of the mind where, while it is not exactly lost, it is hidden by other material and time is required to recover it. Meanwhile I have a vegetable garden—the merely practical and temporal concerns—and in this garden the weeds are growing. I am enough of a farmer to feel troubled about these weeds, but if I attend the weeding job, the Nuggets continue to roll over the dump. And it so happens that I am enough of a miner to appreciate the Value of the Nuggets. For the Gold commands all the lesser values, symbolized by the vegetables, while the latter do not command the Gold.

I choose the Gold before the rest.

LVIII

The Power of Illumination

I HAVE BEEN DIPPING into Whitman during the last few days. With the perspective of the Consciousness I have called 'Satisfaction' and the 'High Indifference,' he has become essentially clear. Most of the remaining obscurity in his writings has also been clarified by interpreting his language in the more obvious and simpler sense. In assuming in his work an involved meaning, as I have done heretofore, I found him baffling, but when I took his words as carrying the more simple and direct meaning, I found a very great increase of clarity. Whitman combines Illumination with a remarkable objective simplicity. It is the Illumination that makes Whitman great. There are some men who are so great on the level of relative consciousness alone that they are effective forces in the world for centuries and even millennia. Aristotle is an outstanding example of such greatness. I find nothing of this kind of greatness in Whitman. If he had had a high order of capacity in the purely relative sense, it would hardly be conceivable that the great or Illumined Whitman could not have made his earlier writings—those written before Illumination—live. In fact, only his Illumined work has power, but it has unmistakably great power. This fact, however, simply increases the value of Whitman as an example of what Illumination means. On the other hand, men like Dante and Francis Bacon are not nearly so good examples for the study of Illumination, for both of these men, particularly the latter, were men of ability and training in the relative field. It is very probable that Bacon would have had a place in history even though he had not attained the Cosmic Consciousness. Hence, the contrast between the Illumined and the merely egoistic Bacon does not have the sharpness that is so marked in Whitman. It is hard to imagine that, without Illumination, Whitman would ever have been known beyond his own immediate circle.

How great, then, is the force of Illumination? An effective measure of It cannot be attained, but some men do show its force in relative 'isolation.' Whitman and Balzac are notable examples in recent times who afford us the marked contrast between the powers of the men before Illumination and what they became afterward. Western history gives us two other conspicuous examples. These are Jesus and Jacob Boehme, one a carpenter and the other a shoemaker. Each of these was a man of fine personal character, but neither of Them was great enough, in the purely egoistic sense, to have left any mark on history. It is unnecessary to remark upon the importance these Men achieved after winning the Higher Consciousness, especially in the case of the former. There are, undoubtedly, other men of this kind to be found, particularly in India, but some of these lived and died in retreats, or lived seen by men but under the vow of silence. Therefore, They have not constituted a recognizable force in history and do not live for the open record. Other men, of greater ability in terms of ordinary egoistic consciousness, who subsequently attained the Higher Consciousness, do not afford good examples, for the contrast between the two levels is not so marked. The difference between these two types may be illustrated in the following way: Nearly everyone can note the fact when a rather ordinary hill is raised to the magnitude of a high mountain as by the sudden action of geologic forces. On the other hand, if an already high mountain, with its top lost in the clouds, were suddenly raised to a still grander height, only a few would be able to appreciate this fact. Finally, only Those who dwell above the clouds can measure the relative altitude of the mighty peaks with just appreciation. So it is with the great Men of Illumination.

The Illumination is one fact. The form which Its partial expression takes within the subject-object field is something quite different. All Illumined Men form one Community; They are one Brotherhood grounded in mutual understanding and fundamental agreement. On the other hand, Their modes of expression in relative terms are as variable as are the differences in the development of personality. In principle, any mode of expression that exists in this world is a possible vehicle of Illumined Consciousness. In formal terms, not all these expressions are consistent with each other. They may even be far from correct in the scientific sense. But they all carry the Reality, in greater or less degree; Reality being understood as that which can be known only by Awakening to another dimension of Consciousness. Hence, any and all of these expressions from the Beyond are of the highest value to men. For a diamond is always a diamond, whether embedded in clay or washed clean, whether a rough stone or cut and polished. At one end of the scale Illumined Men give us diamonds embedded in considerable clay, while at the other They supply us with diamonds well cleaned, cut to mathematically true angles that reflect most perfectly the contained Light, and polished to the last degree of refinement. The latter is, unquestionably, the more finished offering, but all are equal in this, that a diamond is a diamond. So, also, are all manifestations of Realized Consciousness equal, in that they are from a Source rooted in the Beyond or the Infinite.

For my own part, I much prefer the polishing of a Plato to the rough-hewing of a Whitman. But, unquestionably, Whitman is an 'open Way' for some for whom Plato is a closed door. And all Ways that men need are acceptable to Me in the larger sense. But the Way of the rugged and simple man is no more *the* Divine Way than that which fits the needs of the highly cultured and aristocratic spirit. In fact, when it comes to the final showing, the real 'snobs' in this world are not the highly cultured and aristocratic people, but a certain only partially finished group who feed their own pride by glorifying crudity, and insist that the crude way is the best way. The Illumined Man will do what is necessary to meet His people, and, if they require crudity, He will manifest through crudity, but this does not mean that He despises finished and polished workmanship nor those who prefer that Truth should be offered in a beautiful setting.

LIX

Expression and Transcendent Consciousness

FIGURES OF SPEECH or analogies seem to be absolutely essential to express the realities of Profundity. The direct meaning of language does not express the actuality of the Higher Consciousness. We might say that the Actuality envelops the expression but is not directly contained in it. Thus the reader should strive not so much to understand the formal meaning contained in these writings, but to make a certain turn in his own consciousness toward a Matrix that surrounds the expression. He should concentrate upon faint stirrings in his consciousness which he cannot really express, even to himself. They constitute a certain 'plus' quantity added onto the formal meaning. The formal meaning serves as a sort of focal point that entrains the subtle 'plus' value. It is very hard to reach the latter without the use of the focal point until a rather high level of spiritual development is attained. Hence it remains important to employ various means of expression. But if the expression is taken too much in the rigorous or defined sense, the real and deeper Meaning is lost. Therefore, the words of an Illumined Man should never be taken in the literal sense when He is giving a cross-translation from the Beyond. Now, the 'plus' quality at first is almost indistinguishable from nothing or emptiness. It is like a breath that has just escaped, a momentary gleam caught from the corner of the eye that disappears when the full focus of sight is turned upon it. It must be reached for very gently, as one must act in seeking the confidence of a defenseless and fearful creature of the wilds. One should reach out almost as though not reaching at all.

A time will come when This that is so very subtle will be transformed into a Presence more palpable and stronger than the toughest granite. It will manifest a Power so great that It will dissolve not only the immediate field but even the whole universe. But the Great Power is rarely in the beginning a clearly dominant force, and It must be assimilated very carefully or It will disappear in the first stages. In the beginning it may seem that one is walking a tight-rope over unmeasured spaces, and the necessary balance is extremely hard to hold. In the end the rope becomes all Space, the Supreme Support of all universes but Itself in need of no support. Visible man, in that case, has been transformed and has become the all-containing Matrix. No longer, then, does he struggle to keep his balance on a rope, but he finds Himself everywhere and therefore Invulnerable.

LX

The Symbol of the Fourth Dimension

THERE IS A VERY BEAUTIFUL and frequently employed analogy to be drawn from mathematics. It is that of the fourth dimension. Certain cross-correlations between subject-object consciousness and the Transcendent Consciousness are made considerably clearer by considering some of the properties of three-dimensioned and four-dimensioned space. While it is true that this symbol may be interpreted in a sense that gives a false impression, still this error may be avoided by divorcing the notion of 'dimension' from metrical properties which, strictly considered, are significant only in applied mathematics. I have followed this course in the present discussion.

Subject-object consciousness may be likened unto three-dimensioned space. This relationship becomes clearer when it is realized that this kind of consciousness has three and not merely two aspects. For the sake of brevity I have called it subject-object consciousness, but actually it consists of the three following aspects:

1. The self, or subjective moment of consciousness that is aware of the content of consciousness.

2. The object of awareness that forms the external world, whether in the gross or subtle sense.

3. The awareness itself which occupies an intermediate position and has only a psychical existence.

in the two-dimensional world. This process can be carried on indefinitely, and this is done in pure mathematics, so that we have not only four dimensions but actually an unlimited number of dimensions, for there is no logical stopping point. But, for our present purposes, we will go no further than the addition of the fourth dimension, i.e., the space or world having a four-fold degree of freedom.

A very important point to be noted is that while all the relationships expressed by 'degree of freedom' may be correlated with points in an extended space, the extension is not essential to the idea. The same relationships may be expressed by abstract numbers alone, without attaching to the numbers the meaning of measurement at all. Thus we are dealing with notions that are far more fundamental than the notions of either extended space or time.

As is true with every symbol, the formal relationships involved in the above notions become significant by attaching to them the appropriate interpretation. Let us consider, then, what we will mean by 'degree of freedom' and by the phrase 'an infinitely greater freedom.'

'Degree of freedom' will mean here the elaboration of all possible states of a given consciousness-mode, such as sensation. Every possible sensation or combinations of sensations, including percepts and recepts, will form one dimension or degree of freedom in consciousness. As we can place no limits upon these elaborations *in their own direction,* we regard their total possibility as a one-fold infinity. Sensation, together with affection, would give a two-fold infinity, while sensation, affection, and cognition would give a three-fold infinity.

'An infinitely greater freedom' carries the meaning that the elaborations in the sense of a higher dimension cannot be expressed in terms of lower dimensions. Thus, every step from one group of dimensions to the next larger one involves a transcendence that is equivalent to entering an infinitely greater world.

However, cross-representation from the world of a higher degree of freedom to a lower one is possible in a sense, and this is analogous to what is called 'projection' in mathematics. Thus a three-dimen-

151

sional configuration, such as a bridge, a building, etc., can be projected upon a two-dimensional field, such as a sheet of drawing paper, in such a way that an engineer can construct the bridge or building from the drawing and may determine the forms of all his materials before a stroke of physical work is done. But there are certain important things that can be done with the actual constructed object, a bridge, for instance, that cannot be done with the simple plan of it. Thus an automobile can travel across a real bridge but cannot cross on a two-dimensional drawing. This means that the three-dimensional actuality has something that can never be captured within the limits of any two-dimensional representation, however completely the latter may be elaborated.

This leads to the point where we are enabled to apply our symbol. Here the fourth dimension represents the Higher Consciousness, by whatever name we may know It, such as Cosmic Consciousness, Specialism, Christ Consciousness, Transcendental Consciousness, Nirvana, etc. We may call this dimension "Profundity." Now, the actuality of Profundity can be realized only by Awakening in the direction of this Fourth Dimension. It may be 'projected' downward into the three-dimensional field of sensation-affection-cognition, but this projection is not any more the actuality of Profundity than the descriptive plan of a bridge is the bridge itself. But as an engineer by the aid of his peculiar knowledge can employ such a plan to construct an actual bridge, so also through the more or less aroused Consciousness of Profundity a man can use a projected expression from out of the Fourth Dimension to derive values in terms of the Higher Consciousness. In this way even a latent Consciousness of Profundity may be stirred to life.

The sum-total of all possible Higher Consciousness may well involve many dimensions, perhaps an unlimited number, but for mankind, in general, the next step is well represented by the Fourth Dimension.

A very important point to note is that the birth from a narrower dimensionality to a higher is not conditional upon the complete exhaustion of every possibility on the lower level. Man has unfolded on both the sensation and affectional dimensions more than any animal, but much of this has become possible to him just because of the superior advantages he possessed by reason of being cognitively awake. Thus, sensuous art requires, in addition to sensuous capacity, a considerable development of affection and cognition. In fact, great art requires a special development of the affections. Likewise, a high development of character, of the love-nature, or of the moral side of man, requires the cooperation of the cognitive dimension. Any one of these three dimensions may be the most highly developed in an individual man, but the distinguishing mark which separates a man from an animal is the presence of the cognitive capacity, or that power which, among other things, makes rational thought and language possible. A man does not differ from an animal because he *has* affections, for animals as well as men can and do know love, loyalty, passion, anger, etc. But through the combination with cognition, man has increased the possibilities of the affections enormously beyond the highest possibility of any animal. As a matter of fact, it is only a minority of men whose highest excellence is in the pure cognitive dimension, while the majority excel in the affectional or sensational dimensions. The important point is that the lesser wakening which separates a man from an animal and the greater Awakening which separates or distinguishes a God-Man from the ordinary man involves the arousing of an entirely new capacity. Degree of development in terms of the new capacity is a matter of evolution on a higher level, but that which distinguishes an animal, a man, and a God-Man is not a question of *degree,* but of *awakening* to a new dimension of consciousness.

Now, just as awakening to cognitive capacity enormously enriches development in terms of sensation and affection, so also the Awakening to Higher Consciousness tremendously augments the capacity in the already partially unfolded inferior dimensions. The result is that the greater portion of the best in religion, morals, art, philosophy, science, etc., has come from the hands or lips of those Men who have had this Higher Awakening in at least some degree. Here is an effect that the man limited to three dimensions of consciousness can in some measure evaluate and appreciate, even though the Key Power is as yet beyond his understanding. In fact, two of the earmarks of the Illumined Man are afforded by an increase, amounting sometimes almost to a revolution, in the intellectual and affectional functions or dimensions. Now, an animal may well recognize that somehow man can excel it in its own field, as is revealed by the fact that man is a far more dangerous killer than the most predatory animal, but the animal has no idea of the key that gives man that peculiar power. Likewise, ordinary subject-object conscious man, however much he may appreciate the superior excellence of the God-Conscious Man in the former's field, is utterly unconscious of, or blind to, the Key that unlocks the latter's Power. As has been repeated over and over again, man must Awake to understand this, and it is quite useless for him to try to circumscribe that Awakening by attempting to divine what It actually is. When something of It is suggested, as in the present case, by the use of an analogy or symbol, It is not being circumscribed in the sense involved in all effective definition.

I wish again to call attention to the fact that the notion of 'dimension' as employed in this discussion is taken in the sense characteristic in pure mathematics. Dimension, conceived as 'degree of freedom,' involves the notion of 'manifoldness,' but not necessarily that of measurement or metrical property. Strictly considered, measurement belongs only to applied mathematics where extension is pertinent, since it is a property of physical matter. Thus the first three dimensions, as well as the fourth, do not logically introduce the notion of measurement or extension. The manifolds may be given a purely qualitative interpretation, and thus the difficulty involved in thinking of four dimensions of extension is avoided. But the notion of manifoldness is essential and primary. Without this there could be no evolution nor differentiation in any sense on any level. In fact, we could regard all space in the extended sense as merely an illusion, and yet retain the whole of pure mathematics, with all its richness of diversified development remaining unaffected. Verily, if the reader can break down the power which the notion of extension has over his own mind, he will have gone a long way in preparing himself for the Awakening.

154

LXI

The Nature of Ponderable Matter

September 15

A COUPLE OF WEEKS prior to the 7th of last August, the final correlation in the development of an idea broke through into my mind. This idea had such a clarifying effect, relative to the nature of the phenomenal world, that it was decisive in clearing up the remaining intellectual barriers to Recognition. As this correlation was of high importance in my own case, it may prove to be of similar value to others, and in addition may have systematic objective significance. Accordingly, I shall strive to give it a clear formulation.

What is the nature of the phenomenal world? The non-critical Naturalist says that it is the actual 'thing' itself, existing quite independently of the perceiving subject. He goes further and says, not only is it self-dependent apart from the observer, but it is, as well, substantially as it appears to be to the observer. But all philosophy that has attained any degree of the critical sense, as well as modern science, agrees that the facts force a modification of this naive view. Genuine philosophers concur in holding that whatever the real world may be, it is at least modified by the senses so that what man directly experiences is something different. Also, for the twentieth century physicist, ponderable matter, that is, matter and form as given through the senses, is definitely known not to be the actual physical reality. The ultimates of matter are apparently wave-systems of essentially the same nature as electromagnetic or light waves; and, further, these systems cannot be correctly imaged in any sensible model. Only mathematical equations are capable of representing the reality, whatever that may be, in a manner that is consonant with the observed effects.

Closely connected with modern science and mathematics, a school of philosophy has developed in which the world is conceived as composed of externally real existences, but these existences are viewed as other than their sensible appearance. This school is known as Neo-Realism. This philosophy is highly technical and acutely logical, and thus fundamentally quite beyond the understanding of any reader who is not well versed in modern studies on the foundations of mathematics. But for our present purposes only one point is of decisive importance in determining our relationship to this school. This school is in agreement with Naturalism in regarding Consciousness as irrelevant to Actuality. Things are regarded as being what they are, quite independently of any observer or thinker.

If either the Naturalistic or the Neo-Realistic views were the true one, there would be no meaning attaching to such words as 'Recognition,' 'Higher Consciousness,' the 'Awakening,' the notion of the 'Self sustaining the universe,' 'Cosmic Consciousness,' etc., except in a merely psychological sense. Neo-Realism, as well as Naturalism, denies that there is such a thing as a Metaphysical Reality, at any rate in the ontological sense. Our own standpoint is necessarily quite at variance with either of the foregoing schools. While we recognize that Neo-Realism offers much of unquestionable value as a partial view of the sum-total of all possibilities of consciousness, yet we must challenge it as a system claiming exclusive validity.

It is not our present purpose to attempt a systematic criticism of Neo-Realism, but only to make clear that a challenge of that philosophy is implied by practically everything that this book contains. We may, at a later time, undertake a general criticism of Neo-Realism as well as other philosophies that occupy a position that is not compatible with our own, but such critical work is necessarily rather technical, and so does not properly belong here. At this time we merely wish to clarify our own philosophic position in the reader's mind and acknowledge the existence of the critical problem.

Both in India and the West, systematic philosophies exist wherein the ultimate Reality is posited as being pure Consciousness. The apparently inert and lifeless matter comes to be viewed as merely a partially obscured Consciousness. Thus, if we regard a portion of an originally homogeneous Consciousness as partly blanked-out or neutralized by its own other, the result is some degree

156

of relative unconsciousness. This relative unconsciousness is the objective world, or, in other words, the basis of the whole universe as experienced through the senses. An extensive restatement of philosophy and science can be given from this standpoint, but this also is not our present purpose. I desire simply to emphasize the most important ontological features of this view. Now one decisively important consequence of this standpoint is that the experienced universe, including all ponderable matter and form, is essentially an abstraction from, rather than an addition to, the original unmanifested Reality. Starting from an original and eternal non-relative Consciousness, which comprehends time and space as well as all else, all notions such as external manifestation and development must be in the nature of a predication concerning something abstracted or subtracted from the Whole. Among other things, it is clear that nothing can be predicated of the Whole which necessarily presupposes the dominance of time, as for example, process or development. The Whole,˙ since It comprehends space and time, is not conditioned by these. In the end, we find that no relative concept—and all concepts are relative—can be predicated of the Whole, not even Being. In fact, It is THAT which is neither Being nor non-Being, and thus remains essentially unthinkable, though It may be Realized through the Awakening to Identification.

It may now be said that the universe is produced by a process which we may call a partial blinding, and that the reverse process, i.e., that of Awakening, destroys the universe to just the extent that the Awakening has proceeded. This should make perfectly clear the rationale of the statement of the Mystic who says: "I sustain this universe and can produce or destroy it at will." When Shankara speaks of destroying the universe, he does not have in mind a physical cataclysm but a Transition in Consciousness such that the apperceptive Subject realizes Itself as Lord over the universe, instead of being a victim of it. The individual soul that has attained this position may choose continued cognizance of the universe, but the essential power of the latter over the former is destroyed unequivocally.

If, now, we substitute for the term 'relative unconsciousness' another term which is fundamentally equivalent, i.e., 'ponderable matter and form,' we may give the foregoing philosophy a transformation that fits more closely the terminology of modern science. This leads to the judgment that ponderable matter and form constitute a state of relative vacuity or nothingness in the essential sense. It is interesting to note that we are now not far from a position formulated by the young English physicist Dirac, though he reached this view by means of a quite different approach. There is nothing in this standpoint that militates against the relative correctness of any physical determination. The only thing that is changed is the metaphysical interpretation of what those determinations Mean. There is in this no challenge of the scientist, so long as he confines his conclusions to the limits logically defined by his methodology. He remains our best authority in the determination of objective fact as seen from the perspective he assumes. If he generalizes beyond these limits, we need no more than his own logic to bring a counter-challenge. This logic, followed strictly, can go no further than agnosticism relative to metaphysical actuality, and We are content that as physical scientist he should stop there. But We are not content that, as a man, he should linger in that position, for it is barren of enduring Values.

Let us give an illustration of how our standpoint would affect the interpretation of a fundamentally important principle of physics. Long ago our science reached the point where it realized that the vast bulk of the sensible effects associated with matter do not afford the essential determinants of matter. As now understood, 'matter' is defined by 'mass,' and this in turn is manifested through the property called 'inertia.' Thus, where there is matter there is inertia, and where there is inertia there is matter. Newton gave the law of inertia in the following form: "Every body perseveres in its state of rest or of uniform motion in a straight line, except insofar as it is compelled to change that state by impressed forces." The mechanics of Einstein gives this law a different form but does not change its essential characteristic. Now, inertia implies absence of inward or self-produced motion, and hence it also implies essential deadness. In contrast, the fundamental distinguishing mark of Consciousness is the capacity for Self-produced motion. Thus it is that Universal

Consciousness is often represented by the term 'Ceaseless Motion.' But, from this standpoint, the state of relative motion as well as that of rest in a material body, mechanically considered, is simply the absence of *real* motion. Where Consciousness is full, there is no inertia. Only absolute absence of Consciousness—a state of real nothingness—would be absolutely inert. Thus, we would say, the physicist is right in making inertia the prime mark of that which he is studying, but he is wrong if he proceeds to predicate substantial reality of his object of study. Actually he is studying a relative nothingness. This fact does not detract in the least from the practical values of his studies, but simply means that he is dealing with the obverse of metaphysical actuality. Further, once it is realized that he is unfolding the laws governing the obverse of the Real, his knowledge can be employed as a Way to the Recognition of that Reality. I can see how our present physical science is unfolding a peculiarly beautiful Path to Yoga. So I certainly have no quarrel with physical science as such. In fact, I feel quite otherwise.

Today physicists have found that at least much of force is not external to matter. In radio-activity there is an element of unpredictable spontaneity that certainly looks like what We mean by self-produced motion, or energy arising from within. The result is that matter is now seen as not wholly inert, all of which simply opens wider a Door for Us.

Let us, then, take the standpoint that ponderable matter, or the sensuously perceived world, is to be regarded as relative emptiness, so that absolute matter in this sense would be an absolute vacuum. We then see that the relative world, or this seen universe, is produced by a kind of process of negation, and hence from the standpoint of metaphysical philosophy it would have to be regarded as a Maya or Illusion. From this it is not to be concluded that the universe is without value. But it does imply that if a man misplaces his predication of 'Reality,' he would then be caught in an illusion in the sense that produces bondage. None the less, it would still remain true that if he avoids this error he can, through the universe, find the Real. Most of humanity has fallen into the error, and that is the cause of all suffering. But the very agency that caused the fall may be used as a stepping-stone to Recognition. To achieve this, a certain Copernican shift in individual consciousness is necessary. Thus, instead of regarding the sensuously apparent as being substantial, the standpoint should be reversed. Then we would view the seeming emptiness of space, where there is a relative absence of physical matter, as being actually far more substantial than any ponderable matter. We would thus say: "Increase of ponderability implies decrease of substantiality and vice versa." Consequently, in some sense, the laws governing the ponderable become the obverse of the laws governing the substantial.

The foregoing discussion gives us a new angle for interpreting the meaning of the technique designed to arouse Recognition by the systematic denial of all that is ponderable or thinkable. The end of the process is the arrival at a *seeming* nothingness, i.e., pure Consciousness-without-an-object. This stage, plus the identification of one's Self with that *seeming* nothingness, produces at once the Recognition. But at that moment the Nothingness becomes complete Fullness and absolute Substantiality. Then the Realized Man may turn toward the world and assert universally: "I am all things." But now it is the obverse of the ponderable universe of which he is speaking. We may regard this obverse as something like a matrix. This Matrix is a continuum, while the ponderable manifold is discrete. So far as we can see, this resolves the difficulties in the reconciliation between the many and the One in the logical sense. Actually, for myself, this view was the finally effective cognitive aid that made possible the Transition in consciousness.

*   *   *   *   *

I believe that in the foregoing I have discovered a new elaboration in the technique for arousing Recognition. It does not demand the radical silencing of the thought processes. However, in my own case, I did employ silencing in a different sense, i.e., in silencing the affections, so that at the crucial moment there was high order of calmness. There was cognitive activity, but it was so nearly purely cognitive that it was highly dispassionate. The cognitive action was exceptionally keenly discriminative, but it had to be maintained on the outer side only very briefly until something very deep and strong took hold inwardly, and thereafter the activity centered in the personal consciousness ceased to have any really effective obscuring power. It is as though the whole complex nature of the organized man were, from that moment, entrained behind a commanding Power that dominated from then onward. The result is that I do not seem to feel troubled by the residual habits in the personal man that have grown out of the past. There is something more or less automatic in the progressive transformation of them.

LXII

Real Equality

WE ARE NOW IS A POSITION to attach a valid meaning to the idea of 'equality.' It is perfectly clear that in the relative or phenomenal sense no two things, persons, or creatures are equal, one to the other. In fact, of all the milliards of concrete states of consciousness no two are actual duplicates, and, therefore, no two are equal. The notions of equality and inequality involve measurement, in some sense, and thus equality implies that all measurable aspects of one thing are precisely the same as those of another or of others. We do find such equality in mathematics, but not in the sensible world. Further, the notion of 'equality' is incompatible with the notions of 'development' and 'freedom.' For, if there is such a thing as growth, and if self-determinism has any effect upon it, then not all entities would develop in precisely the same way or to the same degree, even though at the hypothetical initial stage there were absolute equality. But if we turn from the phenomenal world to the Matrix of all relative things, creatures, men, etc., it at once becomes apparent that the Matrix of a blade of grass is equal to the Matrix of a man or of a planet. For the Matrix, taken in the inmost sense, is the universal homogeneous Plenum. But even here, in strict logic, we should not predicate 'equality' but rather negate 'inequality,' since in the Great Continuum measurement is irrelevant.

One consequence follows at once, that true Democracy exists only for God-Realized Men. All others, being as yet bound to the relative or subject-object world, do actually stand on a scaled ladder, marking the different stages of achieved development. We can thus see how Carpenter was right in calling his poem "Towards Democracy." It is simply one way of saying "Towards Recognition." Consequently, this Democracy properly has nothing to do with what is possible here and now in the matter of government, men being what they are. So he who would bring about a true democracy in the world, instead of the spurious kind which alone is known to history, should work toward the spread of Recognition among men.

There are only two senses in which it may be said that men are born equal. In the first place, all men, and as well all things from an atom to a star, are equal in the sense that at the heart of everything is the one unchanging and indivisible Spirit. In the second place, all men are equal in the bare fact that to be a man a creature must have awakened into consciousness on the cognitive level. But in the degree of relative development of powers, in any sense, no two men are equal. Further, no two men unfold during life their initial possibilities in exactly equal degree. Thus in the relative sense, there can be no equality among men.

The fundamental fact of the empiric inequality of men does have a vital bearing upon the problem of what kind of organization of society can endure effectively. Institutions built upon a false premise cannot really endure nor can they function effectively. No formulation of a law made by man can change this fact. Nature is what it is, and propaganda to the contrary can merely produce an illusion. Visible man is what he is, and not what an idealist may imagine him to be or wish him to be. Ultimately sound government must orient itself to actualities, however much administrators may labor toward an ideal.

162

LXIII

The Predicament of Buddha

September 16

I TURN to the "Gospel of Buddha" and find these words: "He
—the worldling—will call resignation what to the Enlightened One
is purest Joy. He will see annihilation where the Perfected One finds
Immortality. He will regard as death what the Conqueror of Self
knows to be Life Everlasting."

According to the record, this was said soon after Gautama had
attained Enlightenment under the Bodhi tree. At first the Tathagata
was tempted to keep silence, for it seemed useless to preach a
Message of Liberation which certainly could not be understood by
most men. In the end, Buddha decided to give the Message for the
benefit of those who could understand. But the problem He faced
is a very fundamental one, since it is very difficult for the man who
is bound to subject-object consciousness to conceive of another kind
of Life where egoism ceases. The average man can imagine a heaven
or a hell built upon the subject-object pattern where life is more
intense, whether in a pleasurable or painful sense, but the truly
Emancipated Life is beyond his comprehension. The Christian world
has interpreted the Kingdom of Heaven as simply a sublimated subject-object domain, and thus quite missed the real meaning of Jesus.
Christ brought a Message of Emancipation, just as Buddha did, and
Its meaning was exactly the same, though stated in a form to fit the
consciousness of a different people. Few, indeed, of the Christian
world have ever truly understood His meaning. A subject-object
world experienced after physical death as a highly blissful state is
not Liberation. Essentially it is not different from this present world
right here. Consequently such a world could be represented in terms
of conceptual language just as this is. But such is not the case with
respect to Nirvana or the Kingdom of Heaven.

The impossibility of genuinely formulating and conveying to

163

others what the Liberated State is is not simply the difficulty afforded in trying to give expression to an unfamiliar experience. The problem, in the latter case, may be great but it is not, in principle, beyond solution. It is simply a question of inventing the appropriate concepts and word-signs, and this can be done by men who are sufficiently skillful. But the kind of consciousness that falls outside the subject-object field is more than difficult to express in relative terms. It is absolutely impossible to do so. It is not simply a question of our not yet having developed sufficient skill. The impossibility inheres in the fact that the subject-object form, essential to language as such, can only distort the Transcendent. The 'Kingdom of Heaven' and 'Nirvana' are simply names pointing to a deathless Reality. But that Reality is ever something other than anything that can be conceived in relative terms. Hence it is the negation of everything we know in the subject-object sense. Thus, It is not-evil and not-good, not-large and not-small, not-colored and not-colorless, and so on through all pairs of opposites. More than this, It is not-good and not not-good, not-large and not not-large, not-colored and not not-colored, and so on, also, through all pairs of contradictories. This means that It is not to be found anywhere in the 'universe of discourse,' as understood in logic. Naturally, this must appear as annihilation to the subject-object consciousness.

Yet, in point of fact, It is Infinite Life. It is pure Joy, the utterly satisfying Richness. It is the absolutely certain Knowledge. But It can be Known only through Identity. Once It is Known, even though it be for but a moment, then It is realized as the one and only adequate solution of human misery. More than that, It supplies the basis which, alone, affords an adequate solution of the final problems of philosophy and science. The combined testimony of Those who have attained Realization builds well the case for the Reality of this Transcendent World, and something deep in the heart of every man whispers: "Yes, it is so." If only men would listen to this still, small Voice!

But man must be born again before he can Know. And He who is born again is There, whether or not He remains correlated with embodiment in the relative world. In being born again, he has died to subject-object consciousness, in the essential sense, even though he continues to function in this field. He has died in a far more fundamental sense than is true of the worldly man who merely departs from the physical body. The latter type of transition does not lead out of the subject-object domain. But the Great Transition leads beyond the ordinary heaven and hell, just as much as it does beyond this world.

That which man overcomes finally in the Great Transition is the vehicle of egoism. This is an entirely different matter from that of merely losing the instruments of action and of relative knowledge in a particular zone of consciousness.

LXIV

The Adept World

A RARELY DISCUSSED QUESTION that arises is: "When all the units of mankind are finally Awakened, will the values of the subject-object consciousness be abandoned in every sense?" Theoretically such could be the case, but it is not necessarily so. Between the subject-object world and Nirvana or the Kingdom of Heaven there exists a domain, creatively produced, in which there abides a rare Community of Liberated Souls. Here the Real Man is embedded in the Transcendent, and yet He acts in the subject-object sense. The Members of this Community in part act for the redemption of the still-sleeping mankind, but even supposing this labor of love completed—and some day it will be—yet They will continue to act in the pursuance of a larger and longer-enduring purpose. This is the Great Domain of genuine creativeness. Here abides the Hierarchy of real manifested life, which rises in grandeur from minor levels up to modes of informed Consciousness so vast as to transcend the comprehension of even the greatest Adept.

This is a sort of Life which is more within the range of imagination and appreciation of the subject-object man than the pure Liberated State. There exists an Initiation wherein man may make a choice between this Life and pure Liberation. This kind of Life retains the essential values of the subject-object consciousness, though it is rooted in the Transcendent, and consciously so. There are many Worlds beyond—many possibilities—most of which are quite outside the capacity of the imagination of the present humanity. But Liberation is the Key to these Worlds, and thus it is said that Liberation is not the end but the beginning of Real Life. Liberation is the Goal to be envisaged by the once-born, subject-object man, but when he attains that State He is twice-born and then faces alternative possibilities, one of which is continued expression through a Life that is real in the objective sense, though something quite different from the life in the familiar subject-object domain.

We have here taken a step beyond the usual occidental interpretation of the Nirmanakayas. The latter are those Men who have won to Nirvana, or the Kingdom of Heaven, and refused to 'enter in' fully. Hence They remain embodied, though in a sense too lofty for the grasp of the ordinary understanding. Their choice of that course of action has been portrayed as due to a Compassion for the humanity that remains behind. But it is further stated that this involves a real Renunciation. This is only part of the story. The refusal of Nirvana opens the Way to the ascending Hierarchy of the World Builders—an Hierarchy which reaches upward to the stars and systems of stars. But, in a sense, that is a Life both in and outside of Nirvana. It is grounded in the Divine Indifference, which is as truly a manifested as a not-manifested State.

LXV

Manifestation without Evil

ANY ACTION, in the subject-object sense, does imply duality or polarity, but it is not essential that any particular manifested world shall arouse all possible dualities. In fact, even in this world, as we progress in our knowledge, we discover new dualities and perhaps create dualities that do not appear in the old cultures. The implication is that there is unlimited possibility in such dualistic expression. Other worlds may have dualistic forms utterly unknown to us, and we in our turn have forms quite unknown to them. Thus at present worlds may be existent or may become existent wherein the duality of good and evil simply does not exist. It is said that such is the case. Mayhap man may leave evil behind him forever and yet remain an actor in the objective sense. This opens up some interesting possibilities and shows how there may be an objective life which at the same time remains one of continuous happiness.

LXVI

The One Element

ONCE ONE HAS HAD A GLIMPSE of the Consciousness which I have called the High Indifference, it readily becomes clear that there can be but one ultimate Element. Spirit is not divided from matter in any final sense. This is simply the truth concerning the subject and the object, given in other terms. In that State where I realize Myself as identical with all space and with all objects, there is no division between an 'I' and a 'not-I.' This is equivalent to saying there is but one Element. But the same thing cannot be said concerning the seeming relationships within the shell of the subject-object consciousness. For here the subject has the appearing of being different from the object, but these two stand in some relationship to each other. Likewise, here spirit and matter appear as though divided in some relationship, rather than united. Thus there is a sense in which the Sankhya dualism is valid. There is no transcending the dualism *within the shell*. It now becomes clear why the notion of only one Element misses the understanding of him who has not yet broken out of the shell, and also why 'Spirit' seems to require a definition that delimits It by saying, "Whatever Spirit is, It is other than matter." It is not correct to say that Spirit becomes matter, and vice versa, within the limits of the subject-object manifold.

LXVII

The Current of Numberless Dimensions

BEFORE ME there streams a Great Current of unnumbered dimensions.

This is the High Indifference of All in all,

Producing, sustaining, and consuming all;

Utter and eternal Completeness, the End and the Beginning and the Mid-point.

Within this Current, eddies, swirls, and grand sweeps, blended together.

These, the worlds, the stars, and systems manifold, yet continuous.

Within their midst, a few vortices, hard-cased, seemingly separate.

Therein, consciousness bound in separateness and misery.

There also, this world, forlorn orphan, sick and weary;

Snare of Mara, who, triumphant for a season,

Makes the unreal seem the real, meshing in bondage.

But Time! and the shell will crack,

Flowing on in the eternal gyrations;

Sorrow becoming Joy, and Ignorance transformed into Wisdom.

LXVIII

Concerning Duty

To THE MERELY EGOISTIC MAN, duty appears as in some sense an external constraint. It is a mode of conduct, as defined by the civil law, by the religious authority, by the social body of which he is a member, or by his own rational judgment. Impulses arising from the different aspects of the human nature are often at variance with the pronouncements of such duty. The result is a battle in the man between something that he calls 'lower' and something else which he feels is higher. Duty comes as an imposed discipline and implies more or less hardship although, in general, the fruit of faithfully performed duty is a sense of 'having done well.' As a rule, in the end, this feeling more than offsets the hardship. But it is unquestionably true that the urge to freedom, naturally great in some men, leads to restiveness under the sway of duty. It is also true that, among the variously imposed duties, there is very often an incompatibility, so that if the individual acts in faithful accordance with a given duty, he at the same time violates the requirements of another. This may happen even within the field of duties which the individual himself freely recognizes as proper. So it is impossible to say of a life confined strictly within the path of duty that it is free from conflict.

In the case of an Awakened Man, 'duty' undergoes a radical transformation. Duty ceases to be or, more properly, progressively ceases to have the character of something externally imposed, even in the sense in which we may say that a man's own theoretical judgment of right and wrong is external. On this higher level, duty becomes the spontaneous impulse that flows out of the Illumined Consciousness, so that here the conflict between duty and impulse vanishes. From the standpoint of Illumination, the desired thing to do is the right thing to do. As a consequence, in one sense, the Illumined Man, while He is acting or judging in the Current of Illumination, is beyond duty. But this is true only so long as we give to 'duty' the connotation of 'something externally imposed.' However, in some usages, the meaning of 'duty' has been extended to cover a wider connotation than this.

'Duty' has been employed as a translation of the Sanskrit term 'Dharma.' Now, 'Dharma' carries a meaning for which there is no adequate English equivalent, though 'duty' carries a portion of that meaning. However, the inadequacy of this translation is made clear in the following illustration. It is perfectly proper to say: "It is the dharma of fire to burn." But if we substitute 'duty' for 'dharma' and say, "It is the duty of fire to burn," the effect is quite false with respect to the primary meaning we attach to the word 'duty.' In a similar sense, it is perfectly true that it is the Dharma of the God-Conscious Man to act in accordance with the Divine Impulse that springs up in Him. Clearly this Dharma is not an external constraint as it is at-one with an interior and Divine impulse. Such a Man is happy when acting in accordance with Dharma, and not otherwise. If, now, we agree to give to 'duty' just precisely the meaning attached to 'Dharma' then, it remains true, the Illumined Man does not transcend duty. But in this case, 'duty' would cease to have the connotation of an external constraint.

The problem in connection with the word 'duty' is psychological and emotional rather than rational. Intellectually we can say, "Let 'duty' have the connotation of 'Dharma'," and then proceed to use it in the changed sense. I have done this myself for some time and find no hardship in the notion of 'duty,' the only difficulty being the definition of just what the duty is in a given complex situation where different canons of action come into conflict. When a clear definition emerged, I always felt happy, but much of the time I found it difficult to attain that clarity. However, I find that many individuals are unable to overcome a certain negative emotional complex centering around the word 'duty.' So I suggest that we take over into our language the term 'Dharma,' as we have already assimilated many Latin and Greek words, and use it to cover the meaning for which 'duty' is admittedly inadequate. From an electron to a God there is no creature beyond Dharma, but there is a level where duty is transcended, when understood in the usual sense.

It is a mistake to think that the Dharma of even the God-Conscious Man is without problems. As God-Conscious, His impulse is His Dharma, and thus there is no emotional conflict. But the question "What does that Dharma mean in practical action?" is quite another matter. Absolute solutions of relative problems, outside of mathematics, do not exist. The Higher Consciousness is certain on Its own Level; It does effect an enormous clarification of insight on the subject-object level; and It always manifests as an intent to effect the highest good of all; but in all dealings with human beings unknown variables are involved, even from the perspective of high Adepts. As a consequence, Illumination by no means implies infallible action in the subject-object field. So there always remains the practical problem, which we may state in the form of the question, "What course in action best manifests the inwardly recognized Dharma?" Naturally, for the solution of this problem, the Illumined Man who has, in addition to His Illumination, a broad rational understanding of the science of ethics is also best equipped for making lofty intent to manifest as wise action.

Another important point which should be remembered is the fact that rarely if ever is the personality of the God-Conscious Man enveloped in the full Light of the Higher Consciousness at all times. Generally the period of the envelopment is brief, sometimes of only momentary duration, and in many cases it happens but once in a lifetime. Much of the time, even in the cases of Men who have Known a high order of Illumination, the consciousness sinks more or less into the subject-object field, with a corresponding obscuration of the insight. The lesser impulses, which have their ground in the subject-object man, are not completely transformed in one moment, although the purification of them proceeds progressively. There remains, therefore, a practical need for discrimination among the complex of all impulses that may arise. He who has had even no more than one moment of Illumination does have a modulus for such discrimination, and that gives Him a decisive advantage over other men. But nevertheless He has not transcended the need for discrimination in practical action.

LXIX

Philosophic Reconciliations

ONE OF THE STRIKING CHANGES I find in my own consciousness is a marked increase in the capacity to see reconciliations between ideas that ordinarily seem quite incompatible. From my present perspective, I see a great deal of truth in all of the philosophical views that have come before me, with the possible exception of naive Naturalism. At the same time, it does not seem that any philosophy has succeeded in saying the final word. When translated into words I find that the Recognition takes on a form that is fundamentally idealistic, a view of the Whole which gives primacy to Consciousness. I know of no report from the level of Mystical Consciousness that does not concur in this, and thus, in general, Mysticism does challenge all materialistic schools in the ontological sense. Yet it cannot be denied that even the materialistic outlook does have some relative value.

But within the idealistic group, my own spontaneous expression accords far more closely with rational monism than with the dualistic or voluntaristic systems of idealism. At this point there is no longer an agreement among those who have attained the mystic insight, though the preponderant expression tends toward monism in some sense. We have here to recognize the fact that the form which Realization takes when expressed in the subject-object world is determined by the predilections of the individual man, as these already exist at the time of the Realization. Recognition adds something that is held in common in all instances; but, inasmuch as no individual personality is itself universal, every expression is at best but a facet reflecting the Truth as near as may be. It would seem but the part of wisdom for each individual to recognize this fact and then be true to himself in the personal as well as the Higher sense.

As one who, by temperament and natural inclination, stands close to rational Idealism, it was inevitable that in the past I should have come into conflict with the main thesis of the Pragmatists, inasmuch as the latter have generally sought to establish themselves, first of all, by a challenge of the validity of rational Idealism. William James gives as one of the primary postulates of Pragmatism the principle, "There is no difference of truth that does not make a difference of fact somewhere." This criterion is then repeatedly employed to challenge the view of rational Idealism. I submit my own Recognition as an instance which controverts this challenge. I mounted to the Moment of the Transition in the framework of rational Idealism, and the critical step hinged upon the isolation of the pure apperceptive moment of consciousness itself. Thus Truth, as conceived by rational Idealism of the monistic type, did effect a difference of fact for me. The difference of fact is a new relationship to the subject-object consciousness and a state of far greater peace and happiness than had been known previously. But the cause of this 'difference in fact' was not an experience but the attainment of 'Knowledge through Identity,' which, as I have already pointed out, is neither experience nor formal knowledge but a third kind of knowledge.

From the foregoing a partial reconciliation seems to follow. The Pragmatists are right in asserting that formal knowledge is not enough to determine effective or final Truth, but they are wrong in asserting that such Truth, or the knowledge of it, must depend upon experience. On the other hand, the rational Idealists are right in maintaining that the effective Truth must be absolute and, therefore, cannot be derived from experience, which of necessity must be finite. But they are wrong in so far as they claim to be able to establish this Truth by formal demonstration alone. The effective establishment of this Truth requires 'Knowledge through Identity,' i.e., a direct Recognition on the level of Infinity, which is never attainable by any expansion of experience alone.

LXX

Recognition an Act of Transcendence

I CANNOT too strongly emphasize the fact that Recognition is not a natural result of simple growth or expansion in the subject-object field. It is an act of Transcendence, whereby a Man Awakens to find that, instead of being finite, He is an Infinite Being, has always been so, and always will be so. For a time his consciousness had been obscured and it seemed as though he were a finite being, but in one moment a finite world is destroyed in an essential sense. In principle, he may Awaken regardless of whether he has had much or little experience in a finite world, or of whether he may be highly or imperfectly evolved in the subject-object sense. Practically, it is a rule that a certain superiority of individual development is the antecedent condition of success. But this is so simply because it takes strength to resist the hypnotic effect of the subject-object field. However, it is not an invariable rule. Unquestionably, the Awakened Man of superior individual development after the Transition can offer more to His companions who remain bound within the relative world than is possible in the case of a man of inferior capacity. But all this has to do with expression and not with the fundamental nature of Recognition as such.

The Awakening, when viewed from the relative perspective, is a 'being-born,' and a 'being born' is a 'dying' to the antecedent condition. It is useless to try to dodge this fact. It is simply the anciently uttered and repeatedly formulated Law: "The self of matter and the Self of Spirit cannot meet." I have already explained how the Twice-Born has died to the ordinary life, and yet continues to act through the form of embodied consciousness in an entirely different sense from that which had obtained prior to the Transition. Now the antecedent condition of Awakening to THAT, is a dying to this, in a mystical sense. This is the rational basis of true asceticism. The asceticism may be a conscious and deliberate discipline, or its value may come through accepting what life brings with resignation. But for either to be effective there must be a turning to the Higher Life or, in other words, Aspiration. Now, after the ascetic discipline has finished its work and the new Birth has been accomplished, the old rules cease to be relevant. The new Life is Free, and the course of action in the subject-object world is Self-chosen.

*　*　*　*　*

Note: It has been drawn to my attention that the idea of the antecedent death, preceding the Second Birth, is a notion easily misunderstood and repellent to many natures. Perhaps the idea could be made clearer by noting the fact that it is a dying to what is already a state of relative death, when considered from the metaphysical or eternal standpoint. It is thus a case of a double negative giving a positive. This mystic death is not death of the body, nor the destruction of any principle or function in the constitution of human consciousness, though it does initiate a progressive spiritualization of those principles. In one sense, it is death of *attachment* to matter, or to the world as object. In a deeper sense, it is death of personal egoism. It is entirely useless to cavil at this for we are dealing with a Law of the Higher Nature that has been made clear, at least since the time of Gautama Buddha. To disguise this Law as a concession to psychological prejudice does not change the fact of its actuality. If a man would become consciously immortal, he must die to mortality. The fruit is abiding Joy and Life Everlasting.

LXXI

The Record Continued

I FIND THAT, as the days go by, there is a re-organization and consolidation of life about a new center. The thrill of new Awakening, that at first so dominates and sweeps the personal consciousness, gradually becomes a quiet steadiness on a level of new confidence. I cannot say that I feel any regret for the old life. I do not find any inhibition that would restrain me from dipping into any phase of old experience if I desired and found it convenient to do so. I do not feel the restless urge for outer adventure that formerly I felt so strongly. Not that I cease to feel joy in the wild places, but the service that they rendered does not seem to be nearly so important. On the whole, outer interests generally have become quiescent in the presence of an all-consuming interest in a new activity. Still I do not anticipate that I have turned my back on nature entirely. I shall gladly receive the caress of the wilds when convenience makes that possible.

Most of the ordinary activities in which men commonly find pleasure either never did have an attraction for me or some time ago ceased to have that attraction. Many of these activities I have long found distinctly distasteful. But I do not find myself under anything like an external compulsion to refrain from these. It may even prove expedient to devise some entertainment in which the physical personality may participate, but this personality does not seem to insist. The fact is, that the personality does share in the Higher Consciousness and is not a sacrifice. The sense of sacrifice belongs only to the antecedent stages; afterwards there is a Joy in which the whole nature participates. To be sure, now, as ever, the larger purpose must take precedence over minor interests, but there seems to be a quality of such inner harmony that the sense of conflict in such a choice is almost wholly gone.

In addition to the companionship of those immediately surrounding me, I have, as always, the rich companionship of those who have incarnated themselves in books. Only this has become much richer as I feel more keenly the presence of the men who wrote. Further, there is a tangible inner Communion, and this is something of very rare value. If at present I share in an objective responsibility, it is none the less true that I freely chose it, and so I do as I have chosen to do. Finally, I know that even though I move for a time in the restricted field of the external world, yet the High Indifference is not far away—in fact It is present everywhere and at all times.

There is always the intriguery of new discovery, perhaps just around the corner. Even that which I already Know, in the sense of the profound Abstraction, comes again to me as time goes on in the form of concrete discovery. I find It as It takes form in my mind while I write It down. Again, I recognize It in the words of Men who have attained the Recognition, as They bring to me, in terms

176

of formation, That which I already Know in a profound sense. Also, they unfold new aspects of Myself that are not native to this personal consciousness of mine. It is a very satisfactory life, my brothers, and immeasurably more than life-restricted-to-the-shell has anywhere to offer. If the form of outer living which I choose is not the form some other one would choose, let such a one refrain from thinking he would have to cast his life over my form. Remember that Walt Whitman lived a very different life from that of John Yepes, yet both These were Men of high Recognition and both knew profound happiness. In Its deeps the Life is utterly Free, and in a surprising degree that Freedom is reflected in the outer life.

LXXII

The Problem of Government

September 18

IN THESE DAYS when there is such a widespread 'liquidation' of old governmental forms and the substitution of new forms of extreme illiberality and brutality, one who is interested in the welfare of man can scarcely be indifferent to the problem of government. It is clear that thus far all our attempts in government on a large scale have fallen far short of a really satisfactory success. Otherwise there would not be so much of change and demand for changes.

For a government to be truly successful, it must maintain, in high degree in the social body, three principles, (1) Freedom, (2) Justice, and (3) Efficiency.* Now, none of the forms of government that we have tried so far have afforded enduring success in all three respects. The rule of kings and aristocracies has at times worked rea-

* I do not name 'Order' among these for it seems that Order is a means to an end, rather than an end in itself. Practically, we find Order to be vital for the highest possible realization of Freedom, Justice, and Efficiency, and consequently it is important in the pragmatic sense.

sonably well, but in recent as well as ancient, history we have seen very clearly how badly this form can fail when there is a decay of character and competency in the ruling classes. Under certain conditions, democracy does function fairly satisfactorily. These conditions seem to be the following:

1. That the unit of government is not so large as to be beyond the effective comprehension of the average voter.

2. That the intelligence and sense for responsibility in governmental affairs of the average voter is considerably above that of the average human being.

3. That the governmental problems are fairly simple.

In the modern large nations, with our extremely complex civilization and particularly where there is a considerable heterogeneity of population, these conditions are far from being fulfilled. The signs of the break-down of that form of democracy involving universal suffrage are painfully evident today. Democracy has become too dangerously inefficient, and thus this system is being replaced in an increasing degree by the dictatorial form of power wherein efficiency in certain directions is secured at the price of radical loss of freedom and justice.

It has certainly become clear that an excellent constitution is no guarantee of good government. For the government largely becomes what the ruling class makes it, within certain limits determined by the temperament and character of the people governed. In a government such as that of the United States, this ruling class actually is not the people, as it is supposed to be in theory. In practice it is the class of the professional politicians, who, in their turn, have been checked, balanced, and sometimes controlled by another class whose basis of power is economic. Now the professional politician is typically the kind of man who can command the vote of the average elector. Generally this is a sort of man who stands upon a distinctly inferior intellectual and moral level, though there are some brilliant exceptions. The result is that, though the American government is based upon an admirably designed form, it is today showing the signs of serious weakness that may become fatal. If the right kind of men, in sufficient numbers, could be selected for positions of authority and responsibility, this need not be the case. But with the intelligence and moral character of the average elector being what it is, and the common denominator of the whole being still a great deal lower, it is too much to hope that these positions will ever be filled, in sufficient numbers, with the men of requisite capacity and character. We do not have a lack of men with these qualifications, but for the larger part they are not popular with, or comprehensible to, the average voter. Hence, their services, when made available for governmental purposes, are much more commonly located in appointive than in elective positions. But final judgments in matters of policy rest with those who occupy elective offices.

It may well be that a dispassionate study of the history of the American government will show that the checking and control of the politicians by strong men who wield economic power has been more a factor serving the ends of stability and soundness in government than the reverse. Two factors tend to produce such a condition. In the first place, the only important field on the American scene where men of administrative talent could find opportunity for the exercise of their capacities has been in the business and financial worlds. On the whole, in America there are more men in the business field who manifest the caliber of statesmanship, in the true sense of the word, than there are in the political arena. In the second place, economic necessity, in the long run, requires of the men who achieve and hold economic power that they shall develop the kind of thinking which is characteristic of the engineer and scientist, in some measure at least. It is a kind of thought based more upon fact in the objective sense than upon psychological prejudice. In contrast, the typical power of the politicians is psychological and thus capitalizes prejudice, superstition, etc., as instruments of popular appeal. They often win votes by promising something contrary to the laws of nature, and in the very fact that they are willing to make such impossible promises they reveal a dangerous defect of character. The result is that it may well prove to have been the restraint exercised by business and professional men of high character that has, on the whole, proved to be the most beneficent influence affecting practical American government.

It seems to be pretty definitely demonstrated that excellence of system is a far less important determinant in good government than the presence of wise men in the positions of power. The real problem of government is one not of mechanics but of wisdom. Thus the effective key to the solution of the generally chaotic condition of the world today is finding the men of sufficient wisdom and giving them power. This simply means that the crux of the problem of sound government lies in finding and placing sages at the center of power. The true Sage is a Man of Recognition and is, therefore, One who has transcended the temptations that the world has to offer.* At the same time, He brings to the problems of the world a more than worldly wisdom. There are Sages who, like Buddha, have an ancient understanding of government. Mankind can secure the leadership of such Men. But mankind must call for Them and recognize Their authority when They respond.

In the meantime, I see no real hope in the governmental field. Brief palliations there may be here and there, but no healing of the fundamental disease. It may be that conditions will have to continue to grow worse, that mass-man will try, as never before, to wield decision with respect to problems hopelessly beyond his comprehension, and that, when he has failed utterly, as he must fail, and is entangled in the impossible maze of his own construction, then in true humility he will call for help from Those who alone can give that help. In that day, and not before, the problem of government can be solved. For the inescapable fact is that the problem of practical government is too complex for mere subject-object consciousness, however highly developed. The perspective of the Higher Consciousness is an absolute requisite.

* It is not suggested that all Sages are necessarily wise in the special field of government. There are different kinds of wisdom, and rarely, if ever, does any one individual attain the fullness of wisdom, in all directions, in a single embodiment. The Sages fitted for government are those who have unfolded the sense for the art of administration in an especial degree.

LXXIII

Compassion

O COMPASSION! More than the other loves of men, less than the
    High Indifference;
Calmly standing by and waiting; years, centuries, millennia;
Taking to Thyself the suffering of all; transforming toward Joy;
With Light restraining Darkness; with good, evil;
Refusing release while others are bound; melting differences;
Accepting impurity, giving purity;
Bound by no law, yet acquiescing in bondage;
Available for all as the light of the sun, yet forced on no man
    against his will;
Needing nought for Thyself, though giving to all need;
The Base of all hope for this humanity so low;
Pure Radiance Divine.
Sweet art Thou, unutterably sweet; melting within me all hardness;
Stirring inclusion of the low as the high; the evil as the good; the
    weak as the strong; the unclean as the pure; the violent as the
    considerate; none left out;
Awaking new understanding and patience beyond Time;
Arousing forgetfulness of the petty in the grand sweep of the noble;
Equalizing regard, yet exalting true worth;
Reaching beyond all contradiction.
To Thee I sing, glorious Spirit; grandest God mankind can know.

LXXIV

The Symbolism of the Butterfly

September 25

THE LIFE-CYCLE from the egg, through the caterpillar and the chrysalis, to the butterfly, constitutes one of the best symbols afforded by nature of the progress of the human soul from birth into the world, thence through the development of subject-object consciousness, and then finally culminating in the translation to the Transcendental Consciousness by means of the Second Birth. Since our interest is centered upon the Second Birth, we are concerned primarily with the transition from the caterpillar to the butterfly, rather than with the birth of the caterpillar. The caterpillar represents life on the level of subject-object consciousness, which is life centered in egoism. The butterfly symbolizes Cosmic or Transcendent Consciousness, while the chrysalis is a good representation of the ordeal of the Transition, known in the Christian world as the Passion, culminating in the Crucifixion.

The life of the caterpillar is one confined to crawling on surfaces, and thus it may be said to represent a kind of two-dimensional consciousness. The primary concern of this life is nutrition, and this consciousness can comprehend nothing save in terms of crass utility. Hence, the typical caterpillar philosophy, if for the moment we may assume on the part of the caterpillar enough self-consciousness to develop a philosophy, must be such as would predicate reality and value of that alone which affects sensation, particularly in relation to nutrition. Thus ideas would be significant only insofar as they serve as a means which effect a fuller sensuous life and supply creature utilities.

In radical contrast, the life of the butterfly involves free movement in the air and therefore very well symbolizes a three-dimensional consciousness, as contrasted to the two-dimensional life of the caterpillar. The primary concern of the butterfly-life is mating and depositing eggs, with nutrition reduced to a distinctly subordinate position. Further, the typical nutrition of the butterfly is confined to fluids and thus contrasts radically with the gross nutrition of the caterpillar. The butterfly-life and philosophy may be said to center around creativeness and joy, and so beauty becomes an end-in-itself instead of crass utility. Thus reality and value for the butterfly have a significance not only utterly different from that conceived by the caterpillar but quite beyond the comprehension of the latter.

The chrysalis represents a stage where the caterpillar dies as caterpillar. To the caterpillar-consciousness this must seem like an annihilation or 'blowing out,' as Nirvana does seem to the unillumined subject-object consciousness. But when viewed from the other side, as it were, the chrysalis is the open door to the free life of the butterfly.

The butterfly consciousness has certain very clear advantages. The butterfly, as compared to the caterpillar, moves in a world of an infinitely vaster comprehension. It lives in space with the power to return to surfaces. It is thus in a position fully to understand surface relationships, the whole domain of the caterpillar, but, in addition, knows an infinitely richer world that is utterly unknown to the caterpillar. Further, it knows surfaces in relation to depth, and thus can master problems connected with surfaces that quite transcend the capacities of the caterpillar.

This symbol is a peculiarly beautiful one. The restrictions of caterpillar-life very well represent the limitations of the subject-object consciousness. From the perspective of the restricted subject-object consciousness, the final problems of philosophy remain without satisfactory solution, and often involve unreconciled contradictions. These solutions are attained and the contradictions reconciled by Those who have Awakened to Transcendental Levels. This is due to the fact that the latter have the higher perspective, symbolized by the butterfly, and thus can comprehend the subject-object, or surface world, within the higher integration of space, representing here the Higher Consciousness. But just as the world of the butterfly is inconceivable to the caterpillar, so likewise the integration of the God-Conscious Man is meaningless to those who have no glimpse of

Reality beyond mere subject-object consciousness. Thus, without some degree of Recognition, the philosophies of men like Plato and Hegel seem like something purely abstract and unsubstantial. These higher philosophies admittedly are largely not concerned with the production of mere sensual or experiential values, and certainly give a very subordinate place to nutrition and the creature comforts generally. But when these philosophies are seen from the level of Consciousness on which they are based, they are found to deal most emphatically with substantial actualities. They are written from the perspective of a real Waking Consciousness.

Philosophies of the type of neo-realism, pragmatism, and naturalism are conceived from the perspective of the surface consciousness, symbolized by the caterpillar. At least, this latter form of consciousness dominates. If, now, we restrict ourselves to the subject-object or caterpillar standpoint, the proponents of these philosophies do have the best of the argument. Essentially they understand only the inductive or 'foot' logic of the caterpillar. Their final authoritative basis is either the data of sensation or data derived indirectly through sensation. Their final thesis is that what is objective alone is real. On their own ground, they are apparently unanswerable, but for every Man who has Awakened to 'Knowledge through Identity' they are at once known to be in a false position. A Plato knows, beyond any possibility of doubt, that he is substantially right, but he may well be quite incapable of doing more for the caterpillar type of consciousness than suggest a Reality beyond the caterpillar level. The result is that argumentative conflict between these two great groups of philosophies is largely a waste of time, because there can be no agreement on basic recognitions. Each may prove his case satisfactorily from his respective standpoint, but the effect is simply one of a sort of shadow-boxing that accomplishes very little, so far as convincing the opponent is concerned. The Awakened Man *Knows* the inadequacy of the caterpillar recognition, but cannot prove this to the caterpillar type of man. On the other hand, the latter cannot grasp the Recognition of the Awakened Man unless he, himself, Awakens. The result is a stalemate, unless the caterpillar-man has adumbrations of a Beyond.

184

Of all men who are confined in consciousness to the subject-object manifold, those who see the primary problem of mankind as the one connected with economics are the ones most bound to the caterpillar level. For them, life centers in gross nutrition and the creature comforts, and this is precisely the dominant characteristic of the actual caterpillar. It is a pitifully restricted view. Mere increase of nutrition can only produce larger caterpillars. It can never solve the primary cause of human misery. For man to realize the enduring Joy, he must become so transformed that he enters upon the free life symbolized by the butterfly. It is doubtless true that some human caterpillars need to become fatter before they are ready to enter and pass through the chrysalis stage, but also many are ready now for that Transition and are wasting their time in making themselves into overgrown caterpillars. If the latter think they are serving humanity by continuing in their present course, they are but fooling themselves. When they have Awakened, and only then, can they competently serve that humanity, even with respect to the problems of social and economic organization.

The primary significance of the chrysalis is that entering into the free state of space-life is possible only through dying to the caterpillar level. Mere evolution, in the caterpillar sense, merely produces bigger and juicier caterpillars. There comes a time when man must turn his back upon the whole of the form of life symbolized by the subject-object consciousness, if he is not to be caught in the cul-de-sac of a wasted and barren existence. Of course, from the standpoint of the lower level, this does involve for a brief period an essential asceticism in some form or other. But the end is something infinitely richer than anything contained in the old life, and in addition it is anything but ascetic. Attachment to lesser values serves as a barrier to the realization of greater values. This is a familiar principle, even within the limits of ordinary life. It applies even more forcefully with respect to the attainment of the Supreme Values. Yet many human beings cling to values that are relatively no more than child-toys, and thus refuse to take the steps that open up a Life of Glory, Freedom, and Power. Is not this the supreme folly?

LXXV

Concerning Asceticism

THROUGHOUT THE HISTORY of religion, asceticism has played a highly important part, both as an enjoined discipline and as a spontaneously accepted practice. Several reasons underlie such practices, many of which have been listed and discussed by William James in his "Varieties of Religious Experience." However, I shall add certain considerations relative to this subject that have grown out of my personal experience and reflection.

I am convinced that for most natures and perhaps for all, a certain degree of ascetic practice is necessary if the individual is to attain his highest possibilities. But while this is particularly true with respect to preparing the Way for the Awakening, the same principle applies none the less in the unfolding or developing of power or skill in any field whatsoever. Man wins power in any direction by concentration of effort in the appropriate sense, but this involves inevitably a suppression of diffused activity. Combined with the main interest at any given time, most men feel within themselves counter interests and desires, and if the latter are indulged, the former are sacrificed. Here is a sufficient basis for essentially ascetic practice which may in extreme cases have all the value of the mortifications characteristic of some of the religious disciplines. A man may do this for the mastery of an art, of a science, for the building of a business, etc., just as well as for an objective of the type more commonly classified as religious. If the main interest is so all-consuming that there hardly remains any conflicting interest or desire, it may well be that but little discomfort is felt in the practice. On the other hand, important competing interests may cause the discipline to have the effect of real hardship. But, in any case, mastery in any field does require such discipline.

In the foregoing type of asceticism there is no question of the

186

essential sinfulness of the carnal nature. In fact, a rationale of asceticism may be developed entirely apart from the question of sin. Sin has been given a far too important place in religious thought and feeling. Such sin as there may be is largely incidental and the result of Ignorance and thus fundamentally a delusion rather than an actuality. The result of giving to sin the respect and attention which underlies the idea that it is of sufficient importance to be a worthy object of warfare is that sin is actually given life and power. *We never destroy anything by fighting it.* A force that we fight may be temporarily crushed, because at the time we may be wielding a stronger force. But it remains true that we have won at the price of a certain exhaustion, and meanwhile the opposing force rebuilds itself, partly out of the very force we have expended. Then it comes back upon us when we are weak and may conquer us. No man escapes the action of this law simply by dying physically before the rebound. Somewhere he will live again, and in the next life he may find himself as much identified with evil as in the preceding life he thought himself to be identified with good.

Undoubtedly a strong carnal nature does have to be restrained, and in the case of those who do not have a sufficient balance-wheel of wisdom, possibly extreme effort in restraint may be necessary for a time. But unquestionably it is far better if this discipline is looked upon in the rational spirit of regarding it as simply a form of training. The problem is vastly simplified if the individual, instead of taking an attitude of fighting or suppressing, will undertake to transmute the carnal energy. Every form of energy, regardless of how seemingly evil it may be, has its higher mode or aspect into which it can be transformed. If the effort is focused upon this transforming, the energy is released and becomes a positive power, and this is relatively easy to do.

But after all is said and done, asceticism related to the carnal nature belongs only to the kindergarten stage of the training for the Higher Life of man. The higher and genuinely adult asceticisms are of an entirely different nature. Thus, when a man learns to become detached with respect to his pet opinions or ideas, and is willing to accept conclusions quite counter to his preferences when either evidence or logic points that way, then he is practicing asceticism in a higher and nobler sense. This kind of asceticism does cut far deeper into the real vitals of a man than any restraint connected with the mere carnal nature, and if he can succeed in the higher discipline, then anything remaining in the lesser nature requiring to be purified becomes a mere detail. In the superior discipline, the will has become so highly developed that the carnal nature is controlled relatively easily, provided the effort is put forth.

I would reduce the whole problem of asceticism to the following simple formula: *Let the individual concentrate his effort upon that which he desires most and restrain or transform incompatible desires.* What a man desires most may change as there is growth toward maturity. One implication of the formula, then, is to drop action in the direction of the old desire when the new and more potent desire takes its place. Of course, discrimination must be made between a persistent new desire and the mere temporary uprising of an inferior desire. The rule is to be applied as indicated only in the former case. This course followed consistently will achieve for the individual ultimately his highest good, and sooner or later that will mean the Awakened Consciousness. The advantage in this form of discipline lies largely in the fact that the center of emphasis is placed upon the positive value to be achieved, rather than upon the negative or interfering quality. It makes for a life of greater happiness, and this, in turn, arouses a greater strength, all of which means that success will come the more quickly, at least as a rule. Of course, such a policy of life practice may very well involve one or more radical changes of direction in the life-activity. Thus a man may start his adult life with a desire to attain a great business success, but after having only partly completed this work, he may find that a greater desire takes its place. In that case, he might have to forego great success in the business sense and, remaining content with but moderate achievement in that field, throw the central focus of his energy in another direction. But while this would entail a smaller degree of success in the narrower field, the whole life of the individual, considered in the wider sense, would be more successful. Such a one would escape the tragedy of so many retired business men who, after leaving their businesses, find themselves quite helpless in a meaningless and barren life. From the standpoint of the Awakened Consciousness, all life here below is of value only in the sense of training for the Higher Life and has nothing in it that is valuable as an end-in-itself. So, from the higher point of view, the judgment of what constitutes success in the subject-object field is formed on quite a different basis from that of the usual world-standard. Everything here below is instrumental and only instrumental. So a life encompassing many but partial successes in the subject-object field may actually be making more progress toward the Awakening than a life which is highly successful in one concentrated field. From the higher standpoint, this lower life may be viewed in much the way a music-master views his pupil. The music-master has in mind finished perfection as the ultimate, but in the work-shop of the studio the time is given almost wholly to fragments, such as the technical handling of a phrase, the building of tone-quality, etc. This life here is such a studio and only that. The concert stage is Cosmic Consciousness.

Once a man has Awakened to the Higher Consciousness, he may make a decision that requires the very highest ascetic resolution. He Knows the infinite superiority of the Higher Life in every sense, and, if he had only himself individually to consider, naturally he would choose that Higher Life exclusively. But consideration for the needs of others may lead him to forego this and accept a life in the world while, at the same time, it is not a life *of* the world. As a part of his work he may move rather freely in the field of sensation, emotion, etc., and may even seem self-indulgent to the superficial observer, yet all the while he would be practicing asceticism in the severest sense in the very living in that way. For him there is not any longer a question of resisting carnal temptation, for Knowledge of the higher Joy has reduced all this to husks and ashes, relatively speaking. He simply endures what the carnal man imagines to be enjoyment.

The whole problem of asceticism appears to me, from my present perspective, as merely one of rational judgment and wisdom and is quite divorced from the emotional unpleasantness that is usually associated with it. It is simply good sense to choose the greater value in any conflict of values. Why should this be regarded as an occasion for serious emotional stress?

LXXVI
Poverty and Obedience

October 2

As I READ through the records of monastic practices, I find myself increasingly impressed with the feeling that on the whole there is more inadequacy in this kind of life than there is superiority. Undoubtedly for certain specialized natures a larger human usefulness is achieved under the conditions of monastic life than is the case within the turmoil of worldly existence. Thus, in general, the scholar can be more effective in his work if he has the advantages of monastic insulation. Monasteries were sanctuaries for learning during the Dark Ages. Today the university performs that service very largely, but in its turn it continues some of the more important values of the monastic life. However the value of the monastery in this higher sense requires that the associated members shall be of superior intellectual or spiritual endowment. Further, it requires that the members shall be individuals of sufficient character so that they do not require the prod of worldly life to stir them out of slothfulness. In a word, they must be men who have a value of a superior sort to contribute to mankind that could not be contributed, or could not be so well contributed, in the midst of worldly confusions. But taken as a whole, monasteries have served more as places of retreat for weaklings than as universities for the exercise of specialized capacities. It is this broader use of the monastery that I find inadequate.

The vows of poverty and obedience are very common throughout monasticism, and the rationale underlying these disciplines is easy to understand. The fundamental idea in much of monasticism is a training that will effect a complete surrender of the personal will, so that the individual man will find room for nought save the Divine Consciousness. This technique unquestionably has been successful with some natures, but none the less I am convinced that the literal interpretation of the rules of poverty and obedience is grounded in superficiality rather than in profundity. Of course, I am not bringing into question the necessity for obedience in connection with specific programs of training, or in the case of the performance of an organized work where the directors are alone in a position to decide with respect to courses of action. Here obedience is a practical necessity. I have in mind simply the more general monastic concept of obedience as it has been developed specifically within the Christian Church. In this sense, obedience is intended as a device to destroy the capacity for self-determinism.

It is unquestionably true that private possessions and personal self-will have their origin in egoism, which, in turn, is the basis of the sense of separateness. In its valid sense, the discipline of poverty is a means for overcoming the feeling of exclusiveness that so commonly characterizes the private possession of property. Similarly the practice of obedience is designed to awaken perfect conformity with the Divine Will. But subjective change of attitude toward possessions and the exercise of personal will can have all the value of the literal practice of poverty and obedience. In fact, in this subtler form, the discipline can become much more thorough and afford a better protection against the pitfall of spiritual pride or self-righteousness than in the case of the more literal practices.

In the matter of property, strict analysis will show that there actually is no such thing as private property in the absolute sense. Thus no man owns any external private possession any further than Death permits. Therefore, regardless of social policy, all objective possessions are merely temporary trusts. Now, while it is true that property affords opportunity in terms of indulgence and functioning, yet in even a larger degree it involves responsibility. The more spiritual a man is, the larger looms the factor of responsibility, and thus the acceptance of this responsibility has the value of genuine austerity. In addition, this austerity reaches deeper into the soul of a man than any hardships of poverty. In the case of a man who is not a householder, the ultimate of poverty is hunger, thirst, and exposure to the rigors of weather until death supervenes. This by itself entails only a brief physical suffering. None of this cuts very deeply into a man unless he is of small caliber. But in contrast, when a man feels that his position of power makes him responsible for the well-being of hundreds, of thousands, and perhaps of millions of human beings, he is living under a discipline of such austerity as to make merely personal suffering quite trivial. This is a much more heroic life than that afforded by mere literal poverty.

The same principle applies to the exercise of decision. The willingness to dodge responsibility in this respect is a mark of real weakness and not of strength. So far as man is concerned, the Divine Will acts through the human will. The Universal Will is transformed very largely through the human mind in acting upon the concrete field. Becoming effective in the objective sense is achieved pragmatically. Thus, the higher courage, which marks the really strong man, is revealed in a willingness to assume responsibility for the making of unwise decisions. If the correct course in any situation were always clear, there would be no need in this world for real courage. Accepting responsibility for decision, then, is a much higher and a much more severe austerity than unquestioning obedience.

In the practice that I find unfolding in my own mind, I would make use of the householder form of life as the main objective instrument of discipline, up to the time that the individual is ready for special training. Further, this special training would be of purely technical significance leading toward a definite objective. The essential moral training would be secured through a combination of the problems arising out of actual life, together with the cultivation of a certain attitude toward those problems. I am convinced that on the whole this is a better way to build the higher resignation, at least in the case of men possessed of the western temperament. I would ask students not to dodge temptation but to face it until it was mastered. I would expect the cultivation of conscientiousness combined with detachment. Likewise I would insist upon the practice of self-determinism and would regard him who dares, even though it be unwisely, as the better man than one who obeys blindly.

Conscientiousness has the moral value of poverty. Likewise detachment has the value of obedience. Literal obedience is of importance in connection with technical training for reasons that are quite obvious, but for moral descipline self-determinism is by far the most effective austerity. What We desire is men, and the stronger they are, the better. We do not seek mere mediums. Strength, even though combined with the vices of the strong is preferable to weak goodness. In all men it is the essential value that is important, not the details. For the latter can be handled easily if the central core is sound.

LXXVII

The Higher Consciousness and the Mind

IT IS OFTEN STATED in mystical literature that the activity of the mind is in a peculiar sense a barrier to the Realization of the Higher Consciousness, while at the same time the action of the higher affections is viewed as not such a barrier or as an obstruction in only a minor sense. The primary reasons why mental activity is so regarded are twofold: First, the sheer activity, as such, produces an effect which we may liken unto a great noise that hides the subtle sound of the Voice of the Silence. In the second place, mind-action is a fruitful cause of egoism, and the latter is the basis of the sense of separateness. Both logic and my own experience concur with respect to the contention that action in the objective sense and egoism are barriers. But barriers may be overcome by being surmounted as well as by being removed. Thus a perfect silencing of all activity and a complete eradication of egoism are not absolute necessities upon which the Recognition is contingent. If this were not so, it would seem to follow necessarily that Recognition could never be achieved save in full trance, and thus values from the Recognition could never really descend into the personal consciousness. As was noted in the first section of this book, at the time of the Transition in August, the mind and the senses were active, I was self-conscious, and thus egoism was not completely blanked out. However, both the intellectual and the sensuous consciousness were substantially subdued, and another, a more Universal Consciousness, assumed a position of predominance. Further, prior to the substantially larger unfolding on the evening of the 8th of September, the mind was intensely active. But in this case, the higher level of energy was so great that whatever obstruction was interposed by the activity was easily swept aside. In fact, if the mind had not been as active as it was, there is reason to doubt whether the subject-object consciousness could have remained as witness, or whether there would have been force enough to draw me back into objective functioning.

It seems that the mystics must have employed overstatement in their definition of conditions. This may have been deliberate for psychological reasons, and, in some cases at least, it may have been due to an insufficiently acute power of introspection on the part of the mystic writers. We know that overstatement is one of the principal vices of the Orient, and it is in this region that we find the greater number of genuine mystics. Further, it certainly is true that with mystics as a class psychological factors have been given greater attention than logical or factual correctness.

But the foregoing is not the whole explanation of the confusion. In general, the mystical and occult use of the word 'mind' does not carry the same connotation that western philosophy or the most authoritative usage gives that term. If for 'mind' we substitute the word 'manas,' at once the mystic's statement becomes more correct. 'Manas' is commonly translated as 'mind,' since there is no other single English word that approximates its meaning. But whatever the original or etymological meaning of 'mind' may have been, its meaning, as defined today by the most competent and authoritative usage, comprehends much more than the Indian philosophers and mystics mean when they say 'manas.' Unless this distinction is born in mind, confusion is almost inevitable. For my own part, this confusion caused me some years of needless misunderstanding. What I read violated what I felt intuitively and subsequently demonstrated to be the case. It was not the competent mystical philosophers who were in error, but the translators and the western students of mysticism and occultism.

Another point to be noted is that in the profounder and more complete Oriental philosophy 'manas' is divided into two aspects, a lower and a higher. Now, it is in the lower aspect that manas is called the 'destroyer of the Real,' and thus it is this aspect that must be conquered by him who would attain real Knowledge. This lower manas is united to desire and thus is merely the chief of the organs of sense. It is even called the 'raja' of the senses. Thus conquering of the lower mind means 'conquering the senses through the raja of the senses.' This is obviously important, as the senses afford the basis of objective experience and accordingly make possible a desire that is directed toward the objective and thus away from the purely Subjective upon which the whole objective universe rests.

Now, while the meaning of lower manas is partly comprehended within the western usage of the word 'mind,' the latter is employed to mean much more. Let us refer to the definitions given in a good dictionary. Thus in the "Century Dictionary" we find the following definitions: "That which feels, wills and thinks; the conscious subject; the ego; the soul." This is very much nearer the real meaning of 'Atman' or the 'I AM' than to 'manas,' whether in the lower or higher sense, except that 'egoism' is closely related to manas. Again, we have the following definition: "The intellect, or cognitive faculty or part of the soul, as distinguished from feeling and volition; intelligence." In part, this is close to the meaning of 'Chit' and also, it gives much of the meaning of higher manas, but does not, as such, involve the association with desire which is an essential aspect of lower manas. Third: "The field of consciousness; contemplation; thought, opinion." This covers a wide field of meaning which, most certainly, should be differentiated. In Oriental philosophy, to cover this ground, we have terms, such as 'Nirvana,' 'Sangsara,' 'Samshaya' and 'Mata.' Only with the last meaning, that of 'opinion,' do we begin to enter the lower manasic field proper, for desire and sensation are very apt to form a part in determining opinion. Philosophic usage also connotes by 'mind' qualities such as 'Reason,' 'Understanding,' 'Discernment' and 'Discrimination' and much of 'Intuition.' It would seem that we must conclude that, however close 'mind' may be to 'manas' in its philological background, yet, given the meaning that it now has, it is a peculiarly bad translation of 'manas,' particularly when the latter is taken in the lower sense. Our words 'sensation' and 'desire' come much nearer to the meaning of lower manas, though they also fail to give a really satisfactory translation.

In the broad sense, "The Critique of Pure Reason" is devoted to an analysis of the faculties and functions of the human mind, covering, in the first part, the functions and the forms of the faculty of receptivity, which is fairly equivalent to the lower manas and the senses, while in the second part the spontaneity of the understanding is discussed. This second part covers the ground designated by 'Atman,' 'Buddhi' and 'Manas,' the latter being taken in the higher sense. Kant's 'Intellect' very largely overlaps Shankara's 'Buddhi.' These points are quite important, for Kant's usage is probably more influential than that of any other western thinker.

I have entered into this point at some length, partly for the reason that in my earlier studies the mis-translation of 'lower manas' seemed to require of me a crushing of faculties of the soul that are vitally important for even the Realization Itself, for I was quite familiar with what the word 'mind' meant in western usage. Others may be facing the same difficulty. Literally, to crush or suppress 'mind,' giving to that word the meaning it has in western thought, is to crush or suppress the soul. No true mystic means that, whatever he may seem to say as a result of not being familiar with the English term.

In these discussions I am trying to convey the fundamental meaning of the Recognition and to elucidate the factors favorable to it. As should now be clear to the reader who has understood all that has been written so far, by 'Recognition,' when taken in its full sense, I mean exactly what Buddha meant by 'Enlightenment,' Shankara by 'Liberation' and Jesus by 'The Kingdom of Heaven.'

Pursuing this aim and at the same time retaining as high a degree of accuracy as I can, I divided the modes of human awareness into three types, sensation, affection and cognition. 'Sensation' is made to cover the whole field of reception, such as sensation proper, perception, and reception. 'Affection' covers qualities such as Love, Confidence, Desire, Faith, Joy, and in general all emotional qualities, both positive and negative. 'Cognition' is made to include pure intellection or thought, discernment, reason, etc.

It should be clear that pure cognition as here understood is not sufficient to bring to birth egoism, but for it to do so it must be united with the quality of desire and perhaps other phases of affection and sensation. Actually, with the mass of men cognition is bound to egoism, but a divorce of these two is possible. In the cognitive activity of pure mathematics we do find such a divorce in high degree, for here the desire is almost wholly directed toward Truth and Beauty, with little or no attachment to any preconception of what Truth may ultimately prove to be. Cognitive activity of this type is most emphatically not a barrier to Recognition, and if my experience is any criterion, may well prove to be one of the most powerful subsidiary aids for those who can make use of it. In any case, I must conclude that if by 'mind' cognitive activity is meant, then it is not true that the mind must be stilled in order to attain Recognition. But it is true that the cognitive action must be within a matrix of a high order of *dispassion*.

The higher affections, such as love, compassion and faith, are also most emphatically an aid. But upon this point I do not need to dwell, for here agreement among the mystics seems to be practically universal. Further, this phase of the subject has been much more clearly presented and better understood. This is the Road through Bliss, the Way most widely appreciated and most commonly followed by Those who have attained God-Realization.

By means of pure cognition it is possible to enter through Intelligence (Chit). Or, again, one may Enter through various combinations of the higher affections and pure cognition. Such a course is naturally the most synthetic. But it is not necessary that the balance between the two should be perfect. The individual may be more developed on the one side or the other at the time of the Entering. But once he is grounded in the Higher Consciousness, there is a tendency for the nature to unfold toward balance, so that finally such a Man is symbolized by the 'Great Bird' which has two wings equally developed. And these two are Compassion and Intelligence.

* * * * *

Note: Since writing the above I have made a considerable study of modern work on the psychology of types and this has brought to light further important considerations which I propose to discuss at some length in a later work. At this time I wish to make the following notation: The thinking of any non-thinking psychologic type tends to be negative or destructive when it is not guided by the function which is dominant with the given individual. With such individuals the force of thought may easily seem to be destructive of the real, or Satanic. This makes clear much of the criticism of the mind on the part of mystics. What they have said in such cases is no doubt valid with respect to the kind of thinking with which they are familiar, but they have erred in universalizing what is no more than a peculiarity of certain psychological types. The thinking of the well-developed thinking type has quite a different character, as it is positive and constructive. He, in his turn, is negative or destructive in terms of the independent action of his repressed functions.

LXXVIII

The Atlantean Sage

October 4

THOU ART DIVINE, yet also human, most comfortably human;
Knowing the breadth and the depth and the weakness of man,
Ever remembering the God within the mask;
Trusting with certainty that God,

Regarding not too seriously the mask;
Speaking most often the word of encouragement and comfort,
Yet not neglecting needed rebuke;
Fearing no enjoyment, here below,
Intrigued to forgetfulness by none;
Living in unbroken Joy, balanced by sage judgment;
Wise Teacher ever, yet One who never ceases to learn;
Ancient ruler of men, wise in the ways of men,
Knowing them better than they themselves;
Not scorning convenience, yet ready preference to forego,
Once need makes demand;
With touch tender as a woman's ministering to pain,
Stern, also, meeting enthroned perverseness;
Beyond discouragement, certain of triumph,
Freed from the tyranny of Time;
Ever expecting the best, accepting what is;
Unbounded in nameless majesty,
Beyond the entanglements of earthly man;
One who makes more easy the Path, seemingly so hard,
Discovering unsuspected alleviations of difficulty;
Master of the Inner Powers, melting Darkness with Light,
Transforming enemy-victories into defeat,
Thou Artist of strategy supreme, High Commander on the Staff
    Divine.
How greatly dost Thou awaken the love of those who come near
    Thee,
And confidence in a wise strength;
How greatly dost Thou remove the sting of dread austerity,
Bringing the Beyond within the compass of reasonable achievement.
Honored, I feel, that I should have known Thee,
And count most precious our days of communion.
Ever will I remember that day, on a northern mount,
Crested with pines, mantled with white sternness of winter;
Below us the deep carving streams;
In a little house, remnant of the days of the argonauts,
Now humble and decaying, but rich in memory of great adventure;

Ah! ever will I remember that day when first Thou camest!
I knew Thee, not knowing quite how I knew,
And recognized Authority to countermand the old pronouncements.
Saidst Thou: "In this new day in a newer land,
With customs and perspectives also new,
Old Realities needst must be, in new garments, clothed.
Balancing the strength and weakness of old, there is now another
strength and another frailty.
It is but Wisdom's part to adapt effort to these.
Underlying is the unchanging Truth,
The Way to Recognition manifold.
Be not attached to the method, but to the End."
With much hesitation, I finally learned,
If not largely, still considerable store
Of this new, yet old, Wisdom.
Upon Thy promise I dared and found Thee ever true.
A blessing art Thou to this mankind;
Unknown, save to the few.
May a monument be built to Thee,
Not of inert stone, so easily the victim of Time's ceaseless wearing,
But of the living, growing hearts of men.
In Thee abides a Presence Divine, yet also a man.

LXXIX

The Barriers to Recognition

IN HIS GIFFORD LECTURES, "The Varieties of Religious Experience," William James sought to establish an outline of the basis for a philosophic science of religion. This entailed a search through all the greater religions for the common objective elements of all varieties. He found the two following common elements:

1. An uneasiness due to a sense of something being wrong about human beings as they naturally stand.

2. A solution that in some sense saves man from the wrongness by making the right kind of connection with higher powers.

Neither from the standpoint of my own individual experience, nor from that of my objective studies of religious thought, do I find any basis for questioning the correctness of the above conclusion. Without a sense of something not being right in the life as we find it manifested in this world, there would be no meaning in the programs of the religious movements as we actually find them. So we may say that the typical religious and religio-philosophical problems grow out of a condition which may be designated, in the broad sense, as pathological. Consequently, when this condition is cured in the case of any individual, the latter transcends the need of any religion, in the sense that 'religion' is more commonly understood. Now, in point of fact, the God-Realized Men are superior to all religions in this sense. While it is true that such Men may become founders of religious movements, They are no longer the mere followers of already given religious disciplines. This very largely explains why so often They appear as atheistic to the followers of the various established religions. But the fact is that the God-Realized Men alone have found the solution and are cured of the usual pathological condition that envelops all other men.

What is wrong with man that, instead of God-Realization being the usual state of consciousness, it has been the Attainment of but a bare handful out of the mass? I see four factors which, while they do not cover the whole of the problem, certainly do comprehend it sufficiently, so that if all these factors are mastered, then the important barriers to Recognition will be removed. It may well be that these four factors are so interrelated that in the last analysis they would reduce to one. But, in any case, they would represent four approaches to the fundamental problem. I shall list the four without giving prior importance to any one of them at the present time. These four are:

1. Egoism.
2. Somnambulistic consciousness.
3. Sensual desire.
4. False predication. By this is meant predicating properties of

the subject that are true only of the object, and the complementary error of predicating qualities of the object that are true only of the subject.

1. In 'egoism' we have the 'ahamkara' of the Vedantins. It is the negative aspect of individuality. It is the name for that state of consciousness expressed by the feeling, "I am I and none other." Consequently it is the cause of the sense of separateness, the strife of individuals, groups, and nations, of all destructive competition, and in general of all unbrotherliness. Without egoism there could be no pride, conceit, jealousy nor either the inferiority or superiority complex. Egoism tends to crystallize and hold closed the microcosm of the individual. That it is a barrier to Cosmic Consciousness is quite obvious, for the latter is a State of Consciousness extending throughout the spatial matrix which contains all microcosms. The shell of the microcosm must be cracked or melted so that the individual consciousness may become one with Universal Consciousness. Now, inasmuch as the microcosmic needs can never be completely supplied by the resources of the microcosm alone, the individual so encased must, sooner or later, realize that something is wrong. Just so long as the individual seeks for the solution of this wrongness within the limits of egoism he is doomed to failure. Thus he must overcome egoism and, by so doing, melt the shell of the microcosm and then—but not before then—he is united consciously with the infinite supply that is adequate for satisfying every need.

The mistake has often been made of regarding the mastering of egoism as equivalent to the destruction of individuality. In other words, Liberation is sought as pure Universal Consciousness without any element of self-consciousness. It is possible to do this, but such a course results in something less than the highest destiny of man. Individuality, the essential basis of self-consciousness or the power to know that one knows, can be retained in a form so freed from the dross of egoism that it is blended with Universal Consciousness. In this case, the microcosm is melted, as it were, so that it is no longer crystallized but remains as a fluidic vortex of force, continuous with the Universal Force, yet, in a sense, distinguishable as a vortex. This is the Path that leads to the highest Destiny of man.

Both a strong intellectuality and a powerful personal will or desire tend to build dominant egoism. Now, it is precisely men of these types who have the greatest powers of all those who are still confined within the limits of the subject-object manifold. They supply the greater number of the leaders of men and have great world-influence. Because of the influence and the power of these men, it is of special importance that as many of these as possible should attain to the Higher Consciousness. But owing to their greater development of egoism, they have unusual difficulty in rendering their microcosms fluidic. On the credit side of the ledger, they bring to the task of solving this problem a greater power than most others possess, and if they are successful, they will in general go further than others.

2. In section No. XLIX, I have already discussed somnambulistic consciousness at some length and will not repeat here what I said there. Somnambulism is a barrier through weakness rather than one due to too much strength in the subject-object field. Often it is not difficult to awaken adumbrations of the Higher Consciousness in representatives of this class, but characteristically they lack the power to imprint these adumbrations within the personal consciousness in such a way as to organize them into a permanent value for the relative consciousness. In general, egoism is less developed in them, but likewise so is the quality of individuality, and consequently, if they do effect the Transition without first having strengthened their individuality, they are peculiarly apt to flow into Universal Consciousness without retaining self-consciousness. Thus they require first of all a strengthening of the capacity for self-determinism and self-directed thought. If they can accomplish this, at the same time retaining their greater natural capacity to receive adumbrations of the Higher Consciousness through the action of induction, then they have the definite advantage of being more responsive than most other types to the assistance of Those who have already Arrived. In any case, their course of training differs in important respects from that which is requisite for those falling in class No. 1.

3. Sensuality is the opposite of spirituality. Hence, desire directed primarily toward the objects of sensation tends to carry consciousness outward and away from inwardness where alone the universal

Key is to be found. To follow sensation is to go toward ponderable objects, and this means movement toward essential nothingness or illusion. The primary agent in this movement is the sensual mind, or, more correctly, the lower manas. As has already been shown in a previous discussion,* it is when it is taken in this sense that the Sages have traditionally viewed the mastery of mind as the central problem. As I explained in that section, the real meaning of 'mind,' when so employed, is better expressed in our usage of terms by the phrase, "desire directed toward sensation."

It is perfectly true that sensation can be used as a stepping-stone to Recognition. But this is done by viewing the objects of sensation as symbols rather than as actualities existing in themselves. It is possible, then, to use the direct object of sensation as an instrument to awaken consciousness of that Matrix which is the Fullness that comprehends or encloses the relative emptiness of ponderable objects.

I question greatly whether this technique is practical for any extensive application to occidental humanity in its present stage of consciousness. There is a tradition that a certain ancient race did employ this method as a systematic technique, but that race had a much higher development of sensual purity than is now the case. So it would seem that, on the whole, with men being what they are now, the technique with overly great sensual desire must be in the form of replacing the sensual with super-sensual objects. Gradually, then, the desire can be moulded or directed toward genuinely spiritual objectives.

4. This may be called a barrier that grows out of the nature of subject-object consciousness as such. A man who is relatively free from egoism, as is true of many scientists and philosophers, may have a strong intellectual development and be little, if in any degree, involved in somnambulism, and in addition he may have a strong control of sensual desire, and yet with all this fall into the error of 'false predication.' With respect to this class more than any other, the problem of Recognition falls in the field of philosophy. In my judgment, this constitutes the really crucial problem relative to the

* See Section No. LXXVII.

Liberation of human consciousness from the state of bondage. Accordingly, I shall discuss this barrier to Recognition at some length.

The problem of false predication arises in the following way: The Self, or the purely subjective moment in consciousness is the primary reality of the subject-object manifold. It is the Light, or the Intelligence, or the Consciousness on which the whole universe depends for its existence. It is unitary and above space, time, and causality and, therefore, not subject to conditions. The objective world, including the human body as well as other objects, is dependent and bound within space, time, and causality and, therefore, subject to conditions. It is also multiple in appearance.* Thus it is, in all respects, of a nature both opposite and complementary to the Subject.

Now, it is a widespread habit among human beings to reverse the above predications. So we have the custom, explicitly or implicitly manifested, of predicating self-existence of the objects of consciousness. As a result, things or objects come to be taken as primary, and then it may actually become a problem as to how a self-conscious Self ever became introduced into this world. Many a good scientist has addled his brains over this quite falsely stated problem. The fact is that a problem concerning nature has as its essential basis a conscious self that makes the apperceiving of the problem possible. In a purely blind and dead nature, there never could arise a scientific or any other kind of problem. Of primary importance, then, for the understanding of any problem concerning nature is a knowledge of the Self and of the knowledge-forms through which It acts in cognizing or sensing the world. The most primary fact of all is the Self that thinks and senses. Its presence is the one completely immediate reality that can neither be proved by logic nor found through experience, for it is the absolutely necessary basis for both these forms of consciousness. Thus it is only of the

* I will not at this time develop the logic that supports this position, but that logic is well unfolded in existent philosophy and in addition has the overwhelming support of the testimony of the mystics. For the present I shall ask the reader to assume the essential correctness of the above statement of primary fact.

Self that we may properly predicate self-existence. It alone is that which is the original indubitable 'given' on which all the rest depends. So the real problem is: How does the external universe come to have existence? It is a complete misconception to state the problem in the form: How did the Self come to be injected into the universe?

The Self, then, is the one Reality of which we can be absolutely certain, for It is presupposed as much in false as in real knowledge and underlies dreams as well as waking states. Now what can we predicate at once concerning this Self in addition to self-existence? A simple answer comes immediately: The Self is an unchanging power of awareness. This bare awareness is not affected, as such, by the modes or qualities of the contents of that awareness. Thus, the states of objects, including the body of man, do not affect the Self. For instance, a man may have a sick body, but he makes an absolutely false predication when he says: "I am sick." The experiencing of the state of sickness in the body is a fact, but to predicate this sickness as attaching to the Self is to build the typical binding illusion which holds human consciousness in thralldom. Similarly, man's manifold instrument of body, mind, etc., is limited, but the Self is not limited. Thus to say "I am limited in such and such respects" is to produce but another of the illusions of nescience. It would have been perfectly correct to predicate these limitations as attaching to the individual and personal instruments. The application of this principle should now be clear.

The final consequence of both classes of false predication is the production of a state of Nescience or Avidya. The effect is a sort of superimposition upon the originally given universe of a secondary or false universe which enthralls the bulk of human consciousness. It is this secondary universe that is an Illusion or Maya in the invidious sense. Problems relative to nature and Being, taken from the standpoint of this secondary universe, involve a fundamentally false perspective, and therefore it is impossible to find effective solutions for them. On the contrary, they simply lead into ever greater and greater entanglements, in the effort to elaborate solutions. The fact is, that this superimposed universe has no more real existence than a dream. Now, the whole conscious field of a dream, together with its problems, is destroyed by the simple process of waking-up. This leads us to a very important point in metaphysical logic. Whenever we recognize any state of consciousness as being a dream, at that moment we have discovered that it is unreal, or, in other words, is devoid of self-existence. A man suffers while in the midst of the ordinary dream simply for the reason that at the time of dreaming he believes the state to be real. But this belief in the reality of the dream is caused by a superimposition that the dreamer himself has produced. The awakening is equivalent to a removal of this superimposition. At that moment, the state which was imagined as real, and therefore as having self-existence, is recognized to be no more than a dream. This destroys that particular world or *loka* of consciousness. Now we come to an especially important point. That world or *loka* is not simply destroyed for the future, but it is equally destroyed in the sense that *it never has been.* This does not mean that it is not a fact in the historic sense that at a certain time the individual in question was deluded while in the state of the dreamer. It simply means that the self-existence or actuality which was imagined as true of the dream never was in reality a fact. The same principle is true of the secondary universe in which the bulk of mankind lives somnambulistically. When a man Awakes to the Higher Consciousness he destroys this universe, both in the sense of futurity and in the sense of realizing that it never has been. Right here we are dealing with one of the most important principles of the higher epistemology and logic, but also one that has been very widely misunderstood. It is not the field of subject-object consciousness, as such, that is an Illusion or Maya *in the invidious sense,* but the secondary universe. It is this that the Oriental Sage has in mind when He speaks of destroying the universe, but He has simply failed to make himself clear to the western mind.

There is a considerable group of western students who, through an imperfect understanding of the oriental doctrine of Maya, have developed a philosophy in which 'Illusion' is predicated of the whole field of relative consciousness in a sense that is valid only of the secondary universe. The result is, that instead of destroying an illusion by their technique, they have simply succeeded in imposing a new kind of illusion and produced for themselves a state of auto-hypnosis, which results in a deeper state of dream-consciousness than is true of the average individual. In this deeper dream-state, only the evidence which seems to confirm preconceptions is recognized readily and the acceptance of contrary evidence becomes almost impossible. It is a state in which real discrimination is paralyzed. It is practically useless to try to help any individual who is in this state, until the force of auto-hypnosis exhausts itself.

Properly understood, the whole doctrine of *Maya* is entirely compatible with the idea that within the relative or subject-object consciousness there can be a correct view of the universe. But this view is correct only in so far as it is taken as true with respect to the subject-object base of reference. Critically self-conscious modern science is well aware that its knowledge is not valid beyond the limits imposed by the base of reference that has been assumed. From the standpoint of Recognition, there is no criticism to be made of a science built upon a background of such critical understanding. Confusion arises only when generalization goes beyond the theoretical limits of the base of reference. From the perspective of Transcendent or Cosmic Consciousness, the problem of nature and Being takes quite a different form. But this fact does not imply a challenge of the relative reality of a body of knowledge developed by sound method within the relative field.

Once one recognizes the fact that the relative world, or primary universe, is a valid part within the Whole and is relatively real, then the problem of cross-translation from the level of Cosmic Consciousness to that of subject-object consciousness is realized as being of high importance. The possibilities of cross-translation are admittedly limited. The immediate content of the Higher Consciousness cannot be cross-translated, but certain formal properties can be through the use of systematic symbols. In some respects it is like the old problem of the evaluation of irrationals in terms of rational numbers. The ultimate content of the irrationals cannot be given in the form of the rationals, yet, in the radical signs, we have symbols representing the essential unity binding the two sets of numbers. Just so soon as the mathematicians abandoned the effort completely to reduce the irrationals to rational form, and accepted the radical sign as an irreducible symbol of profound meaning, then they did succeed in integrating in their consciousness two quite differently formed domains of reality. This integration meant that the two domains were found to be logically harmonious, although that which we might call the 'affective' content was discrete. Cross-translation, in something of this sense, is possible with respect to Cosmic and subject-object consciousness. In fact, if the consciousness-equivalents of the entities and operations of pure mathematics were realized, we would find that, in that great science and art, cross-translation in a lofty sense already exists. The Root Source of pure mathematics is the Higher or Transcendent Consciousness, and this is the reason universal conclusions can be drawn with unequivocal validity in pure mathematics. The greater bulk of mathematicians fall short of being Sages or Men of Recognition because their knowledge is not balanced by genuine metaphysical insight. But they do have one-half of the Royal Science. Up to the present, at any rate, the Fountainhead of the other half is to be found mainly in the Orient. The union of these two represents the synthesis of the East and the West, in the highest sense, and is the prerequisite of the development of a culture which will transcend anything the world has known so far.

It is a mistake to regard the primary universe as being in some sense a great error. With respect to this point some of the exoteric Vedantins have not seen clearly, for they have said that the universe was a Divine Mistake. At the same time, from the transcendent level of the High Indifference, it is a mistake to give the universe a teleological interpretation. But from the subject-object standpoint, we can see purposive value in it, and so long as we confine our predication to the latter base of reference, this value is real. But a radical error is introduced when purposiveness is extrapolated as predicative of the High Indifference. In the highest sense, the universe is neither a mistake nor a purposive necessity. But it is an empiric fact, and it is the part of wisdom to accept it as such. The actual primary and empiric universe is not an ontological necessity. It is rather to be regarded as an existent and creative actuality, within the limits of ontological possibility. Ontologically, the universe might have been other than what it actually is, but empirically it is what we actually find it to be. To understand the fundamental meaning of the universe, one must rise in Consciousness to the level beyond Creative Ideation.

The state of subject-object consciousness, in the sense of the primary universe, is not to be regarded as pathological. However, the genuinely illusive secondary universe does involve a pathological or hypnotic type of consciousness. This is the universe that is produced by Ignorance and is destroyed when Ignorance is destroyed. When We speak of this world as being a sort of asylum or hospital, We have in mind earth-humanity en masse. We are not including all beings who are functioning within the subject-object manifold. The state of this humanity is abnormal, and thus is in a condition not typical of other humanities. This mankind, through a failure of discrimination, confused the subject and the object, producing thereby the false predication. To this was added the innate creativeness derived from the Divine Spark, resting at the center of every man. The combination of these two produced the secondary universe, which is not other than an illusion in the invidious sense. Actually, it is a hell that was so created; and, so far as most human beings are concerned, this life right here is the worst hell they will ever know. It would take considerable perverse skill to produce anything much worse. The only hope for individual and collective man lies in his utterly destroying his perversely produced secondary universe. Then, and only then, does he take up once more his course of development along the lines of genuine evolution.

In the philosophical sense, the crux of the problem of the effective destruction of the secondary or superimposed universe lies in the awakening of the power of real Discrimination. This is essentially the act of rigorously distinguishing between the Self and not-Self, or, in other words, the careful differentiation between the properties true of the object of consciousness and the qualities true only of the Subject. The practice of this discrimination has the value of a de-hypnotizing force, and once it is carried far enough, the man Awakes. This Awakening is equivalent to a discharge from a hospital. The methods that do actually effect de-hypnotizing for different individuals vary considerably, as has already been noted. But in the end, all methods, when they have been carried to the point of effective results, lead to true Discrimination, and thus it is Discrimination that remains the ultimately effective agent for Liberation. That is why Recognition is more than a *means* to Liberation; it actually *is* Liberation.

Religion, in the forms commonly known in this world, is but a treatment designed to meet the needs of sick souls. The really healthy soul has no need of religion, in this sense, for such a one is not only Divine but in addition recognizes that fact. He is thus identical with the Object of religious worship. The 'wrongness,' almost universally felt by men in this world, is not something produced by an original Divine Plan, but is the production of a perverse creativeness on the part of man himself through the method already noted. Once the wrongness is corrected, there remains a continuation of evolution in the relative as well as in the Cosmic sense, in which the development is normal. This normal evolution does not have evil and misery as constituents of its make-up. On the contrary, it proceeds within the matrix of essential happiness and understanding. Thus Real Life begins only after man has Awakened.

LXXX

The Nameless

October 7

ABOVE, BELOW, to right, to left, all-encompassing,
Before and after and all between,
Within and without, at once everywhere,
Transforming and stable, ceaselessly;
Uncaused, while fathering all causes,
The Reason behind all reasoning,

Needing nought, yet ever supplying,
The One and Only, sustaining all variety,
The Source of all qualities, possessing no attributes,
Ever continuous, appearing discrete,
Inexpressible, the base of all expression,
Without number, making possible all number,
Containing the lover and the beloved as one,
Doing nought, remaining the Field of all action—
The actor and the action not different—
Indifferent in utter completion;
Diffused through all space, yet in the Point concentrated,
Beyond time, containing all time,
Without bounds, making bounds possible,
Knowing no change;
Inconceivable, yet through It all conceiving becoming;
Nameless ever and unmastered;
THAT am I, and so art Thou.

LXXXI

The Record Continued

October 15

AT THE CLOSE of the noon-day meal of last Sunday there occurred the third significant event of this series. I had made a certain inward call, but had not anticipated the nature of the response. Presently there was evident an unusual field of energy of a quality I recognized from previous experience, but of an unprecedented degree of intensity. All who were present were aware of this field. I felt a tension which led to a spontaneous straightening of the spine, in a vertical position, and an exerting of the will in a very positive sense. Everyone reported feeling a quality of extraordinary Peace, but in addition I felt the Presence of most unusual Power.

I felt quite sure that I recognized what this Presence was, but it must remain nameless. The quality of the State was similar to that where I reported the thinking of thoughts of extreme abstractness and also to that which enveloped us on the evening of September 8th.

One quality of these fields of energy is analogous to that of a certain physical experience with which a number of individuals are familiar. When a moderately sensitive individual is placed in the electro-magnetic field of a powerful generator he will feel a curious kind of tension, quite difficult to describe. He may even find it necessary to set his will very positively. He may not know why he has to do this, and the willed response seems largely spontaneous. Now the energetic Field of subjective Presence is similar, but is more subtle and may be much more potent. All of this simply supports the idea that Consciousness or Life is in some sense electrical. However this Energy may manifest in a number of different forms, of which terrestrial electricity is merely the most gross. This idea also helps to show how the phenomena of terrestrial electricity furnish analogues of certain of the actions or functions of the Higher Consciousness, such as that of induction.

The Presence of last Sunday continued with decreasing intensity throughout the rest of the day and since then has not seemed far away. One directly traceable consequence took the form of a rewriting of the experience of September 8th. The cross-translation of this inward State afforded peculiar difficulties, and my first effort was far from satisfactory. The rewriting last Tuesday was far more successful and is, I believe, the most difficult piece of formulation that I have so far attempted. However, I composed this quite readily, but all the while my thought was on an exceptionally high level. I was under strong drive while writing and was unusually impatient of interruption before its completion.

During the last two days, I have become aware of a peculiar change of attitude on the part of my personality, in a fundamental respect. This new attitude seems to be more in the nature of a gradual growth rather than a sudden development. Heretofore, and up to some point in the past two months, I have felt that there was such a thing as self-sacrifice. I have always felt that, wisely employed, it was a necessity, not only for the development of the higher moral life, but likewise even for the exercise of a merely decent moral code. My refusal to leave the world-field, when the opportunity to do so came, had the value of self-sacrifice, but the chosen course seemed to be the only honorable one to follow. In this there was a very real renouncing involved. But, in contrast to this, at the present moment I do not feel that any course that I may choose to follow involves self-sacrifice. Studying this as objectively as I can, I must say that it is a very curious state. Admittedly, some courses of action remain relatively uncomfortable or difficult when compared to others. But, regardless of whether I am personally uncomfortable or comfortable, there does not seem to be any self-sacrifice involved. I find myself disposed not to predicate meritoriousness or its reverse of any course of action I now choose. I rather tend to judge whatever action may be chosen as more or less sound, or more or less wise, and so on. Folly seems to be the only possible mistake. Bear in mind that I am not presenting this outlook as a thesis relative to what should be, but simply as a report of a self-analysis of a state I now experience. Whether or not it is an enduring state, only the future will reveal.

The fact of this state of feeling with respect to self-sacrifice leads to a reflection concerning its significance. I can trace it directly as an effect of those hours of consciousness correlated with the High Indifference. There certainly is a persisting effect that is radically changing my attitude toward life. Now here is the logic as I see it. In the High Indifference the 'I AM' or the 'Atman' is transformed, as nearly as I can express it, from a bare point of pure subjectivity to the whole of Space. The result is that I am not peculiarly involved in what happens to any one point in that Space, even though that point is this personal self-identity which I call myself, spelt with a small 'm.' A plus at one point in that Space is immediately balanced by a minus at another. However, since I am not confined to any one point but comprehend all points at once, I do not experience the effect of a 'lessness' or of a 'moreness,' no matter what the course of action at any time may be. If self-sacrifice may be regarded as in some sense a 'lessness' at a given point, it is, at the same time, a 'moreness' at some other point or points. I, in reality, being the whole Space, comprehend at once both effects. Clearly, from the perspective of such a level, self-sacrifice is an impossibility. Literally no circumstance can reduce Me, and equally no circumstance can exalt Me, and this remains true even though the personality were crushed out of existence on one hand, or were given the highest honors on the other. I do not see how, logically, any other state of feeling would be compatible with genuine Indifference.

All of the foregoing simply further develops a quality I have found to be characteristic of the Recognitions I have had. They tend toward an integration of the whole nature, and thus the conflict between the affections and the logical demands of thought, a condition so common with most men in the usual state, is progressively eliminated. This is real purification and may well be more important for the eradication of misery than any other factor.

Is this State of fundamental Indifference in which I find myself a desirable one? I find it so. I would not choose anything else that I have known or heard of in preference to It. Yet, before my individual consciousness had been correlated with It, no reference to indifference that I had ever heard or read had succeeded in making it seem attractive. It seems that one's whole basis of valuation undergoes fundamental change. From a distance, the State looks like negation, but when Realized it is Known to be more complete than any antecedent state. But it may well be that only by Realizing It does it become possible to prefer It to all others. I have no sense of being forced into This against my will. Perhaps, even now I could retreat from the effective memory of It, but that would be absolutely the last thing I would wish to do. I see no reason at all why anyone should fear it. There are States of real spiritual Bliss that do not involve this High Indifference, and it is possible for men to Realize that These are worth infinitely more than any of the offerings of the subject-object consciousness. I know of nothing that would cause men to abandon such States against their wills. If, when the Hour comes, some wish to continue on to the more comprehensive Consciousness, they are at liberty to go as far as they can. It is not a

215

matter of outer constraint. Meanwhile, let me add my testimony: The State of the High Indifference is supremely worth while.

Concern is the earmark of a state that is incomplete. When completeness is realized, concern vanishes. The High Indifference is the hallmark of utter completeness. Action or inaction within the High Indifference is not the effect of concern. Concern may still be the basis of motivation within the personal consciousness, but at the same time in his deeper Consciousness the individual is quite aware of the irrelevancy of the concern. As the High Indifference is no more a state of inaction than It is of action, relative consciousness naturally puts the question, "What is the cause of action on that Level?" But the very form of this question makes an answer impossible, for a modulus of relative-world conduct is extrapolated into a State where it has no relevancy. Perhaps something of the truth may be suggested by saying that all Motion, in the highest sense, is spontaneous and is therefore not to be explained in terms of causal connection. Somehow, the Supreme and causal worlds are simultaneous facts. The Supreme IS, the causal world *apparently* is, and yet it is not. Let him who can resolve this apparent absurdity.

LXXXII

The Point-I and the Space-I

October 17

A NEW WAY OF APPROACHING the subject of Nirvana has come to my mind which may be helpful in clarifying certain difficulties relative to the nature of this State. The usual idea of Nirvana seems to be that It is a sort of blissful State produced by an extinguishing of personal life through the elimination of the will-to-live and the desire for enjoyment. Since ordinarily men find themselves unable to conceive of consciousness unrelated to personality and the various cravings associated with sentient life, Nirvana appears to be something like an absolute non-existence or an annihilation in the full sense of the word. If, on the other hand, it is granted that Nirvana is some sort of State of Consciousness, it is often thought of as something undesirable. There is much misconception in all this. Anyone who has ever touched even the hem of Nirvanic Consciousness would not regard It as an undesirable State and most certainly would Know that It did not imply the cessation of Consciousness, although It is a kind of consciousness quite different from anything to be found within the relative field. Now the difficulty seems to me to grow out of a misunderstanding of what is meant when we say 'I,' and I believe that I can say something that will make this matter clearer.

Approached from the usual standpoint of relative consciousness, the 'I' seems to be something like a point. This 'point' in one man is different from the 'I' in another man. One 'I' can have interests that are incompatible with the interests of another 'I,' and the result is conflict. Further, the purpose of life seems to center around the attainment of enjoyment by the particular I-point which a given individual seems to be. It is true that in one sense the 'I' is a point, and the first objective of the discriminative practice is the isolation of this point from all the material filling of relative consciousness, and then restricting self-identity to this point. For my own part, I finally applied this technique with success. But, almost immediately, at the moment of success, a very significant change in the meaning of the 'I' began to develop. A sort of process of 'spreading out' began that culminated in a kind of spatial self-identity. I found that the 'I' had come to mean Space instead of a point. It was a Space that extended everywhere that my consciousness might happen to move. I found nowhere anything beyond Me, save that at the highest stage both 'I' and Divinity blended in Being. But all of this process involved both an intensifying and broadening of Consciousness, and most emphatically not a narrowing or 'pinching out' of it. For our present purposes, we may leave aside the State of Being, where both the subject and the object disappear. There remains, then, an 'I' in two senses, which we may call the point-I and the Space-I. There is enough in this to clarify the fundamental problem of Nirvana, taken in the simpler sense, leaving out of account States called Paranirvana and Mahaparanirvana.

As a matter of formal properties alone, it should be clear at once that life-values take on very different forms when viewed respec- tively from the perspectives of the point-I and the Space-I. The point-I involves discreteness, separateness, difference, etc., and, as a consequence, there are possible attainments and failures to attain This gives a certain meaning to desire-led action, resulting in all the features so common in ordinary life. In contrast, the Space-I is con- tinuous, not-separate, not-different, etc. At least in a potential sense, the Space-I spreads over all possible consciousness-values. It thus stands above the need of experiencing (enjoyment). For the Space-I, consciousness-values are not attained by action, desire, etc., at least not in the common meaning of those terms. Consciousness may be focused anywhere within the given Space, and at once the corre- sponding consciousness-value is realized.* The important fact is that the Space-I does not have to strive in anything like a competitive sense to achieve any value. In a potential sense, the Space-I is all values at once; and by focusing, it makes any value whatsoever actual. Now, the Space-I includes all point-I's. Hence, in principle, any individual who has Realized his identity in the Space-I finds himself present in all point-I's. This also gives to him, in principle, the resources of all point-I experiences, and not merely those of one isolated point-I. It is easily seen that in such a Space-I there is no room for, nor meaning in, the separative affections of mere point-I consciousness. Further, the Space-I is a State of infinite completeness, as compared with the consciousness of any point-I or the compound effect of any number of point-I's. Of course, such a State is one of Bliss immeasurably transcending anything possible for any point-I. It is the Space-I Consciousness which is Nirvana.

Now, to have transcended the point-I state and achieved self- identity in Space does not imply that no further evolution is possible. We are already familiar with the idea of one space being compre- hended in other spaces of higher order. The Higher Evolution may

* Just what is meant by this "focusing" brings up an interesting philo- sophical problem, but I shall not enter into this at the present time.

218

be said to be a progressive Spatial integration, each advancing step being literally an infinite transcendence of the preceding stage. Thus, if point-I evolution may be said to be represented by finite numbers, the Space-I evolution would correspond to transfinite numbers. In this higher series of Transcendence, we very soon reach the limits of the most advanced pioneer of this humanity and, in fact, do not have to proceed very far before we have reached the utmost limit of man as man. Beyond the latter are fields that form the normal Level of Beings quite different from man as he is commonly conceived to be.

Formal mathematics has reached a long way ahead of the consciousness that is actually possible to man. Man will have long since ceased to be human, in the restricting meaning of that term, by the time he has Awakened in terms of Consciousness at the most advanced Levels represented by mathematical concepts and symbolic formulae. Mathematics thus constitutes a thread to the Beyond that has never been lost, even when mankind sank to the greatest deeps of materialistic consciousness. But there are very few who have realized just what that Royal Thread is.

LXXXIII

Sangsara

October 28

THOU MONSTER, spawned of Ignorance impregnated by human
    ideation;
Appearing glamorous, promising all,
Yet deceiving ever, rewarding fidelity with empty cups.
Like a beautiful lake thou appearest,
Offering rest and refreshment to the traveler weary;
But a mirage thou art, ever receding,
Leading on and on to desert barrenness.

219

Appearing again as multi-colored rainbow,
Promising the gold never to be found.
Intriguing with a seeming joy and victory,
Jeering at thy victims as they,
Compounding sorrow and defeat, die disillusioned.
Empty art thou, void of all value,
Ghost of that which might have been;
Beguiling all onward till, caught in thy web,
They struggle, helpless and forlorn;
Demanding full loyalty, rewarding with illusion's drug,
Dream-stuff, turning to ashes on the morrow of waking.
Binding in ceaseless travail thy victims,
Draining the substance of the soul,
Leaving man ever poorer and poorer and poorer.
Thee, I challenge to mortal combat,
To a war that knows no quarter,
Thou vampire, draining the life of this Great Orphan.
In that battle may there be no truce,
No end, until the Day of Victory Absolute.
Thou reduced shalt be, to a dream utterly forgotten.
Then man, once more Free,
Shall journey to his Destiny.

LXXXIV

Nirvana

FELT DIMLY in the soul, by world-man unconceived;
Unknown Goal of all yearning;
The Fullness that fills the inner void,
Completing the half-forms of outer life;
The Eternal Beloved, veiled in the objects of human
    desire;

Undying, Timeless, Everlasting;
Old as Infinity, yet ever new as upspringing youth;
Pearl beyond price, Peace all-enveloping;
Divinity spreading through all.
'Blown-out' in the grand conflagration of Eternity,
Death destroyed as a dream no longer remembered.
Life below but a living death,
Nirvana the ever-living Reality.
Divine Elixir, the Breath of all creatures;
The Bliss of full Satisfaction;
Uncreated, though ceaseless Creativeness;
Ecstasy of ecstasies, thrilling through and through,
Freed from the price of ignoble pleasure;
The Rest of immeasurable refreshment,
Sustaining the labors embodied;
The one Meaning giving worth to all effort;
Destroying forever all sorrow;
Balancing the emptiness of living death,
With values beyond conceiving.
The Goal of all searching, little understood,
By few yet attained, though free to all.
Sought afar, but never found,
For closer IT lies than all possession;
Closer than home, country or race,
Closer than friend, companion or Guide,
Closer than body, feeling or thought,
For closest of all IT lies,
Thine own true SELF.

LXXXV

Conceiving and Perceiving

October 31

WHICH IS THE CLOSER to Reality, the percept or the concept? In this we have a rather simple form of a very old question that has divided schools of philosophy from the time of Plato down to the present day. In an earlier time, before psychological analysis had developed as a recognizable field of research, the question took the form, "Which is more real, the universal or the particular?" But the underlying issue is fundamentally the same. Clearly, percepts give individuals or particulars, while every concept is either a generalization in some degree or an universal. At least in western philosophy no standpoint has emerged that has dissolved the issue this question has raised, although the form which the issue assumes is certainly not fixed. In Plato's time we find the contention reflected in the contrast between Plato and Democritus on the one hand, and between Plato and Aristotle on the other. In the Middle Ages it is reflected in the division between the Conceptualists and the Nominalists. The Conceptualists held that the universals were real and existed before things. In contrast, the Nominalists held that universals, or more properly generalizations, were merely abstractions from individual or particular existences which alone have reality. Later, at the beginning of the modern period, the division is represented by the Rationalists and the Empiricists. The former found primary reality in universal rational entities, such as those which form mathematics, while the Empiricists held that the data given through the senses was primary. Immanuel Kant found a road which in a measure united these two currents of thought, but, again, the division flows out of him in the form: "Which is the most primary or real, the *a priori* element in knowledge or the *a posteriori*?" The subsequent current of thought, most influenced by Kant, certainly did give primacy to the *a priori* element. This current fruited in the Absolute Idealism

222

of Hegel. In contrast to this school, today we have the Pragmatists who emphasize empiric utility in some sense as the mark of truth and reality. This latter form of division is sometimes contrasted as "Intellectualism vs. Vitalism." At this point the question takes the form, "Which is the most primary, Consciousness or Life?" Finally Spengler gives the problem a new form by introducing the words "Physiognomic" and "Systematic." The Physiognomic is a mode of awareness or living process grounded in Life and Time, both of these being taken as original. The Systematic is a conceptual construction which conceives the Real in terms of Space. Spengler himself admittedly is grounded in the Physiognomic, but he concedes that other temperaments may be grounded in the Systematic. This latest presentation of the question takes two possible forms: (1) "Which is original and primary, the Physiognomic or the Systematic?" (2) "Which is most primary, Time or Space?"

The analysis of the basic problem which underlies all these various questions may be approached either from the genetic or the logical standpoints. Depending upon the line of approach, the conclusion seems to follow almost predictively. There does not seem to be any doubt but that in point of time cognitions of universals arise after experience. If the process in time is assumed as real and original, then it follows that percepts and particulars are really prior to concepts and universals. But it is entirely possible to regard space and number as more primary than time, and this is certainly the position of the modern physicist who has reduced nature to a four-dimensional manifold wherein the time-dimension has essentially the properties of space, and the final picture of physical reality becomes a group of differential equations, or in other words a system of relationships in terms of number. Further, in a more specifically philosophical sense, the genetic development may be viewed as simply an occasion for making a pre-existence manifest. Thus experience merely becomes the stimulus or catalytic agent that awakens sleeping Knowledge, but is not itself the source of that Knowledge.

The conflict of these two currents of thought has played a part of unquestionable value in philosophic development. Either stream by itself, almost certainly would have become crystallized long since.

But the interaction between the two series of schools has led to greater refinements of understanding and profounder recognitions than could otherwise have been the case. Rarely, if ever, is a man converted from one school to the other, once he has become philosophically self-conscious. The arguments of one school fail essentially to convince the proponents of the currently opposite school. It would seem that the reason for this would lie in the fact that none of the arguments reach as deeply as the insight in which any philosopher is grounded. This insight is original, and the fundamentals of the system that spring from it follow necessarily. But the conflict between the implications of the different systems leads to mutual growth of self-consciousness in the two types of recognition.

This primary division in philosophy itself is reflected in a still broader field where philosophy is contrasted to mysticism. While there is such a thing as philosophical mysticism, or a mystical philosophy, the general rule is that mystics are typically not philosophical in their outlook. The latter class certainly does find the Real in something that is nearer the percept, or the physiognomic, than it is to the concept of the systematic. Poetry, symbolism, and what is called 'living the life' afford their characteristic instruments of expression. In contrast, all philosophers, of whatever school, actually do work with concepts and more or less universal ideas. Now, in their higher manifestations, both Philosophers and Mystics are Awakened to the Higher Consciousness. Buddha and Shankara on the one hand, and the great Persian Mystics on the other, afford outstanding examples of these two groups. As a consequence, we see that this division runs deeper than ordinary subject-object consciousness, and in some sense extends into the Beyond. There must be something very fundamental in this.

The division is traceable further in the complemental and opposed Greek notions of Eros and Logos, with their more modern equivalents of Love and Wisdom. In Occultism it is reflected in the complemental contrast of Buddhi and Manas or that of Ananda and Chit. As already noted in a previous discussion, each of these pairs represents modes of more ultimate realities, designated as Atman and Sat respectively. The ultimate Reality, when brought

224

into expression, requires the mediation of one or the other of the respective modes, or a combination of the two. Whether or not any living man has achieved a perfect equilibrium between the two modes is a question which I find impossible to answer definitely at the present time. It would seem, however, that if the incarnation known as Gautama Buddha was not a case of perfect equilibrium in this sense, at any rate it comes nearer to it than any other case of which we have clear historic record. Shankara's predominant expression is clearly philosophical, while that of Jesus is notably mystical. But there is a subdominant mystical element in Shankara, and likewise a subordinate philosophical element in Jesus. All three, Buddha, Shankara, and Jesus, do seem to represent, when taken as a group, more balance than other historic incarnations. By uniting these Three and regarding them as one Reality in Three Persons, it would seem that we have the most synthetic spiritual manifestation lying within the limits of historic records that have any degree of exoteric definiteness.

My own contribution to this problem grows out of a Recognition of a third kind of Knowledge which I have called "Knowledge through Identity." This Knowledge, on Its own level, is neither conceptual nor perceptual and consequently can neither be defined in the strict sense of the word nor be experienced. Through Awakening, man can Recognize himself as identical with It. It is only when the Awakened Man seeks to achieve a correlation between that Knowledge and subject-object consciousness that any question arises as to whether It is nearer conception or perception. To me It seems nearer conception, but in a subordinate degree I also express It in the physiognomic or mystical form. But considering this problem objectively or logically, I am quite unable to say that actually Knowledge through Identity is nearer conception than It is to perception. I do not see any practical escape from what might be called a coloring of the colorless, just so soon as the Inexpressible is reflected in expression. The most perfect vehicle of expression is, inevitably, a distortion in some measure. The alternatives are, therefore, either to refrain from all expression, or consistently to employ the instruments of expression which the individual has actually evolved, being careful, however, to warn all that the expression is only a reflection of THAT which on Its own level remains ever inexpressible. Expression helps as a Road to THAT, but where a given expression helps certain temperaments, quite a different form is needed for others.

LXXXVI
A New Word

November 7

IN THE EFFORT to give expression to Values which have their source in the Transcendent World, a serious difficulty is encountered, owing to the inadequate supply of words having the appropriate meaning. One result is, that very often the writer or speaker asserts ineffability in a wider sense than is necessarily the case. The Transcendent as such is inexpressible within the relative manifold, but there is an intermediate domain, between the Transcendent proper and the more restricted subject-object consciousness, where partial expression is possible. If this were not so, it would be entirely useless to write or say anything on these subjects. But when we come to the question of how far expression is possible, there is no definite answer. The problem seems to be much like that of the evaluation of an irrational number in terms of rational numbers. We know that a perfect evaluation is a theoretical or absolute impossibility, but at the same time the evaluation can approach perfection without limit. In actual practice, the mathematician proceeds in this evaluation just so far as is significant for his purposes, and stops there. With respect to the expression of the Higher Values, there is likewise no theoretical limit to the process of approximation. The absence of the conceptual tools or the limitations of the intellectual capacity of a given individual determine the limits for him, but do not define the limits of possibility for other individuals. This is all

a question of relative skill and equipment. The higher approxima-
tions are, admittedly, very difficult to produce and they are, progressively, less and less easy to understand as they are extended into the
unknown. Yet the process in approximation releases ever more and
more power of an increasing inclusiveness. So work of this kind is
important for mankind as a whole, even though those who *directly*
benefit by it are necessarily quite limited in number.

For the expression of the Transcendent, the Sanskrit is unquestionably the best of the fairly well known vehicles, for in this language there are many words representing metaphysical significance,
for which there are no equivalents to be found in western languages.
But outside a limited group of specialized scholars, an extensive use
of Sanskrit is impractical. A few Sanskrit words may be introduced
with appropriate explanation, and that is all. One who confines himself to the more common portion of the English language is restricted to the Anglo-Saxon and derivatives of Latin and Greek.
Without the aid of the latter derivatives, the writer would be all
but incoherent, once he reaches beyond very simple levels of thought;
and, even with all three resources, a certain straining of the meaning of words is often unavoidable. A great deal of the actual expression which one encounters in his various readings involves a very
careless use of words, and the result is often one of needless confusion. I believe that this confusion should be avoided wherever
possible. Part of this confusion grows out of a usage of words that
is neither in accordance with their etymological meaning nor with
current dictionary definition. Often this can be guarded against by a
more careful selection of words and word-combinations and, where
this is impossible, by taking pains to define the new usage of a given
term. Sometimes new words may be coined in accordance with the
established rules of word-building. It is not good practice to employ
this device if adequate word-tools already exist, but where it actually clarifies meaning it would seem to be beyond criticism.

I have coined a new word that seems to supply an unfilled need.
It is the noun, 'introception,' with the verb form, 'introceive.' This
word is from the combining forms 'intro,' meaning 'within,' 'into,'
and 'in,' and 'capere,' meaning 'take.' Hence it has the primary mean-

ing 'to take into or in.' The principal meaning for which I find this word useful is: 'The process or mode of consciousness which penetrates to profundity through the affective function.' Thus, it is the kind of insight aroused through music, poetry, and the fine arts in general. Both the words 'understanding' and 'perception' have been, at times, stretched in their meaning to carry this significance. But such usage is not consonant with the current meaning of these terms. 'Understanding,' properly, is related to cognition, while 'perception' is grounded in sensation. An idea or a concept may be understood; a sensory datum, either in a subtle or gross sense, may produce a perception; but the quality of consciousness, associated with the affections, is something of quite a different sort from either of these.

In principle, inward penetration is possible through any of the three modes of consciousness, or various combinations of them; but, practically, perception as a complex of sensation—not intuition—is rarely a Road in this cycle. Thus, in general, man Enters through understanding, or introception, or *intuitive* perception; or rather with one or the other of these as the predominant mode of his consciousness. With most individuals who reach the Outer Court of the Path, introception or intuitive perception is more developed than understanding, and thus he who would directly influence the greater number of people should speak mostly to the introceptive or intuitively perceptive consciousness. On the other hand, those who have attained a considerable development of power are likely to have exceptional understanding, at least in some fields. Thus, he who would effect an influence with the latter group must appeal, in large measure, to the understanding.

*   *   *   *   *

Note: Subsequently, I have broadened the meaning of introception so as to designate a third function of consciousness defined as: "The Power whereby the Light of Consciousness turns upon Itself toward Its Source."

LXXXVII

The Conflict between Space and Time

November 13

WE ARE INDEBTED to Spengler for having given us one of the clearest and most significant statements of a very ancient and profound conflict; one which even underlies some of the old stories of the wars of the angels. It is a conflict traceable through many phases of human consciousness and beyond. It has its sources in the very beginnings of manifestation itself, and is transcended by man only when he has again found himself in the pre-cosmic consciousness. It appears under many disguises and assumes variable forms, but its most basic representation is a conflict between Space and Time.

As space and time are commonly conceived, the notion of a war between these two hardly seems intelligible. For we have formed a habit of regarding these as purely formal pre-existences, quite independent of matter and consciousness. This is not the standpoint of Idealistic philosophy nor of theoretical physics, since the epochal contributions of Albert Einstein. However, it is a view practically and commonly held, and it must be discredited before meaning can be attached to conflict between space and time.

As should be clear by this time, I do not regard space and time as external to consciousness, but rather as modes and forms determining the play of relative consciousness or, in other words, as setting the stage for the drama of evolution. Neither space nor time are limitations imposed upon the ultimate Reality. On the contrary they have their origin within that Reality and are simply the most primary circumscribing forms that serve the purpose of delimiting consciousness or nature as this appears to human consciousness. The most basic forms, whether in terms of perception, conception or of law, involve the notions of space and time. These underlie logic,

229

relationship, periodicity, causality, etc. Not all modes of relative consciousness in equal degree involve these primary forms. Some are nearly altogether, if not wholly, temporal in their nature, while others are predominantly, perhaps exclusively, spatial. Thus perceptual consciousness is on the whole in closer connection with time than with space, although the spatial quality is peculiarly strong in the case of the sense of sight. In contrast, concepts are very strongly spatial and, in their more developed forms, essentially reduce time to a kind of spatial extension. In general, the closest union of concepts with percepts occurs in connection with the sense of sight or the world of light.

We can see at once one of the manifestations of the space-time conflict in the war between perception and conception. It has already been shown * how this conflict has led to the most fundamental division between the various schools of philosophy. Which of these two is closer to Reality? This is a very old question which has not only divided philosophers, but likewise caused conflicts between classes and groups carrying powers of the one kind or the other. The old war between religion and civil power is one phase of the issue, and this persists strongly, even in our own day. If we are to understand these age-old struggles, with all their practical bearing upon the happiness and well-being of man, it is necessary to determine and understand the significance of their primary source. To attain this we cannot stop short of acquiring some understanding of space and time in their primary relationship to consciousness.

Time is involved whenever we speak of 'becoming,' 'periodicity,' 'life,' 'birth,' 'decay,' 'evolution,' 'progress,' 'loss,' 'gain,' and so on through a multitude of terms implying process in some sense. On the other hand, space underlies notions, such as, 'law,' 'all at once,' 'essential identity of cause and effect,' 'freedom from sin, guilt, or karma,' 'immortality,' 'logic,' 'calculation,' 'reversible time,' etc. Tragic time or the time that is one with embodied life, birth, death, etc., is irreversible. It is tragic because of the irreversibility. That which has happened cannot be recalled; the unused opportunity of the moment

* See Section No. LXXXV.

is gone forever; death closes relationships, etc. If time were ultimately real, it would never be possible to transcend the tragic drama of life. In such a case, to be sure, creative becoming would have genuine reality, but as the becoming always involves a complemental destroying, the joy of the former would always be dogged by the pain of the latter without hope of any ultimate resolution of this pain. Spengler, on his part, recognizes this tragic quality of chronological time. He realizes that it entails essential pessimism, but glories in acceptance of that pessimism, holding that it is the nobler part and the more heroic to accept this frankly. He definitely asserts the primacy of time and thus predicates its ultimate triumph in the conflict with space.

Contrasted to Spengler stand the religious, the scientific, and the larger part of the philosophical thinkers. Outstanding among these are Buddha, Shankara, and Jesus. Let us isolate the fundamental viewpoint of these Men. When Gautama was aroused from his youthful sleep as an indulged Prince, the inciting cause was the witnessing of sickness, poverty, and death. These He readily saw as inevitable consequences of Becoming. He also saw that they were far more effective in producing misery or pain than any of the complemental life-processes were in producing happiness. Hence the final balance of the time-process was suffering. He anticipated Spengler in realizing that the world-life or Sangsara was primarily tragic, and accordingly He held a pessimistic view concerning this particular field of consciousness. But unlike Spengler, He refused to acquiesce in the tragedy. He searched for and ultimately found a power superior to the tragic field of Sangsara. This Power was a State of Consciousness that transcended the whole domain under the sway of time. This State of Consciousness is known to us today by the symbolic designating name, Nirvana. Now, while it is true that in the highest sense Nirvanic Consciousness transcends space as well as time, it is nevertheless approachable by human consciousness as being of a space-like quality. Nirvanic Consciousness implies a comprehension of beginning and end at once, thus destroying the tragic quality of time. But 'comprehension' is essentially spatial. Further, the differentiation of levels of Nirvana also involves a fundamentally spatial notion. It is possible for embodied man to attain some degree of Nirvanic Consciousness while still possessing embodied consciousness. That such can be the case and at the same time be known to be the case here in this world implies that there is some degree of overlapping consciousness. This overlapping is necessarily spatial in the fundamental sense as revealed in the fact that the little more than inchoate reports of Nirvana are space-formed but in the radical sense not time-formed. Buddha brought a message of Liberation and Immortality, and hence in the proper sense he is optimistic. But the significance of the immediate step He offered mankind lies in the fact that He opposed the tragic time-world with a more potent Space-World. Liberation and Immortality are space-notions, freed from time-bondage.

The significance of the work of Shankara is precisely the same, though His approach and methods are different. In effect He set up the notion of the monism of continuity—a spatial notion—in opposition to the discreteness of the universe. He asserted the unbroken and unbreakable continuity between the Soul (Atman) of man and Divinity (Brahman). He denied unequivocally the reality of the discrete world or seen universe. Now, the primary instance of discrete manifoldness, carrying within it the tragic quality, lies in the three-fold division of time, i.e., past, present, and future. Herein lies the root of multiplicity and the cause of all misery.

However large may have been the development of an optimistic attitude toward the world-field in the later centuries of western Christianity, it still remains true that the original Message of Jesus was just as completely other-worldly as were those of Buddha and Shankara. Repeatedly Jesus said: "My Kingdom is not of this world." He never asserted that Immortality, or the Kingdom of Peace, or the Saved Life was realizable as a mere world-field existence. Temporal power, which is always peculiarly time-centered, remorselessly fought Jesus and His followers for several centuries. True, He said: "Render unto Caesar the things that are Caesar's." But he completed this clause by adding: "But render unto God the things that are God's." And, indeed, He challenged Caesar-power far more fundamentally than any mere invading host. Such a host might have conquered even Rome, but this would have meant merely a change in the group that functioned the Caesar-power. Political wars never overthrow Caesar as a principle. But Jesus challenged the power of Caesar at its very roots, and so the Roman political sense was quite correct from its viewpoint in attempting to exterminate all that Jesus represented.* Jesus was willing to let Caesar play with the bodies of men for a brief period of time, but He claimed the Souls of men, realizing well that the Soul is the only part of man that really counts. Without control of human souls the power of Caesar is a vain and empty thing. Realization of this fact is the explanation why great or ambitious temporal rulers so commonly seek to abrogate Divine prerogatives. Caesar succeeds in controlling man only so long as he can accomplish the binding of the soul of man to the body, and then dominate the latter. Therefore, He who can free the soul takes the enduring kernel and leaves to Caesar but the husk.

Jesus did most emphatically challenge the time-world, but in His case it was very largely that world as represented by Caesar-power. He offered an other-worldliness, a prime characteristic of which is immortality. Now, nothing that is subject to time-wearing is immortal. The essence of time-wearing is the negation of persistence. Only that which is not subject to time endures. That which we find through self-analysis to have the quality of durability in man is not under the sway of time. This realizable fact of a persistent element in human consciousness, when properly understood, is definite proof

* That dialectic materialism is but a permutation of Caesar-power is afforded empiric demonstration in the development in Russia. The religion of other-worldliness was crushed along with independent money power. In their place was substituted an unchecked political power. We are thus afforded an excellent example of the rawness of Caesar-power when it has a free field of action. Rarely have there been manifestations of the sheer brutality of naked force of sharper delineation than is afforded by this example. The other totalitarian governments manifest the same quality. The differences between Fascism and dialectic materialism are only superficial. Essentially they are only counterpointal manifestations of the same spirit. In a peculiar sense they incarnate anti-Christ. Theirs is the time-bound spirit manifested with an exceptional degree of purity. Perforce they are at war with the Liberating Spirit of the Spatial Consciousness. But in the end they will fail as they are identified with the lesser power.

of a trans-temporal Reality underlying man. Jesus simply sought, as His predecessors before Him had done, to Awaken in men a Recognition of this trans-temporal Reality. That Recognition means 'being born again,' which, when achieved, at once destroys bondage to the time-world, including the dominion of Caesar.

All Caesar-power, whether in the specifically political sense or in the military form, is essentially a manifestation of the time-power. Nietzsche, as one of the prime exponents of time-power, saw this point clearly, and both frankly and aggressively taught anti-Christ. He exalted the time-violence of the will and hated the potency of the Christly non-resistance. All rulers whose souls are identical with political power are consciously or unconsciously disciples of Nietzsche, and with respect to them, all men and women who incarnate something of the Christly principle stand in counter relationship.

*　　*　　*　　*　　*

The time-principle dominates in the case of consciousness manifesting in primitive forms. It is thus in the massive or numerical sense preponderant, for not only is the bulk of human life under its sway, but as well all of sub-human life. In the historic sense, Spengler is right when he says that spatial comprehension comes into dominance only as a culture flowers. It is born and sustained in this world only with difficulty. But, on the other hand, it wields the ultimately victorious force. The cosmic integration of Sir Isaac Newton is a good illustration of the power of the spatial principle. He gave an especially strong impetus to the conceptual grasp of the universe under law. By supplying a command over a planted time-mystery that had held humanity in its thralldom before his day, he effected a substantial degree of liberation for human consciousness. A considerable sector of time-mobilized nature now stands definitely conquered by man as a result of the spatial understanding introduced by Newton and other men like him. But as a biologic fighting animal Newton would have proven peculiarly ineffective. The impact of the massive brute-force, which constitutes the ultimate instrument of

234

Caesar-power, would be easily fatal to Newton and those of his type. Yet the science of which these men are masters has caused even the Caesars of this day to be nervous in the exercise of their own peculiar power. Adaptation of space-power to brute force threatens to become a boomerang, offering not victory, but mutual annihilation. It is utterly foreign to the native genius of Caesar as a type to be able to master the key to space-power so that he may employ it with safety. This key may be effectively mastered only by a peculiarly developed and rare type of man that from the standpoint of the standards of Caesar would be regarded as effeminate and weak. On a lower level, it is the same contrast that is afforded in the case of Jesus when He is contrasted with the political power of His day. A simple and saintly Man for a few years wandered up and down the roads of Palestine and spoke a few words also simple in form, though often obscure in meaning. Yet temporal and priestly power hated Him, as few men have been hated, and did all that it could, even over a period of centuries, to seek the destruction of the living stream that incarnated His words. Yet this Caesar-power, with all its impressive showing of material power, was forced to give way until ultimately it formally surrendered. Is not all this highly significant as revealing the hidden potency of Space-power?

It is true that the time-power, under the form of the Caesar-principle, does attain some degree of subsequent victory. In the instance of the history of Christianity this was manifested through an apparent surrender of the former, followed by a subsequent adaptation of the new Force to its own purposes. In its purity, the Power, represented by Men like Jesus on the one hand, and by the philosophers and scientists on the other, is spiritual and is manifested through intellectual and moral vehicles. Subsequently, when through 'boring from within' the Caesar-power gains control of the movements that originated in a spiritual impetus, the latter becomes largely crystallized and bound through being formalized in elaborate ritualism, genuflection, and convention. The emphasis of formal religion is then placed upon the story of the life of the Teacher, rather than upon the meaning of the Teaching. Finally, in greater or lesser degree Caesar succeeds in capturing the force of space-power to serve his ends. The extreme manifestation of this we find in the wars of Christendom that Caesar succeeded in having fought in the name of the Prince of Peace!

But while all this reveals a certain tactical victory for time-power as incarnated in the Caesar-principle, the latter has actually incurred an important strategic weakening. The new power that Caesar has invoked actually contradicts him. This weakens Caesar's hand in the end. The result is that no political force in the West has ever been as fully successful as was Genghis Khan, who was an almost pure incarnation of the time-force in the political field. Today, Caesar is very much weaker than he seems. Sheer necessity forces him to restrain his will in the face of the knowledge of the technician. This simply means that the technician, together with the intelligences back of him, wields the ultimately higher power. Caesar may bluster and storm, but the quiet knowledge of law on the part of a few keen and some profound minds is a fatal curb upon his potency. To be sure, Caesar has a certain Samson-like power which he could will to use, but, like Samson, he would be crushed himself in the resulting debacle. So, all in all, if we compare the extent of Caesar-power before the Christian era with that which now exists after the leavening work of the thought of Jesus, supplemented later by that of the philosophers and scientists, we find Caesar in a much weaker position relatively. While he wields greater potencies than ever before, yet he is matched by powers of a still higher order. And temperamentally Caesar is disqualified to meet these higher powers. He can win in a temporary sense by destroying civilization and re-enslaving man, but he does not understand, and therefore cannot control, the powers which alone can lead to the genuinely higher culture wherein man attains more and more freedom.

*   *   *   *   *

In our day, the conflict between space and time is exemplified especially in the war between science and technology on the one hand, and politics on the other. Further, since money-power by psychological affinity lies close to technology, it must be aligned with

236

science and technology in this conflict.* There is a deep reason for this conflict which should be understood as the issue is vital and of great current importance.

The space-power, whether represented in philosophic religion, technical philosophy, science, technology, or money-thought—in the modern sense—requires a careful use of a very vital instrument, i.e., concepts together with their enrobement in language. In order to attain understanding in any of these fields, particularly in those involving the use of the more subtle and intricate ideas, many years of careful discipline are required in the use of concepts and language. While a high order of imagination is required both for understanding and for creative activity in the higher phases of this domain, yet without the training in concepts and language this imagination is impotent. The requisite correctness and precision in the use of concepts is sometimes extreme. Even with an original endowment of natural talent or genius for these fields, the necessary skill is attained only by the most exacting kind of effort. Sometimes the pre-condition of the sufficiently precise concept is protracted labor on the part of very high talent. Naturally, such a vitally important and difficultly achieved instrument comes to have a value that is all but sacred. For it must be remembered, without these concepts no functioning in this domain can be effective. To give this point a more concrete form, I call attention to the fact that the machines of this age could not have been originated, then started into operation, and be kept in motion without the appropriate concepts and the men who had mastered them. There is but a handful of such men existing, but they make the machine-age possible. In contrast, a brute force which is far from intelligent can easily stop the

* Financial thinking combines both the political and the scientific spirit. In the older process of trading, a superior skill in deception was an important factor in success, in which case the difference between business and politics was less marked than it is coming to be at present. But as financial thinking has acquired greater maturity and has to operate in settings of ever greater and greater technical complexity, soundness and reliability have grown in importance as the conditions of success. Thus we are witnessing in business the evolution of financial engineering, and thus money-power is becoming less and less political in its spirit.

237

machine. In this latter fact lies a danger to our civilization that is second only to that of war.

In contrast, the exercise of time-power does not require the mastery of carefully developed concepts. In the form of political power, the final instrument is brute force, and this in turn is controlled by psychological means. Now, the psychological use of language obeys radically different canons from that required in scientific language. Correctness and precision have no meaning here. The man who uses language as a psychological power may be utterly self-contradictory, his ideas may have the loosest sort of relationship with their supposed objects, and yet he may be highly successful. What he is actually doing is effecting a control of a certain kind of force through the exercise of an emotional key. Such a man may have a moral code and his private motive may be excellent, but his attitude toward concepts is amoral at best. On the other hand, the space-power type of man has a highly developed moral sense with respect to the use of concepts. Naturally, he is outraged through and through by this political and psychological use of concepts and language.

A profound consequence of this conflicting use of concepts and language is that there can be no sympathy between political power and technological power. In fact, the clash between the two domains may well be underlaid by a subtle hatred. Inevitably, the technician must view control by political power as an invasion by something inferior and certainly something inimical. As a result, political power, if once dominant, can crush and destroy the fruits of technology, but cannot lead toward, much less command, further and better achievement.* On the other hand, money-power can achieve and has achieved managerial control of technology, but the reason for this is that, in spite of surface frictions, there is a fundamental sympathy between these two due to a similarity of attitude toward, and use of, concepts and language. Neither does the other a deep and unforgivable violence. Finance, on the higher levels, requires the engineering type of mind, and all engineers, whatever the differences

* In this connection, it is a significant fact that in the totalitarian states where political power is dominant, the most imporant technological development has been in the adaptation of technical instruments for war.

238

in their specialties, can understand each other in a fundamental sense. So it is possible for technology and money-power to co-operate, but both are outraged in their deeps by the loose, and in some respects, irresponsible modes of procedure of the political mind.

An illustration may make possible a clearer understanding of the irreconcilable nature of this conflict between technology and money-power on the one hand, and a dominant political power on the other. Of very fundamental importance for both of the former is the rule that standards of measure should remain invariable. Invariables may be regarded as a phase of fundamental concepts by which alone is it possible to achieve calculated control of variables and unknowns. It is therefore a necessity for effective functioning in these fields that standards should not change, or if they do, that they should do so in accordance with a perfectly determinant formula accessible to all. As a consequence, arbitrary political manipulation of standards has the effect of outrage—for it cuts under the whole structure which is dependent upon careful calculation. The revealed attitude of political power in this matter simply illustrates how impossible it is to achieve real cooperation between dominant political power and technology. Further, this runs deeper than mere personal reaction. The political mind is quite incapable of understanding the necessities of technology.

*   *   *   *   *

That space is the greater power as compared with time is indicated by my own Recognitions. While the most inward State of all stands in a position of superiority with respect to space as well as time, there are intermediate stages, in some of which the space-quality is recognizable while the time-quality is not, but in others there is added to the space-quality a sort of modified time-quality. It is significant that the last expressible mode or quality of Consciousness, as the penetration proceeds inward, is something that can be indicated only by words such as 'depth,' 'height,' 'inwardness,' etc. These words with their corresponding concepts are manifestly of the spatial type. They have nothing to do with time. It is true that I have used above the term, 'penetration,' and this word clearly carries the connotation of 'process,' a time-quality. But process is not a part of the content or quality of the Consciousness Itself. There is no sense that the seeming penetration required an acual lapse of time. In the metaphysical sense, it is not correct to speak of the Recognition as an event, however much It may seem to be so from the standpoint of relative consciousness. I simply Awakened to an eternal Thereness—which in a mysterious sense is Hereness as well —that had absolutely nothing to do with Becoming. It is true that the self-consciousness in playing the part of witness did pass through a series of notations of states and analyses of them, and thus it still remained in some sort of time-field. But the witnessing self-consciousness must be carefully distinguished from the Primeval Consciousness witnessed. Now, the Primeval Consciousness is enrobed in a Space-Field, in some sense, at a level where no time-element is recognizable. This seems quite clearly to imply that, as compared with time, space wields the more ultimate power.

It should be clear by this time that I am constrained to assert a position at variance with that maintained by Spengler, who saw time as the father of space. Spengler recognized all cultured consciousness as essentially space-like and also realized that culture ever turned upon time and embodied life with a view to conquering them. Thus the Crown of all culture is well represented by Buddha.* The Message of Buddha is one of Liberation from all life-process with all its tragedy. But Spengler granted to such a Message only a temporary success. He thought he saw the time-life current ultimately undermining the Liberated State and melting It all in the stream of Becoming. Undoubtedly such must seem to be the case to a consciousness confined to the perspective of the historic stream, since all that persists for history is necessarily in time. However Spengler has only been able to trace that which has not yet been conquered by space. That consciousness in which the desire for

* The word 'Buddha' has a three-fold meaning. The popular understanding is that it refers uniquely to the historic personage known as Gautama. But fundamentally it means "Enlightenment" in a transcendental or₁ world-conquering sense. All who have established self-conscious identity with the synthetic non-dual consciousness are Buddhas.

240

sentient existence has not yet been conquered is manifestly still in thralldom to time. But the Higher Consciousness, in which this desire has been destroyed has disappeared from historic observation. No one speaking from the perspective of a Spengler can possibly know anything of this. On the other hand, it is possible to Awaken to a Level of Consciousness wherein the Realized Man may Know that it is Buddha and not Spengler who represents the ultimately Triumphant Principle.

Viewed from the relative perspective, it seems quite clear that the gains of the Force for Liberation are numerically quite limited so far. But it should not be forgotten that these gains are absolute, for the Liberated Soul is outside the jurisdiction of time, whereas consciousness-bound-to-time-bodies is always subject to attack by the Force of Spatial Liberation. The Caesar-principle, being the child of time, is subject to Nemesis, while the space-power is not. Herein lies the basis for the profound optimism which makes it possible to say with certainty that ultimately all souls will be Emancipated from time-bondage.

*   *   *   *   *

I have developed the present thesis in terms of a conflict or war between two principles. Obviously, this is valid only from the relative perspective or as it appears in the time-stream. Metaphysically considered, there is no victory to be achieved, for Primeval Consciousness never has in reality been bound. Time-bondage is only an effect existing for relative consciousness. *Arriving* at a State of Liberation has meaning for self-conscious consciousness, but not for Primeval Consciousness, which, like Space, is unaffected by the presence or absence of events.

SPACE remains the highest Divinity that is in any sense knowable, however dim that knowledge may be. Beyond lies the Eternally Unknowable, surrounded by impenetrable Darkness, Silence, and Voidness.

LXXXVIII

The Final Record

November 16

IT IS NOW one hundred one days since the great day of the Ineffable Transition and three months since I began the record that is now drawing to a close. It has been for the writer a most extraordinary period. He has known what it is to enter a State where he found himself complete; where the problems that weary the soul find their resolution; where there is a Joy unutterable; where there is found the satisfying and certain Knowledge; where there may be known the Companionship that gives the value of deep Communion; and where there is real Emancipation. He knows today, with the certainty of immediate Knowledge, that there is a hidden Kernel of utterly satisfying values within this husk of outer life. He has found the solution of the great metaphysical question, and so for him the Quest of life is finished.

There remains a work to do. There are almost unimaginably enormous fields of knowledge lying below and within the inconceivable Cognition, and for the unfolding of these possibilities veritable ages are required. There is the work of leaving a record so that some aid may be given to those others who also seek to travel this way. This writing is a part of that task.

*　　*　　*　　*　　*

This would seem to be the time for making a general survey of the culminating effect of the past hundred days, so as to afford a basis for the evaluation of the event that I have called the Ineffable Transition. Its value to me in my inner life is clear and beyond doubt, a fact which, it seems, should be obvious to anyone who has read this book. Ever must I say: It is the Value beyond all other values. There is no counter-interest which relative life can offer that in the smallest degree would lead me to wish to turn my back upon the

242

Transcendental World. There is nothing remaining here below that intrigues me, though some phases of outer life still remain more enjoyable than others. I desire that other individuals should Realize that which I have come to Know; and if I can be of assistance toward that end, I shall be glad to do what may be done. But the message I would carry would be that of another World, of another Life, and not one of mere amelioration of the world-field life. In this, my own conviction fully accords with the central theme of the Message of Jesus, i.e., that man must be Born again and enter into Real Life in another "Kingdom" or on another Level of Consciousness. For myself, I have now demonstrated, what others have already told, that it is not necessary to die here, in the physical sense, in order to be born again in that other World. But it does seem clear that, so long as man occupies bodies formed of the gross material of this plane, he can Realize the Transcendental World in only a penumbral sense. Gross matter opposes too much resistance to that Consciousness not to serve as something of a barrier. Yet by a partial refinement of the materials entering into the composition of the compound human form, it is possible to achieve variable degrees of cross-correlation between the Transcendent and the outer relative life. Here we come to a question that requires for its solution a considerable exercise of discrimination. Let us consider this problem briefly.

The grosser the encasement of man, the deeper he can descend into the sphere of evil, dark, and confused consciousness without endangering his continued existence upon this plane of life. But also, the grosser the encasement, the greater the insulation from the Current of Higher Consciousness. As a counterfact, it is to be noted, that the more subtilized a human body may be, the greater is its potentiality in serving as a carrier of the Transcendent or Cosmic Consciousness. Other things being equal, the highest possible cross-correlation would be achieved by a man who had a body so subtle that it was just barely able to endure life on this plane. There is here, then, the action of two counter principles between which a working balance must be achieved in order that the Other-World Consciousness may have some degree of objective manifestation. The records of the cases of Cosmic Consciousness show the balance to have been achieved at quite various levels. In the western world, Plotinus seems to have had the greatest conscious command of inward penetration. But he lived in retirement and had so profound a distaste for the grossly physical that it is said he was ashamed that he possessed a physical body. He gave His values to the world through a philosophical vehicle and through a few personal disciples. At the other pole is a man like Walt Whitman who frankly loved the physical and lived much of the time in distinctly adverse environments. Whitman certainly was able to do what would have been quite impossible for Plotinus. But, on the other hand, the Light is manifested in far greater clarity in the case of the latter, and He had a power to penetrate the inward States as the result of his own conscious effort, something Whitman did not have.

Which of these two achievements constitutes the greatest offering to the world? I do not believe that there is any absolute answer to this question. It all depends upon the need of the hour, the stratum of humanity which is influenced, and the native capacities of the individual who has attained the Cosmic Consciousness. One type of man may achieve a wider breadth of direct human contact, another can manifest the Light in greater purity and completeness but can reach relatively only the few who are better prepared to receive. Both services are needed.

For my own part, at this moment I have not yet consolidated a working balance. The better attuned I am to Inwardness, the harder I find it to endure the harsh world-forces which I find striking in various subtle ways, difficult to describe. In contrast, if I harden myself so that I can endure those forces more easily, I find that the Inward clarity is distinctly clouded. My inclination is to retreat to the wilds and work from there. What working basis will prove to be both possible and desirable has not yet been determined. At present, though living in a semi-retreat but within the psycho-sphere of a great center of population, I find the impact of the world-force difficult to meet, and it has been a strain on the organism. Whether or not I can build outer ruggedness without destroying the requisite inward sensitiveness remains for the future to determine. For my own part, it would only be with the greatest reluctance that I would accept a clouding of inward capacity in order to extend the range of direct personal contact. To accept that course, I would have to be convinced that the social values achieved were worth the cost.

During the past three months I have focused nearly all my efforts upon the problem of expression and, as might be expected, the principal objective effects of the Transition are focused upon the faculties exercised in such work. I find a distinct increase of capacity in terms of understanding and introception. Never have I produced so much material in so short a time, and much of this deals with concepts that are difficult to capture.

I find a new kind of concept being born into my mind. It is not yet sufficiently tangible to give it a clear delineation, and it is questionable how far present word-forms and even logic may serve for enrobing it. If our more familiar concepts may be thought of as granular and capable of fixed definition, this other kind of concept might be called fluidic or functional and not possessed of fixed definition. As nearly as I can describe it, I would say that this new concept is something like this: An idea enters or is born into the mind, but at once the counter idea achieves recognition. Then the original idea takes on a sort of flowing quality which seems to proceed toward the level that synthesizes both it and the counter idea. There is something in this that suggests the dialectic form of Hegel, but the movement is fluidic rather than in a series of discrete triadic steps. In some respects these concepts seem like vortices in consciousness, as there is a certain quality that suggests a turning inside out that proceeds continuously. So long as I do not try to express this thought, it carries a high order of clarity. It does not involve a defiance of logic, but it seems to require further logical laws, not yet recognized. When I attempt to give this thought expression, I have difficulties. It tends to disappear, and I often feel something like a nascent dizziness. It leaves me with the feeling that what I write or say is only partly true, try as I will to be as correct as possible. Thus these sentences both reveal and veil at the same time. It is not an easy Sea in which to think, when one tries to retain correlation with the outer consciousness. Whatever success I do attain in navigating in this compound of the Sea and relative consciousness, I owe very largely to the years of training in higher mathematics. Often I feel tempted to fall back upon the relatively inchoate expression of poetry where the conceptual demands are less exacting.

This effort has entailed quite a considerable demand upon the forces of the physical organism. Since the beginning of this writing I have scarcely lived in the field of the action and reception senses. As a consequence, they have been despoiled in a degree of the values that otherwise would have accrued to them out of the Transition. This simply illustrates the importance of the effect of focusing. The Higher Consciousness, in a greater or lesser degree, is formless and thus is in the nature of a general Power which may be made effective in whatever direction It is focused. So far, I have concentrated principally in the field of thought and consciousness-correlation; and thus quite naturally it is in this region that the main effects are to be noted. I chose this course spontaneously and deliberately, for this is a region toward which my interest gravitates naturally. Others, differently constituted, would not have had the same experience.

*   *   *   *   *

As the final and crowning word of this record, I wish to state my appreciation, and give my tribute, to her who has journeyed by my side in this quest of the ancient yet ever new World; that World which is at once the Source and final Home of all creatures. The completed human being is both man and woman, but on this objective level of consciousness the true balance of these two is not found in one embodiment. So here in this world, the best that may be attained is not achieved by one alone. Man and woman, each in his separate nature, have peculiar powers, and that which is visibly true here also has its higher analogue in the Greater World. Whereas the strongest impulse of man is a passion for Freedom, woman in contrast conceives and cherishes Form. Corresponding to these two types of genius are the grand principles of Liberation and Compassion. It is not in accordance with the nature of the exclusively masculine principle ever to turn back from the Liberation of the great and free Space. But the feminine nature never forgets the needs of embodied

246

form. It is the Woman in Men like Buddha and Christ that has made them Masters of Compassion, as the Man in Them made them conquerors of Mara. Emancipation for an individual soul is but a partial achievement, for the weal of units is not the Liberation of mankind. It is the others, whom man alone might easily forget, that woman never forgets.

In many ways, down through the years, Sherifa has never allowed me to forget the call whispered through the suffering of others. For my own part, I was content to unite with Space alone, but the justice of her claim for these others I could not deny. So, if at the final moment when Consciousness rested Free in the High Indifference and it was too late to form a genuinely new decision, for no desire is born There, if at the final moment, previously formed decision ruled my return to action in this bound-world below, it was the words and love of Sherifa, who never forgets those others, that were ultimately decisive. There is, within this book, a short poem to "Compassion" (Section LXXIII), for which, while I supplied the words, Sherifa gave the Soul. Left to myself alone, it is highly probable that I would never have troubled to embody in words this that is written here but, rather, would have sailed on in an utterly satisfying Consciousness. So, if this book has values for other human souls, if, because of it, some other wanderers are led to seek for the Great Pearl, then thanks are due most to her who never forgot them. It is true that I brought to the task a certain skill and the advantage of some training, but withal I inclined to be far too aloof and indifferent to care to put forth the effort. But the Compassion instilled from her heart would not let it be so. Thus this book is sent forth as our common offering to those others who, soul-sick and weary in the meshes and mazes of Sangsara, yearn for the Light.

May Peace and final Victory come to all those who, having found the emptiness of life external, hunger for the Life that is Everlasting.

OM TAT SAT

LXXXIX

The Supreme Adventure

AT LONG LAST the forest lay behind,
Before stretched a desert, bleak and empty,
Beyond, a mountain, dim in the dancing haze,
Reaching upward, defeating all measure.
I sat resting in the shade of the forest-rim,
The last cool stream at my feet.
Deeply I drank refreshment and pondered:
Long had the journey been and weary
In the maze and the dark of the forest,
Oft had I drifted down false lanes,
Oft had courage been shaken,
Yet I never quite failed to try again
And at last the dim trails were finished.
Behind lay desires, vain and incomplete,
Ambitions inadequate, yearnings now stilled;
Before, reaching all but endlessly,
A dreary waste, trailess and void of sign.
It seemed I beheld the Goal, dim in the distance,
But, again, It seemed not there.
Was uncertain possibility worth the effort?
Could anything be worth the cost
Paid, and yet remaining to be paid?
Oh! for the rest without ending,
If not the rest of Victory,
Then the surcease of defeat,
But in any case rest.
Thus I pondered while a new strength grew
And resolution again was born
Of the ashes of burned desires and yearnings.
Methought: "Better onward continue,
Else all this effort uncompleted

Useless would lie in the void of vain endeavor.
If thought of achievement thrills no longer,
Yet 'twere better to complete the half-finished.
Behind lie values exhausted and lost,
No longer potent to 'rouse the soul
That, in vision, a Beyond hath glimpsed.
Onward alone lieth hope
To fill the void."
At last I arose, resolution firm,
Gathered my staff and compass—
Sole possessions of the final hour—
And strode me forth beyond visible trail.
Ere long the forest behind me vanished,
Consumed in refracting desert haze;
Then all about the emptiness of burning waste.
On I journeyed in time-expanding void,
Unafraid, but weary with the seeming endlessness;
On I journeyed o'er rock and sand and thorn,
Alone in the stillness that is not Peace;
On I journeyed, thirsting ever more and more
For refreshing waters of the forest past recall;
Yet on I journeyed as thirst grew numb,
The mountain, haze consumed, as the forest.
And time, my tread less resolute became;
The void without become likewise a void within,
All endeavor unavailing.
I sank me down upon a rock,
Caring nought, accepting what might be.
Then spoke the VOICE,
In accents strong, cheering, comforting,
Calling from out the Beyond,
Telling of the Glory There,
Recalling the need of forest wanderers.
Within me a new courage grew, a new determination.
Once more I 'rose, onward moving,
Feeling more clear, though not yet seeing

The ancient Mount of untellable Majesty.
The desert journey, all but finished,
Now lay behind.
Already the slopes, mounting in steeper gradient,
Promise of final fulfillment offered.
Steeper grew the Way, but easier,
Strange paradox of a World, inverting former values.
Quickly I ascended, filled with strength
Born downward from Beyond.
The haze grew thin and vanished.
Then, before me, immeasurable Largeness,
Buttresses of the ancient Mountain;
Height rising on height, beyond all vision.
Filled anew with cheer and rich assurance,
Fast I climbed, until at last
Above me stretched the awful cliff,
Transcending the final reach of thought.
Here I lingered but briefest hour,
Extracting from thought its inmost core,
Seeking the Power above all powers.
Success crowned effort beyond all hope
And, as it were, in Time's briefest instant,
Outreaching time and space and cause, I rose
To unthinkable heights beyond unthinkable heights,
Finding at last the ancient Home,
Long forgotten, yet Known so well.
Gone was the forest-world, a new World mine;
Joy untellable, Knowledge all-consuming,
Eternity stretching everywhere;
Not anywhere aught but I
Sustaining all universes,
Their origin and consummation.
Darkness of ineffable LIGHT
Enveloping all.

II

Darkness, Silence, Voidness, utter,
At once, Fullness in every sense;
Deeps beyond seeing, beyond feeling, beyond thought;
At the inmost Core of all I AM,
Sustaining all, not different from all.
Untellable ages, a moment of time,
All time, but one moment there.
From the inmost Core, descending—downward, outward—
Distances immeasurable I came,
'Till finding the Thought unutterable,
Here, lingering, I dwelt for a season,
Thinking what I could not say,
Understanding transcending human conceiving,
Pure Meaning close-packed and o'erflowing,
Containing of libraries the substance all
And more, ne'er yet told.
Filled to the brim, I descended, down through the haze,
Which, ever inclosing the world below,
Holds dispart the Mountain Top
From the nether world of outer life.
Gone was the desert and forest-maze,
Scenes of age-old wanderings.
The Way to Heights ineffable a mystery no more,
A new mystery spread below.
Seething multitudes rushing to and fro
O'er far-reaching plane;
Bent over, searching the earth,
Grubbing here and there, ne'er still,
Driven as slaves, joyless and dull,
Seeking the Gold, finding dross.
One here, one there, standing in pause
Looking upward, eyes dim with pain,
Yearning, questioning, searching,
Not Knowing, yet hungering.

These, aliens all in a foreign land;
Their Home forgotten, yet dimly recalled
As the memory of distant dream.
I stood upon a lofty Field
At the edge of thought articulate,
Pondering the scene below,
Recalling the days I, too, was there
Seeking blindly for I knew not what;
Remembering effort—misdirected, barren of harvest.
All these my brothers are,
All these, not different from Me;
I, Free, yet not wholly Free,
While these, bound, remain, travailing.
Questioning, I pondered their sad estate,
Wondering how might release
For all be won.
Then gazing about me, on that lofty Field,
Beheld I a Glorious Company
Of Men, rare, Divinely Noble,
All striving ceaselessly in deep Compassion
With multitudes far below.
From These, methought I saw
Rays of Light, out-reaching and down,
Search-lights seeking quickened hearts and minds.
Then peering close, beheld I those who,
Pausing, raised their eyes in questing, hungering search,
Each enveloped in Search-Light Ray.
Along these Beams a Call forth-send
Arousing to fuller wakefulness
Ancient Memory.
Some, responding, gropingly to seek began,
Hunting the dim-felt but unseen Light,
Greatly tripping, meandering hither and yon,
Yet falteringly drawing nearer and nearer.
Then spoke the Voice, well loved,
From out an ancient Day, another Life,

Uttering words of counsel sage.
"Thou would'st of this harvest share,
Of souls drawn Home to Peace and Joy?
Then seek again the way
In yon fields below.
None knows the final secret of human soul,
So ever We try and try again,
In every way, old memory to 'rouse.
Go forth and try thy way."
So again I pondered the trials I knew,
The effort wasted, endeavor fruitless,
The final Success, the Key thereto.
Methought:
" 'Tis needless, the journey so hard should be.
A little turn here, another there,
And many a barrier and morass deep,
Easily surmounted will be.
I shall tell of the Way
Which at last I found,
That others in a clearer Light may See."
So I drew a chart, the best I knew,
And here it is for all
Who, wandering in forest and desert drear,
Wish that a clearer Way might revealed be.

Addenda

A—Two Years Later

January 30, 1939

A LITTLE MORE THAN TWO YEARS has elapsed since the completion of the foregoing writings. Although immediate publication had been my intention, yet through one factor or another, this has been delayed. This has proved to be, on the whole, a fortunate circumstance, as the delay has afforded me the opportunity to view the whole cycle from the perspective of temporal distance. As a result of this longer view, it is possible to report a more objective evaluation of the whole event than I could effect at the time when I was more occupied with the freshness of the new Presence. In addition, during the interval I have devoted considerable time to the search of both oriental and occidental literature which had a bearing upon the more metaphysical states of consciousness. As has been noted in the body of the text, there were certain features in the second Transformation for which previous studies had not prepared me. Fortunately, through recent translations and publications of selections from the Northern Buddhist Canon that have come into my possession during the interim, I have been enabled to give the content of that transformed Consciousness something on the order of an objective verification. Presumptively, a brief report of both the evaluation and the verification will be of value to the interested reader, and so I am including them as an addendum to this book.

It is entirely natural that a western student, nurtured in the tradition of physical science, should ask for a scientific treatment of any material which he is expected to consider seriously. Unfortunately, the immediate or intimate elements or states of consciousness do not lend themselves to any such treatment, for our science is oriented

255

exclusively to objective material. Value and meaning are elements of consciousness which cannot be observed. They can be realized through introception, but this, for any individual, is an intensely private matter. It is impossible, by western scientific method, to observe the inner consciousness of any individual other than that of one's own self. The objective behaviour of the organization of an individual, who reports the realization of an unusual inner state of consciousness, may be observed in the scientific sense. But only the crassest kind of extravert would affirm that the inwardly realized value and meaning can be appropriately measured and appreciated through the study of observable behaviour. So the question of the status of any reported inner state of consciousness falls quite outside the range of the methodological technique of western science.

However, I cannot help but feel sympathy with the reluctance of the critical western student to accept statements relative to the mystical states of consciousness, on the basis of faith alone. For my part, I ask anyone not to believe blindly, but merely to be open-minded. There is no final verification save through immediate realization. All that I, or anyone else, can do is to build a presumption which may be sufficient to lead the student to seek private verification himself. This last statement is strictly true with respect to the student who approaches the subject in the critical intellectual spirit exclusively. If, on the other hand, the individual seeker is willing to dare on the basis of faith, in the spirit of the true pioneer, something more can be done for him. In the body of the text I have spoken of the power of 'induction' or 'contagion.' Since writing that I have had rather extensive experience with this power, and have found it even more potent than I then realized. On innumerable occasions, when, either spontaneously or deliberately, I entered the Field of the Current, responsive individuals, who were present, were carried into the same Field in greater or lesser degree. I have secured several written reports of these induced states, and, in many instances, have been astonished by the mystical depths revealed in them. I have a number of reports which would compare more than favorably with the bulk of those given in Bucke's "Cosmic Consciousness" or in William James' "Varieties of Religious Experience." Here is a method of individual verification that approaches something of the requirements of a scientific check.

But strict scientific methodology requires that the observer shall, himself, stand apart from that which he observes. Admittedly for many purposes this aloofness is of superior value. But it may be applied only to strictly objective material, and never to the content of inner consciousness itself. In the latter case, the observer must become his own object. Further, he must permit himself in the aspect of observer to occupy an inferior status as compared to Himself as the observed. This is apt to prove quite a strain upon the pride of the scientific mind, for the typical scientist has a distinctly over-weening superiority-complex with respect to his observing function. It is difficult for the scientific mind to acquire real humility in this respect; yet, if it is acquired, it becomes possible to investigate even the transcendent Level of Consciousness.

Yet, even for the individual who maintains the attitude of the aloof observer, I have found at least one phenomenon that can be isolated from the subject's report of the inner content of consciousness. This is the phenomenon of the psycho-physical heat. In the early days, following the first Transformation on August 7th, I soon had my attention attracted to this phenomenon. Personally, I had the sense of Fire, but through identifying myself with this Fire rather than with the organism, I rarely had the experience of heat. Fire is not hot to itself. But those near me very soon began reporting an experience of heat which was often so extreme as to be far from comfortable. This was an effect for which I had not been prepared by my previous studies. Since then, I have found several references to it in Tibetan Buddhism, but in these cases it was a deliberately developed phenomenon for the purpose of the very practical protection from intense cold. Ascetics, living in caves well above the timber-line, would either have to find some unusual protection from the cold or perish. But, in my case, there was no thought of seeking heat, and so the phenomenon was quite spontaneous. However, the most significant fact is that it is an effect that has been experienced principally by those who have been in my vicinity rather than by myself. Further, it is not an hallucination or the effect of suggestion. Often the observer can detect a noticeable flush or the breaking forth of perspiration. In addition, the body of the subject is frequently warm to the touch. It is, however, a very curious kind of warmth. To the touching hand, the surface of the body may not seem notably warm but, rather, it is felt in the forearm, a little above the hand. I have felt a similar warmth when touching the terminal of a high-frequency electro-magnetic current. The terminal itself seemed cool, but the arm became warm.

Now, in this effect of the psycho-physical heat there is something that deserves scientific study. What is it? What is its cause? For my own part, I am convinced that in this we are in the presence of a manifestation of the Libido, in the sense Dr. C. G. Jung has employed the term in his later writings. But I have proved to my satisfaction that it is a force which is subject to considerable conscious control. In the Tibetan Yogic Manuals there is a decidedly elaborate technique outlined for the development of the psycho-physical heat. Part of this technique consists of posturing and certain breathing practices. There are also fairly elaborate rituals and visualizations listed. In my own case, I have found none of this necessary. Often the inciting cause has been apparently nothing more than a rather abstract philosophic discussion or analysis of the various components of consciousness when suddenly the heat-effect was produced and experienced by the vast majority of those present. For my own part, in such cases, I have generally not been thinking of the heat-effect at all, but merely of the content of the thought I was developing. In the case of the philosophic discussions in the seminars or philosophic clubs of the university, I never experienced anything like this, nor have I heard of anyone else testifying to it. No; the heat is a witness of the presence of something more than merely the intellectual content of consciousness. I repeat: This is something that can be observed and should be studied.

* * * * *

At the present time, about two and one-half years after that 7th of August, the Door of Consciousness that then was opened still remains open. There is, however, a difference. In the beginning, the

Higher Consciousness occupied the position of the central focus of my individual awareness. At present, It is more like a peripheral Matrix back of and surrounding the central focus of awareness, which in its turn is occupied the preponderant portion of the time with relative contents. My private center of consciousness seems to occupy a sort of intermediate zone, between the relative and non-relative. I find myself able to turn either way, but I am never as completely occupied with either mode of consciousness as formerly. When speaking or writing concerning the Higher Consciousness, even when enveloped in the Field of the Current, my private consciousness is more occupied with the problem of the situation than with the immediate value of the Higher Consciousness Itself. The effective psychical state for this kind of functioning calls for a very fine balance and a distinctly positive will. Thus there cannot be a self-abandonment to the affective or noetic value of the Consciousness at such times. I have indubitable evidence that a considerable number of individuals has received distinctly superior values from this kind of functioning. There have been some instances bordering on ecstatic trance, though the rule has been the experiencing of ecstatic or noetic values without any trance effect. When functioning on the platform or in the classroom, I enter considerably less into the ecstatic effect than is clearly evident in the case of several students. The work-effort of the functioning occupies by far the most of my private consciousness.

I find that the Higher Consciousness is partly spontaneous and partly under the control of a will that I can direct. The transition from the relative to the non-relative functioning is quite subtle. The pre-condition is an affective calmness. Any notable disturbance of my emotional state nullifies my control. However, the technique for paralyzing the affective disturbance does not seem to be difficult to master. All that is required is a certain exercise of the will that quickly erases the emotional complex. Then in a setting of substantial calmness and detachment, all that is needed is a turn of consciousness-focus which seems something like the manipulation of a butterfly-valve controlling alternative passages. All that seems necessary is the intent to do this with appropriate application of the will.

I find it quite impossible to describe the detail of the process, but then there is nothing surprising in this, as I find myself equally unable to describe the process of energizing the muscles of my arm when seeking to perform some physical function. It is much easier to move one's arm than to describe all the psychical processes involved in the act. I find that the position of the body or of any parts of the body is entirely a matter of indifference, except that the body should be sufficiently comfortable not to divert the attention. I pay no attention to the breathing process. In fact, such experiments as I have made with the tantric techniques have been barren of any result worth while. I also find the use of mantramic intonations quite unnecessary, though on occasion I have used a few mantrams with success. But in the latter case, only those mantrams that carried a meaning with which I already concurred intellectually have had any value. On the whole, when I make use of this technique, I secure the quickest results from aphorisms that I have composed myself.

Sometimes the shift of the 'butterfly-valve' occurs without my personal consciousness intending it. Thinking, reading, or talking about the Higher Consciousness, more often than not, will accomplish this. Sometimes I am so occupied with the content of the idea that others, who are present, are aware of the shift before I am. I can continue the process of mentation after the shift, but the thought assumes a greater depth-quality and there is a definite slowing of the rate of idea-formation. There is a necessity of 'stepping gently' in order to avoid the breaking of a very fine balance.

The shifting back from the non-relative to the relative level of functioning is also under my control, but this shift involves a much more gradual process in the subsidence than is the case in connection with the initiation of the State. There is something in this analogous to residual magnetism. An iron bar may be almost instantaneously magnetized by turning on an electric current through a surrounding coiled wire, but a degree of magnetism may remain for some time after the current has been turned off.

The Field of the Higher Consciousness does make some demand upon the resources of the psycho-physical organism. Something like work-effort is involved with a resultant subtle fatigue. Wisdom requires that the function shall be restricted to the resources of the psycho-physical organism. However, the total effect upon the latter after the passage of time is an improvement of the general health-tone.

I find it necessary to use my own methods, which I have myself discovered or, at least, modified, if they were first suggested to me from some other source. I am unable to say whether this is a general rule or merely a peculiarity of my own psychical temperament. At any rate, I find the matter of technique to be highly individualistic.

As to the location of my private consciousness, it seems to be in a very solitary place. In a sense, I seem to stand between two worlds, one a Realm of Ecstasy, the other, a world of pain. The latter is this world of ordinary consciousness. I see into this lower world far more clearly than ever before. I see uncleanness of which I scarcely dreamed formerly. Empiric human nature is a sadly defective thing. At the central core of every human being is a very precious Jewel, but all too often it is covered with a case of unclean mud. The Jewel is to be trusted and valued, but not the case of outer human nature. To see realistically is a painful thing, and I do not recommend such a view to one who places a high value upon his personal comfort. It would be devastating to one who had no vision of the Jewel, unless he happened to be a lover of the mud. The only thing to recommend the life between the worlds is the fact that it affords the possibility to do something about the mud. The Inner Fire can so transform the psychical mud that it too may become part and parcel with the Jewel. It is a very significant fact that the diamond is chemically the same as soot and that the ruby is a compound of the commonest metal and the commonest element, both of which are important components of common clay.

This solitary place is one of pain and Joy. It unites qualities that tend to pull apart. From this place it is possible to shed Joy while accepting the offering of pain. It is useless to pretend that the function is a comfortable one, though there are deep satisfactions. It is not comfortable watching men sowing the seeds of pain, when another and joyful life is near at hand, just waiting to be accepted. It is not comfortable to have to stand by waiting for pain to perform

261

its purifying office. It is not comfortable to resist the desire to leave forever this dreary and empty world. And yet, what else can one do when he knows that he has the means of release which can change the state of the few or the many who will accept?

* * * * *

In the body of the text I have already noted the fact that in the Recognition which I have called the "High Indifference" a quality of Consciousness was realized for which previous studies had not prepared me. The only conceptual pattern which would correspond to this State was one which placed Nirvana in a relative status with respect to the objective universe or Sangsara. In contrast, my former studies had led me to the belief that Nirvana was the absolutely non-relative State. My intuitive perception on the level of the culminating Recognition was very clear, but intellectually I desired verification. In the search of my old sources I drew a blank. It was only when, at a later date, I came into possession of "The Tibetan Book of the Dead," "The Tibetan Yoga and Secret Doctrine," edited by Evans-Wentz, and "The Buddhist Bible," edited by Dwight Goddard, that I found the verification which I sought. It is quite evident that the Enlightenment of Buddhism is not identical with the Nirvanic State of Consciousness—which is simply the counterpole of objective consciousness—but a still more profound Consciousness that is neither objective nor subjective. At present, it appears to me that simple logic should have made it clear that the ultimate synthetic Consciousness could not stand in polar relationship to the objective world. It must be THAT which equally includes or nullifies both poles, thus enveloping subjectivity as well as objectivity. However, I had failed to think my thoughts through in this respect, thus having to wait upon the Realization before making the discovery. How much time is lost because of intellectual laziness!

The ultimate synthetic Consciousness is beyond the reach of thinking, feeling, sensation, and intuition, but depends upon another Way of Consciousness which simply has no recognition in western psychology and philosophy. The Buddhist name for this Way of Consciousness is Dhyana, which is a good deal more than 'meditation' as

262

generally understood. It is a latent function of consciousness that so far has been only rarely active among men. Its study is quite beyond the reach of western psychologic methodology, since the latter is oriented to observation rather than to introception. But it is possible, by the appropriate means, to arouse Dhyana to action and in It alone lies the Door to Enlightenment. The functioning of Dhyana is a mystery. Instructions in the practice of Dhyana exist, but anything that can be described is only a collateral objective aid that may be of use to certain psychological temperaments while it fails with others. It is simply impossible to describe the essential laws which govern the functioning of Dhyana, while the collateral aids which work with one psychologic type may have to be radically modified when applied to a different type. The psychical structure of the East Indian and especially of the Chinese is radically different from our own. Hence, merely to transplant methodologies which have been successful in the Orient into the Occident is a case of using the "right method with the wrong man." It is only the combination of the "right method with the right man" that works. This means that for the West the whole problem of devising the effective collateral aids has to be resolved in new terms. We shall have to employ the powers which we have unfolded in superior degree, rather than depend upon those which, while strongly developed in the Orient, are weak with us. Today this is a pioneering problem.

But while the problem of method varies with the type and even with the individual, the Goal is eternally the same. One does not have to be a Mystic to see that this must be so. The very fact that we instinctively integrate all men by calling them 'humanity' or 'mankind,' and all creatures by uniting them under the concept of 'living forms,' reveals an instinctive recognition of underlying unity. It is only because of an underlying unity that it is possible for men to communicate with each other and be understood at all. Thus there must be a common denominator, and all those who find this common denominator, no matter who or where they are, will find exactly the same thing. This Common Denominator is the Goal of Dhyana.

Necessarily, the Common Denominator is nameless, since genuine naming always implies defining. It can be symbolized, but such a symbol merely points to the indefinable Reality. This necessity should also be clear, for the definable is merely that which can be comprehended by thinking. It is, therefore, less than the thought-power. On the other hand, that which comprehends the thought-power, as well as all other functions of consciousness, is ever beyond delimitation by any function or group of functions.

Several symbols for the Nameless do exist. In the first place, I symbolized It by the "High Indifference." Subsequently, I have called It "Consciousness-without-an-object which is also Consciousness-without-a-subject." But no one can really think such a Consciousness, for then at once It would have become an object, a something comprehended by the subject-object consciousness. In Buddhism It is known as "Shunyata" and this is variously translated as "Voidness" or as "Suchness." It is also frequently referred to as the "Dharma-kaya." The Chinese have symbolized It by "Tao." Perhaps as good a symbol as any is SPACE, provided the Space is understood as being unaffected by either the presence or absence of a universe within it. Thus, the space of the Einstein-relativity would not serve as an adequate symbol, since this is affected by the presence or absence of concentrations of matter.

The identification of the Common Denominator under diverse symbols is largely intuitive, but it is aided by observing the way in which they are used and by the statements made concerning the corresponding Consciousness. Very readily, I found that both "Tao" and "Shunyata" have the same symbolic reference as "Consciousness-without-an-object and without-a-subject." But while I find myself in ultimate agreement with the central Core of Taoistic and Buddhistic Enlightenment, I often find the discursive approaches of the Oriental far from convincing. There is reason to believe that I have to credit the Chinese mind with much of this difficulty. For, so far as I know, all of the profounder Buddhist philosophic statements have first been translated from the Sanskrit into the Chinese or Tibetan, with the English translation taken from one or the other of the latter. Now the Chinese conceptual processes are radically different from our own. On the one hand, they involve a much greater sensuous richness than is true of our conceptualism; but, on the other hand, they are peculiarly lacking in the concepts necessary for abstract thinking. According to Lin Yutang, there never has been a development of the higher mathematics among the Chinese, and there could not be without a radical alteration of the Chinese conceptual base. In addition, the Chinese genius, unlike the Indian, has always been weak in the direction of metaphysical speculation. What, then, must happen when the formulation of the crowning insight of the most metaphysical of all races is translated into the Chinese language? It seems that there must be an inevitable transformation of *thinkable* meaning. Then, when on top of this there is a further translation from the concrete Chinese imagery into the abstract form of western language, further distortion seems unavoidable.

In the case of direct translation from the Sanskrit the problem is not so great, though there still exists the difficulty growing out of cross-transference from a metaphysical to a non-metaphysical genius. However, the rationalism of Shankara is enough like our own thinking to be fundamentally intelligible. But from the standpoint of our current conceptual style, Shankara is far from satisfactory. His method of reasoning is too scholastic, and scholasticism has been outmoded with us for the last two or three centuries. Further, Shankara's problem was enormously symplified, as compared with its analogue in the West, since he could establish his case for the Brahmin community by reference to Vedic sources. We of the West do not accept the Vedic tradition, and thus Shankara's argument is undermined at its base, so far as Occidental effectiveness is concerned. Consequently, the whole approach to Dhyana, in a form that will be acceptable to the western psyche, must be carved out of new material.

The latter problem has come to occupy the principal place in my present consciousness. Much of the time during the past two years I have been engaged with this problem. I have in course of preparation another work in which I believe I have achieved a partial contribution in this direction. I believe that at least some sectors of western consciousness are now ready. At the present time, contributions in the form of "Analytic Psychology" by Dr. C. G. Jung form a real advance in this direction, but no one man's statement can be compre-

265

hensive. However, "Analytic Psychology" is reaching close to the Door, at least in the hands of its chief representative.

I am convinced that the greatest achievement of western genius has been in the development of the abstract thought which has its crown in higher mathematics. The freeing of thought from dependence upon the sensible image is an accomplishment of the very greatest difficulty. Until thought has won this power, it cannot penetrate into the Realm of Imageless Consciousness. Now, once it is realized how much has been accomplished in this direction in the field of higher mathematics, it is easy to see what a powerful instrument in the practice of Dhyana we have forged. In my own experience, thought on the level of Imageless Consciousness was possible by employing the intellectual capacities unfolded during the years of mathematical discipline. The demand made upon the imagination was a close replica of that required in the study of the higher analysis and the non-Euclidian systems of geometry. I believe that the purified western intellect at its highest state of development can carry thought further into the Realm of Profundity than has been possible up to this time. Feeling no longer has the "edge" upon thought.

What I have said so far applies to but one wing of Enlightenment. Full Enlightenment requires the development of Eros as well as Logos. It is just in the dimension of Eros that the West is peculiarly weak. The strong emphasis of Love in the Christian discipline is psychological proof of this. It is only a people weak in love who have to give the Eros-principle strong emphasis. In this we have the compensating action of the psychologic unconscious. Our love is weak and, when developed, often only sentimental. Otherwise the development of our intellect would not have been so destructive, a characteristic well illustrated by the world-situation since 1914. As a result of our weakness in the dimension of Eros, practical Dhyana will have to stress the appropriate compensating discipline. For the one-sided Enlightenment through the understanding is weak in Compassion, and thus falls short of the highest possibility. However it is possible from the perspective of the one-sided Enlightenment to arouse the complementary phase through the action of the will upon the latent seed of Love.

266

The culture of the Higher Love is difficult. For it is much harder for feeling to win detachment from the object than it is for thought. It is a lofty achievement to be able to radiate Compassion without thought of return and with full willingness to grant complete freedom to the object. Yet until Love has reached this height, it remains sentimental. And to the merely sentimental lover, Compassion may seem cold, though in reality It is the warmth of the real SUN.

Just because thought is the highest cultured occidental function, I believe that the intellect must lead in western Dhyana. But it must be trained not to abandon the weaker Eros. Here is where the West will face its greatest trial. For a race-horse and a donkey do not make a good team. In such a set-up there is bound to be much conflict, with the race-horse trying to get away and the donkey becoming stubborn. Yes, right here is where the West will have its troubles. I perceive that this conflict is just the place where the Analytic Psychologists will render us the greatest help, provided they are sufficiently spiritualized themselves.

*   *   *   *   *

To the devoted followers of traditional disciplines it may appear presumptuous that I should question old techniques and substitute a new symbolic interpretation. But in answer to any who feel this way I need only quote the words of acknowledged Sages. All clinging to traditional method and interpretation is but a subtle form of attachment and, therefore, a barrier to Enlightenment. Any method that works is pragmatically justified, and no method as such is a sacred object. Then with respect to interpretation, I need but recall the fact that there is no such thing as an exclusively true symbolic representation of an unthinkable Reality. All too easily a valid symbol may through the power of attachment acquire the force of an heretical dogma. Further, the validity of a symbol is a relative matter. Though the unthinkable Reality is eternal, yet every symbol is a time-existence and subject to the process of aging. The power of every symbol is relative to the peculiar psychical complex of an age and a people. Just that symbol is most effective which serves as the best corrective of the psychical complex of the given situation. Symbols are not designed for the benefit of Those who have Awakened, but for those others who are in need of a corrective of their present states of consciousness.

But while there are many valid symbols having quite different appearance in form, yet all these have certain features in common. The most important common feature can be given very easily in abstract terms. For this purpose I call attention to a simple logical principle. Everything that can be experienced or thought exists through contrast with its contradictory, otherwise no particular element of consciousness can be isolated from the totality of all consciousness. The whole universe of all possible experience or thought can be divided into any particular object, state, or function, and its contradictory. Let the letter "A" stand for any such object, state, or function, then the whole universe of possible experience or thought is either "A" or "Not-A." But the ultimate Reality of Enlightened Consciousness lies in neither of these compartments, and thus we say that IT is neither "A" nor "not-A." A whole life-time could be devoted to listing all possible values of "A" and applying the principle in each individual case, yet all the meaning that would be conveyed by such laborious effort would be contained in the preceding two sentences. Such is the power of abstract thought. As one reads the more philosophic Buddhist Sutras he finds large numbers of pages devoted to the detailed application of the above principle with almost endless repetition. Undoubtedly the repetition builds a psychological effect that is potent, but the essence of all this can be given logically in a sentence or two.

Now, just what is THAT which is neither "A" nor "not-A," when "A" is given any thinkable or experienceable value? To the pure thinker IT seems like nothing at all. Thus IT is called "Voidness," for thus IT appears to the consciousness bound to relativity. But through the Door of Dhyana IT is found to be substantial Fullness, quite beyond the comprehension of all possible experience or thought. Modern sub-atomic physics affords us an illustration which is as beautiful as any that I know. When two material entities of which the one is just the negation of the other, such as a positron and an electron, are brought into conjunction, the result is mutual destruction.

268

In their place is a flash of radiation that spreads indefinitely throughout all space. If, now, our capacity for physical observation were limited to the field of the electron and the positron, we might conclude that the result of the conjunction was absolute annihilation. But we are now able to see that this is not so, but rather that the destruction of matter in one state has resulted in its continuation in a totally different state. So, also, is the effect of the mutual cancellation of all dichotomies of experience and thought. The flash of radiation that spreads indefinitely throughout all space is the symbol of the Enlightened Consciousness.

By keeping in mind what has been said in the last two paragraphs, the rationale of the various methods of practicing Dhyana, as well as the basis of the various symbols for Noble Wisdom, become clear. But while the rationale is simple, the practice is generally very difficult. To achieve the mutual cancellation practically is to effect the mystic Death, and this always requires faith and courage. It is also possible that success will result in individual unconsciousness. Hence, the actual practice of Dhyana is to be recommended only for those who are prepared. The essence of the preparation is the building of the capacity to maintain consciousness apart from all objects. This kind of Consciousness is present all the time surrounding the functioning of the relative consciousness. It can be isolated through Self-analysis while observing the phantasmagoria of the appearing and disappearing of the objects in the stream of time. It is THAT which remains unaltered through all change. When awareness has learned to turn its focus upon this ever-present Matrix of Consciousness so that Consciousness becomes its own object, the power to remain individually conscious through the mutual cancellation has been achieved. Then the time has come for the Transition from the embodied to the Radiant State. There is nothing simpler than all this, and yet there is nothing more difficult.

B—Glossary

Note: (Sk) after an entry means that the word is Sanskrit.

Advaita (Sk). A term applied to a Vedantist sect founded by Shankara. The literal meaning is 'non-dual.' Generally, the system of thought developed by Shankara is regarded as the most thoroughly monistic of all philosophies. However, in the strict sense, the inner core of this philosophy is neither monistic nor non-monistic. Hence, to call it non-dualistic is more correct.

Ambrosia. In the Greek mythology, a celestial substance capable of imparting immortality. (The word means 'immortal, undying.') Often thought of as food or a drink. The Sanskrit equivalent is 'Amrita.' In the most common usage, this term is employed in a figurative sense. Such, however, is not the case as the term is used in this book. The Ambrosia is an actual Substance and at the same time a Force and a Transcendent Consciousness wherein the subject and the object are blended. Any real depth of penetration into the Transcendent Consciousness will bring the individual into an immediate blending with this Ambrosia. It has a quality which is recognizably substantial and at the same time fluidic. But It is fluidic in somewhat the sense that electricity is fluidic, more than in the sense that an ordinary gas or liquid is fluidic. It is quite easy to see how the experience of the Ambrosia should have suggested 'wine,' and then, the 'cup,' the 'chalice,' the 'caldron,' and the 'Holy Grail,' as symbols representing It. Thus the search for the Holy Grail is the search for Immortal Life. The 'Blood' or the 'Royal Blood' is another symbol carrying the same meaning. Here the meaning indicated is 'Life' which, in the sense of the Royal Blood, is clearly Immortal Life. The symbolism of the Lord's Supper refers directly to the Ambrosia. The 'Bread' represents the substantiality and the 'Wine' or 'Blood,' the fluidic, life-giving quality. To enter Cosmic Consciousness is to partake of the Ambrosia, and this bestows Immortality, though this is by no means all of Its significance. Further, this is not simply the primary immortality in which all things share, but a self-

271

conscious and therefore individual immortality. This immortality is achieved by man and not merely inherited automatically. In this book the Ambrosia is often referred to as the 'Current.'

In the "Analytic Psychology" of Dr. C. G. Jung, the term 'Libido' acquires, in its most refined development, a meaning that comes close to that of the Ambrosia. Thus it becomes possible to speak of the Libido as Divine.

Ananda (Sk). The literal meaning is 'Bliss,' 'Joy,' 'Felicity,' 'Happiness.' It is an aspect of the Ambrosia. Hence, the expressions, 'Current of Joy,' 'Current of Bliss,' etc. One of the outstanding characteristics of the Higher Consciousness lies in the fact that the different qualities under which It manifests to subject-object consciousness are not definitely separated but are blended. Bliss, Immortal Life, and Knowledge, in the higher sense, are not three separate facts but, rather, three aspects of one fact, or Reality. Ananda, however, lies closer to the affections than to cognition. Hence, Transcendence attained primarily through the affections manifests more as Bliss than as Knowledge, but the division here is not absolute.

Atman (Sk). The 'Self,' the 'I,' the 'I AM' and the 'subjective moment of consciousness.' In the highest sense this is the Universal Spirit or the Supreme Soul of the Universe. When this higher meaning is emphasized the term 'Paramatman' is commonly employed. The Atman is sometimes used in the sense of the 'Divine Monad' and the seventh or highest principle in man. There is, however, a lower usage in which this term is applied to the personal ego. The anatman doctrine of Gautama Buddha, in the more comprehensible sense, refers to the personal ego, and amounts to a denial of the self-existence of this ego. However, there is a higher and more metaphysical application of the doctrine of anatman which constitutes one of the most difficult and profound ideas in all metaphysical thought. Superficially, it would seem that the anatman of Buddha and the Atmavidya, or Knowledge of the Self, of Shankara involve a contradiction. However, such is not the case as it is a matter of difference of emphasis and also of approach to the same Transcendent Reality. The Atman of Shankara is here spelled with a capital 'A' while that of Buddha is spelled with a small 'a.' This affords a key to the reconciliation of the two doctrines. However, the inner Core of Buddha's Teaching is more profound even than that of Shankara, but it is more difficult to understand.

272

Avidya (Sk). Ignorance or the opposite of Real Knowledge. This is not 'ignorance' in the familiar sense of 'lack of information.' All consciousness or knowledge, however highly developed, so long as it is restricted to the subject-object manifold is Avidya. Only Those who have Awakened to the Higher Consciousness have transcended Avidya or Ignorance. Avidya is the real cause of human suffering, bondage, and evil. Likewise these are destroyed when Ignorance is destroyed.

Bhagavad-gita (Sk). One of the best known of the Hindu religious scriptures. It is almost wholly in the form of a dialogue between Krishna, who represents the SELF, the Atman, or Cosmic Consciousness, and Arjuna, who symbolizes the egoistic man of action. It gives a brief résumé of the Roads by which Union or Yoga may be attained. This is one of the most important manuals that point the Way to Cosmic Consciousness.

Buddha (Sk). Lit., "The Enlightened." This enlightenment is Transcendental Knowledge in the highest sense. It is the State of Knowledge wherein the Real Self is known for what it is. It is the Consciousness that is detached from all that is evanescent and finite or merely phenomenal. The State of Buddhahood is the Supreme State of Holiness.

It is a custom within the Buddhist community to call a man who has attained Enlightenment a Buddha. Most commonly, Gautama, a Prince of Kapilavastu, is known as *the* Buddha, after His attainment, but there were Buddhas before Him, and others have attained Enlightenment since His time. But He who was born Gautama is the greatest of the Buddhas who have appeared within historic times.

"Buddhism" is the name given to the religious movement that had its origin in the life and teachings of the great Buddha. But, more strictly, "Buddhism" means the unchanging Doctrine or Dharma which underlies all that is evanescent.

Buddhi (Sk). In the microcosmic sense this is the Spiritual Soul of man and the vehicle of Atman or the Spiritual Self. Buddhi may also be thought of as disembodied Intelligence, the Basis of Discernment, discrimination, and the apprehension of pure Meaning. It is also Compassion, in the highest sense, the very Soul of the Law of Harmony or Equilibrium. In the macrocosmic sense It is the Universal Soul.

Chit (Sk). Abstract Consciousness; pure Consciousness which is not consciousness of an object.

Chela (Sk). A disciple. The relationship of a Chela to his Guru is far closer than than of a pupil to his teacher. In fact, this relationship is the closest of all human relationships. While a Chela generally receives more or less instruction, the essential function of a Guru is to effect a Transformation in the consciousness of the Chela so that what we have called 'Cosmic Consciousness' may awaken in the latter.

Consciousness. In its most immediate sense the state of 'being aware.' In the broad, though common, sense, consciousness is the state we are in when not in the state of dreamless sleep. Quite often this term is used in the sense that should be restricted to self-consciousness, or the consciousness of being conscious. Consciousness that is not self-conscious is very often regarded as unconsciousness. The whole question of what consciousness is becomes a very subtle matter, once an individual goes beneath the surface of meaning.

Consciousness of the Self. This is consciousness of the subject to all consciousness, but, in the highest sense, this is not consciousness of the subject regarded as an object. It may be called "consciousness turned toward its source or the positive pole of consciousness." It is extremely difficult to attain this consciousness, for very easily it reduces to consciousness of a subtle object. To attain consciousness of the Self in its purity is to Awaken to Cosmic or Transcendent Consciousness. Sometimes the foregoing is the meaning implied when the term 'self-consciousness' is used, but more commonly the latter means 'consciousness of being conscious.'

Cosmic Consciousness. In the strict sense, this is Consciousness on the level of some Cosmic Plane of Being and so is not a consciousness of form or phenomena. However, the term is employed in this work in a somewhat looser sense, more closely approximating that given by Dr. Bucke in "Cosmic Consciousness." In the latter sense, any consciousness attained by awakening out of crystallized subject-object consciousness is called 'Cosmic Consciousness.' It thus covers a zone intermediate between subject-object consciousness and Cosmic Consciousness in the strictest sense. See "Transcendent Consciousness."

Current of Bliss or Joy. See "Ambrosia."

Dharma (Sk). The Sacred Law or Doctrine; often used in a sense somewhat analogous to that of 'duty.' But this latter interpretation is deceptive. It rather carries the meaning of true alignment with Essential Being or Reality in thought, feeling, and action.

Dhyana (Sk). The Door to, or Vehicle of Prajna or Transcendental Wisdom. It may be thought of as a higher function of consciousness, not within the range of study of current western psychologic methodology. Often translated 'meditation,' but this is deceptive as most meditation deals with a content, while Dhyana is a Way of Consciousness that transcends content.

Egoistic Consciousness. This is the consciousness of one's self as distinct from other selves. The feeling of 'I am I and none other.' It is opposed to the State of Consciousness known as Buddhahood, wherein the sense of self as distinct from other selves is destroyed. Egoistic consciousness is a fundamental barrier to Liberation or Enlightenment.

Elixir of Life. See "Ambrosia."

Emptiness which is Fullness. Transcendent Consciousness appears as though It were emptiness from the standpoint of subject-object consciousness, but when transcendentally Realized is Known to be utter Fullness.

Gautama (Sk). The sacerdotal name of the family of the great Buddha. See "Buddha."

Guru (Sk). A Spiritual Teacher. Essentially not a teacher of information but one who guides and nurtures the Awakening of the Chela or Disciple.

Guru-current. Used in the sense of a general spiritual influence or force which tends toward the Awakening of Spiritual Consciousness in the aspirant.

Hegel. A philosopher who is the leading representative of the German Idealists. His school is also known as Absolute Idealism.

Ignorance. See "Avidya."

Kant, Immanuel. The leading German philosopher and considered by many as the greatest philosopher of the West. He is the chief representative of the critical spirit in philosophy. By this is meant the recognition that before a valid construction in terms of knowledge is possible it is necessary to study critically the nature and limits of knowledge as such.

Karma (Sk). In the general sense, the principal of Law in action. More specifically, it is the idea of moral causality carrying a meaning which, in part, overlaps the western idea of causality and, in part, the idea of destiny.

Krishna (Sk). An Indian Saviour of about 5,000 years ago. This name appears in the Bhagavad-gita as a symbol for the Higher Self. In the latter sense, 'Krishna' is a principle somewhat analogous to the mystical 'Christ' of St. Paul.

Liberation. Consciousness in the State of Freedom from bondage to form. It is the same as Nirvanic Consciousness.

Loka (Sk). A field or sphere of consciousness, force and substance subject to some principle of modification. Thus, the form of consciousness defined by Kant's "Critique of Pure Reason" would be a particular Loka of consciousness. Consciousness cast under another form would be another Loka, etc. The Hell, Purgatory, and Paradise of Dante are three Lokas of consciousness. In the ultimate sense, we must regard the consciousness of every individual as a Loka. The term has both broad and narrow meanings. Liberated or Nirvanic Consciousness is not a Loka, however, as such is a pure Consciousness freed from the imposition of form.

Manas (Sk). Very commonly translated as the 'mind,' since this is its literal meaning. However, 'mind' in western usage, particularly in philosophy, has come to have a much broader meaning than 'Manas,' so this translation is confusing. See the discussion in Sec. LXXVII. 'Manas' also has the meaning of 'Higher Ego,' or the sentient reincarnating principle in man. It is Manas that makes man an intelligent and moral being. It is the prime distinguishing characteristic of man when he is contrasted to the animals and certain orders of unintelligent spiritual beings.

Mara (Sk). The personified force of evil or temptation. It is the adversary of him who seeks to enter the Path that leads to Freedom from bondage to embodied consciousness. In other words, Mara is the great barrier to Cosmic or Transcendent Consciousness.

Maya (Sk). Illusion. It is the power which renders phenomenal existence possible and, hence, is lord over the flux of becoming. The counter principle is 'Reality,' predicated only of that which is eternal and changeless.

Nectar. See "Ambrosia."

Nirmanakaya (Sk). A mysterious form of embodiment which may be assumed by One who has attained Enlightenment and still retains correlation with relative consciousness. This is the most objective phase of the Trikaya, the other two phases being the Sambhogakaya and the

276

Dharmakaya. The doctrine of the Trikaya is quite involved and simply cannot be understood by the unillumined relative consciousness. In one sense these may be viewed as the three Bodies of a Buddha, but, in another sense, they are impersonal metaphysical concepts. On this Level there is not the sharp division between principles and entities that is characteristic of relative thinking. One view, quite current among western students, regards the three Kayas as alternative states of consciousness which may be chosen in an exclusive sense. Thus the Dharmakayas are regarded as distinct from the Nirmanakayas. But the profounder reality is, that a full Buddha is conscious on the level of all three Kayas and thus is, at once, a Dharmakaya, a Sambhogakaya, and a Nirmanakaya. An Entity who has won this triple Crown unites in himself the possibilities of the Non-Relative and relative worlds. We may conceive of an incomplete Enlightenment which reaches only to the level of the Nirmanakaya, or of another form of Enlightenment which attains the central Core of Shunyata combined with a refusal to accept any correlation with relative consciousness. In this case we would have an exclusively Dharmakayic State. In such an instance we do have a contrast between the Dharmakayas and the Nirmanakayas. Such Dharmakayas are incapable of affecting the destiny of relative consciousness, save through Those who have won the Triple Crown. But the latter are as much Dharmakayas as they are Nirmanakayas. Thus, in principle there is not an exclusive division between the three Kayas.

The Dharmakayic State is spiritually the highest of all but, in the humanistic sense, the Nirmanakaya is especially honored because it is through the Nirmanakaya, and only through It, that the redemption of mankind is possible. However, the Light of the Nirmanakaya is derived from the Dharmakaya and thus it is not the contrast between Dharmakaya and Nirmanakaya that is important but rather the contrast betwee the pure Dharmakaya and the combined Dharmakaya, Sambhogakaya, and Nirmanakaya. It is this combination that links the Transcendent with the relative.

Nirvana (Sk). While the meaning of this term is not unambiguous as used in literature, sometimes referring to pure subjectivity and at others including Shunyata, it seems the better practice to restrict it to the former meaning. Nirvana thus stands as the opposite of objective consciousness but is comprehended by Shunyata which comprehends objective as well as subjective possibilities. Nirvana may be regarded as Consciousness-without-an-object-but-with-the-Subject while Shunyata is Con-

277

sciousness-without-an-object-and-without-a-subject. Both are formless as to content. This latter fact affords a basis for uniting the two States under the notion of "blown-out," the literal meaning of Nirvana. But this leads to confusion, as the difference between pure subjectivity and Shunyata is as great as the difference between pure subjectivity and objective consciousness. To be sure, neither State can be imagined by relative consciousness, but considerable clarification is achieved by building a thinkable logical model.

We may regard Nirvana as Liberation, Shunyata as Enlightenment. Not Nirvana, but Shunyata is the summum bonum. There is reason to believe that the West may find Enlightenment more acceptable than Liberation. While pure subjective Liberation is peculiarly close to the religious feeling of the Hindu, it fails of being vital to the more active consciousness of the Occidental. But Enlightenment occupies a neutral position between these two. Since the central emphasis of Buddha was not Liberation so much as Enlightenment, He stands as the one genuine spiritual World Teacher that has been known in historic times. Shankara spoke to the Hindu and more especially to the Brahmin community, while Jesus was oriented to the more objective occidental spirit. Thus neither of these two are synthetic World Teachers. They stand rather as specialists. Hinduism can never be effectively transplanted into the West, nor will Christianity ever be a really effective force in India or China. But in Buddha and the Dharma of Buddha there is a common uniting ground for both the subjective and objective geniuses. Thus it is that while the Advaita Vedanta of Shankara is only slightly different from Buddhism on one side, on the other the western scientist finds much in Buddhism that sounds like his own thought. Yet, all the while there is a marked contrast between the Vedanta and the western scientific spirit. I repeat, Buddha is the only known World Teacher.

Nirvani (Sk). One who has attained Nirvana, hence, an Emancipated Soul. In general, the perfected individual becomes a Nirvani only after death of the physical body, but there are some, of whom Gautama Buddha is the great example, who attained this State while still living.

Nirvikalpa Samadhi (Sk). The highest form of ecstatic Consciousness possible to man. It may be regarded as a kind of Nirvanic Consciousness, modified by reason of the individual retaining correlation with a physical body. It is a State of Formless Consciousness. It seems to be the rule that this State is only attained in deep trance, but it is

278

possible to attain It without trance, though in this case there is a decided dimming of the outer consciousness. While Buddha did not condemn the trance state, He did not regard it as necessary and advocated Realization without trance.

Philosopher's Stone. That principle by which the base nature is transmuted into the Spiritual and Divine. Other usage of this term exists, but the above is the profounder meaning and is the sense employed in the text.

Realization. The Awakening to the Transcendent or Cosmic Consciousness. As used in the text when this word is given this meaning it is spelled with a capital 'R.' Realization is not a development of consciousness in the subject-object sense. It implies a radical event involving a shifting of the level of consciousness.

Recognition. Used in the text with essentially the same meaning as 'Realization,' this term emphasizes the implication that Awakening is a return to that which had been 'known' but which had been forgotten, perhaps for ages. The use of this word in this sense does imply a theory of knowledge that diverges in important respects from the more current theories. It implies that Real Knowledge is not derived from experience, but rather that experience is the occasion or the catalytic agent which arouses the Recognition of inherent Knowledge.

Relative consciousness. The ordinary kind of human consciousness involving the relationship of a knower to a known, the perceiver to a perceived, etc. It also involves knowledge of objective terms in relation to each other. It stands in radical contrast to Cosmic or Transcendental Consciousness.

Samadhi (Sk). The ecstatic state wherein the individual awakes to some more or less transcendent level. It may or may not involve the trance state. There are several degrees of Samadhi of which Nirvikalpa Samadhi is the highest. It is the means of cross-correlation between various levels of consciousness, in no two of which does consciousness manifest under the same form. The meaning of Samadhi is not sharply differentiated from that of Dhyana, save that Dhyana is the Door to Prajna or Transcendental Wisdom, while there are lesser forms of Samadhi that open doors to levels of consciousness substantially less than Transcendental Wisdom.

Sangsara (Sk). A Buddhist term including the same meaning as the 'world-field,' used in the text. It has, however, a wider connotation as it includes all levels of consciousness in which there is an awareness of an object, combined with the delusion that the object has an existence independent of the observer. Thus, the dream-state, while not a part of the world-field in the narrower sense, is part of Sangsara. The relatively subjective realms such as the various heavenly worlds, the purgatories and the hells are also part of Sangsara. Even relatively high orders of Seership, like that of Swedenborg, penetrate no further than superior aspects of Sangsara. However, Enlightened Consciousness includes the possibility of awareness of objects, but the difference in this case lies in the fact that the dependent existence of the object is Realized. Such awareness of objects is not Sangsaric, as it does not imply bondage to the object.

So long as the independence of objects is believed in—a state that implies bondage to objects—Sangsara appears as the Adversary, i.e., Mara, Satan, etc. But just so soon as this delusion is destroyed, Sangsara in this sense vanishes. This vanishing of Sangsara applies to the past as well as to the present and future, for it ceases, not only to be, but as well ever to have been. This is a mystery to relative consciousness which is rendered intelligible only by the transformation of consciousness-base known as the Awakening.

In psychological terms, Sangsara is a detached psychical complex and thus constitutes a threat to psychical integration. Left to itself, the Sangsaric state leads to exhaustion of the life-stream and real unconsciousness. The practical function of the various racial and world-Saviours is the effecting of pragmatic interlocking of the detached complex with the Root-Source of Life and Consciousness. In the case of the Disciple this function is a more or less conscious correlation, but with the mass of men it operates through the psychologic unconsciousness. Without the function of the Saviours the state of most men would be quite hopeless. The Saviour-Function may be viewed as religious, philosophical, or psychological. The form of interpretation is a matter of indifference, provided it is such as to render the function acceptable to men.

Sankhya (Sk). One of the six Indian schools of philosophy; originated by Kapila. It teaches a dualistic system in which spirit and matter are regarded as co-eternal and not simply aspects of a common and absolute base.

SAT (Sk). This term represents Absoluteness rather than the Absolute. It is the ever-present, eternal, and unchanging Reality, THAT which is neither Being nor not-Being, but the Base of all that is. It has the same reference as Shunyata, Tao, Dharmakaya or Consciousness-without-an-object-and-without-a-subject.

Self-consciousness. In the highest sense this is "consciousness of the Self." More commonly, it is the consciousness of being conscious, implying the recognition that there is a perceiving subject but not, necessarily, the Recognition of the pure Consciousness of the Self. Self-consciousness distinguishes human from animal consciousness.

Shankara (Sk). This is the name of a Brahmin philosopher who is generally regarded as the greatest of the Vedantic Sages. He is the founder of the Advaita (non-dual) philosophy. His philosophy, together with that of Buddha, is regarded as the most thoroughly monistic of any ever promulgated. At the Core there is no difference between Buddha and Shankara, but the latter supplied a more comprehensible philosophic statement. However, Shankara attained superior comprehensibility at the price of a partial veiling of the pure Dharma. Buddha represents the superior synthesis while Shankara attained a superior expression of one wing of the Buddhist Enlightenment.

Shunyata (Sk). Literally Voidness. It is the same as the Dharmakaya. The Voidness is such only to relative consciousness. Actually It is the one substantial Reality. The question is often raised as to the wisdom of speaking of ultimate Fullness as Voidness, since psychologically the latter term often produces difficulties. But there is a still greater psychological difficulty, which grows out of the fact that any image of fullness which can be presented to relative consciousness suggests objective content. The result is the substitution of one Sangsaric state for another and this is not Enlightenment. Real Enlightenment implies the radical dissolution of all anchorage to the object and hence the aspiration of the student must be directed to THAT which is never an object in any sense. To relative consciousness this can only mean polarization to seeming Voidness.

Subject-object consciousness. The same as "relative consciousness." In this term the subject-object character of ordinary human consciousness is emphasized.

Tamas (Sk). The quality of indifference in the inferior sense. It is thus the polar opposite of the High Indifference, which is a State of perfect affective Fullness or Balance. The quality of Tamas tends toward real death or unconsciousness.

Transcendent Consciousness. In the present work this is a very important term and requires special discussion. In the broadest sense, the Transcendent stands in radical contrast to the empirical. It is that which lies beyond experience. Hence Transcendent Consciousness is non-experiential consciousness; and, since experience may be regarded as consciousness in the stream of becoming or under time, the form is of necessity a timeless Consciousness. The actuality of such Consciousness can never be proved directly from experience when the latter term is taken in this restricted sense. Thus It is either a philosophic abstraction or a direct mystical Recognition. In this work Its actuality is asserted on the basis of a direct mystical Recognition. This term is not here used as a synonym of 'Cosmic Consciousness,' but is reserved for pure, formless, mystic Consciousness. On the other hand, mystic Consciousness which gives a content in terms of subtle form or in terms involving any kind of multiplicity, I call 'Cosmic Consciousness.'

Since the appearance of the "Critique of Pure Reason," many philosophic students have maintained that Kant has definitely shown the impossibility of any Transcendent Consciousness or Knowledge. (The transcendental element in the apperceiving power of the Self is distinguished by Kant from the 'Transcendent.') If we were to assume that the Kantian analysis comprehended all possible functions of consciousness, apparently the foregoing conclusion would be unavoidable. But the whole problem rests upon the actuality of the function of Dhyana, which was outside the Kantian analysis as well as beyond the reach of western psychologic methodology. Since my whole case rests upon the affirmation of the actuality of the function of Dhyana it is not answered by a simple reference to the older criticism. On the contrary, a valid criticism, in this respect, would first have to establish the point that there is no such function as Dhyana. This could only be done by one who was in a position to prove that he was familiar with every possibility of consciousness and found no Dhyana function. Negative proof is possible only when every possibility is delimited; and, while this method is often successful in mathematics, there is always presupposed an explicit definition of the whole field of discourse under discussion. But from the standpoint of the present epistemology, this is arbitrary. A possibility is proved either by experience or Realization, but a theoretical delimitation of all possibilities is quite another matter.

I am quite well aware that the scientific imagination has shown great capacity in inventing objective interpretations of all observable phenomena. It is also an extra-logical canon of science that the presumption of truth is to be given hypotheses that do not violate established forms of interpretation. But, logically considered, this is no more than a reference to the authority of style or custom. For my part, I do not share in this superstitious reverence for style and custom and offer respect only to the logical spirit of science. But all this applies only to observable phenomena. When we consider the meaningful content of consciousness we are definitely outside the reach of western scientific methodology, though not, therefore, beyond the range of all possible science. Now, it is only when dealing with meaningful content that it is possible to reach the realm of Dhyana.

Transcendent Knowledge. This term implies the assertion of a Knowledge the actuality of which modern empiric philosophers would deny. It is true that there is no such thing as a transcendent subject-object knowledge. But it is not in this sense that the term is used here, but rather as "Knowledge through Identity." The following question then arises: What is the difference between Transcendent Consciousness and Transcendent Knowledge? The distinction is admittedly subtle. We might say that It is the Transcendent Consciousness as reflected through the knowledge quale. Thus a Transcendent Consciousness manifested through an affective quale would not be Transcendent Knowledge. The assertion of the Reality of this Knowledge implies that Knowledge may descend from the Transcendent to the relative domain. It does not imply that all knowledge necessarily has that source, as certainly in some sense some knowledge comes from experience. Following the Indian usage, the descending Knowledge would be Vidya, while mere empiric knowledge would be avidya.

Vedanta (Sk). This is the group of systems that form a philosophic interpretation of the Upanishads. The earliest Vedantic system originates with Vyasa, and is at least 3,300 years old. Its most systematic and philosophically adequate formulation was given by Shankara, about 2,500 years ago. The latter is known as the Advaita Vedanta, the most consistently monistic philosophy in existence. It is in the latter sense the Vedanta is referred to in this work.

The Vedanta, like the Theosophia and the Gnosis, implies descent of Real Knowledge from a Transcendent Level.

Appendix

LII. THE HIGH INDIFFERENCE. The Event, interpreted in this section, constitutes the culminating point of the whole cycle. It occurred almost exactly thirty-three days after the initial Transition. It was quite unexpected and there was no premonitory excitement as in the first instance. I had had a warning to be on the watch for something involving a time-cycle of thirty-three, but I had no hint as to whether it was a matter of years, months, weeks, or days. I had already discounted the idea that it was only a question of days. In any case, up to the 8th of September I had not noted the fact that nearly thirty-three days had rolled around. In fact, my attention was almost exclusively occupied with the stream of ideas to which I was giving formulation. Certainly I was not seeking anything more and had not the faintest idea what something more could possibly be. Thus this second Transformation was thoroughly spontaneous or autonomous so far as any conscious effort or seeking on my part was concerned.

The interpretation of this culminating Transition afforded extraordinary difficulties. The result of the first effort was far from satisfactory. At the close of the second period of thirty-three days, again I found myself in a state of exceptional lucidity. At that time I undertook a fresh interpretation and was much more successful. This is the formulation that is given in the above discussion. It is an universal characteristic of all mystical states that they cannot be conveyed adequately in any conceptual formulation. The reason for this is clear once it is realized that the essence of the mystical state is a Consciousness that does not fall within the subject-object framework. In contrast, all language presupposes that framework. Thus, the idea, which of necessity is an object of consciousness, cannot contain or represent in the usual sense a consciousness-value where the subject and the object become co-extensive. But the more usual mystical state has an effective content which can be suggested sufficiently well so that anybody can sense that it is desirable. For states that are blissful, happy, or joyous are quite naturally humanly desirable. Because of this, and so far as I can see only because of this, it is possible for the typical egoistic man to desire and therefore seek mystical Realization. But when we deal with the notion of a state of Consciousness which, in additon to transcending the subject-object framework, is also marked by being neutral with respect to Bliss and its opposite, it appears that here we have something that lies quite outside the range of either human conception or desire. That, in addition, such a state should have the highest superiority and could even be preferred to a state of Bliss, certainly seems fantastic to say the least. Yet I can testify that such is the case. However I have found from experience that every effort I have put forth to make this fact convincing to other individuals has been unsuccessful. Indeed, I find that those individuals who come closest to the meaning which I am seeking to convey tend to be appalled. Others simply are not aware of the implications, save perhaps in a detached or academic sense.

At times I have debated the wisdom of releasing for publication the report of this more profound state of Consciousness. Two considerations have finally led to a positive decision. In the first place, lack of understanding automatically protects those who have not yet attained the affective maturity to face the Reality. In the second place, it is just this culminating Transition that supplies the keystone in the philosophic statement that is coming to birth in my mind as a result of the whole cycle. It is because of this cycle of Recognitions, and only because of them, that the resultant philosophy stands on a much more fundamental basis than mere speculative system-building. It is not a philosophy of mere arbitrary concepts, but a reflection in the form of a philosophic symbol of a realized Reality. Thus, to exclude the report of the actual unfoldment in Consciousness would be to leave the resultant philosophy suspended in the thin air of pure abstraction.

None of my previous readings in Theosophic or Vedantic sources had prepared me for anything like the state of Consciousness which I have called the "High Indifference." Up to that time, my familiarity with the Buddhist teachings had been mostly confined to translations of selections from the southern Canon. I knew that Buddhism taught the doctrine of Anatma and Nastikata, that is, the unreality of the Self and of God. But I had understood this in the sense of the unreality of a personal or individual self and of the unreality of any anthropomorphic God. I had not realized that there was a still more profound interpretation of these doctrines. It was only considerably subsequent to the cycle of Recognition that I came into possession of the translations from

Tibetan Buddhism, edited by Mr. Evens-Wentz, and the "Buddhist Bible," edited by Mr. Goddard. In the literature thus made available, for the first time I was enabled to verify the content of the Recognition called the "High Indifference." The two-fold egolessness of the more philosophic Buddhist Sutras conforms with my own mystical discovery. The most profound depth of consciousness transcends the Supreme Self as well as the egoistic self. Likewise, the reality of God is co-extensive with the reality of the Self. Thus, so long as there is a seeming of a Self there is a seeming of God that has equal reality. God is the Other of the Self that with most men abides only in the psychologic unconscious. But from the highest level of Recognition it is seen that there is no independent reality to be attached to either the notion of a Supreme Self or a Supreme Being. In a derived sense both are real, but in the ultimate underived sense there is neither a God nor a Self but simply pure Primordial Consciousness.

Like many other students, I had formerly supposed that the notion of Nirvana pointed toward the most ultimate possibility of consciousness. The Realization of the High Indifference revealed the actuality of a more comprehensive Consciousness. At the time I was rather dumbfounded by this discovery, and made an almost frantic search for confirmation in the literature that I had available at the time. I saw quite clearly that Nirvanic Consciousness stood in polar relationship to objective consciousness, and therefore was not really synthetic. But I felt that there should be some reference to this super-Nirvanic state somewhere in mystical literature. Ultimately I did find the reference, but only when the translations from Tibetan Buddhism came into my possession. The word "Nirvana" is not always used in the same sense, and this is a source of considerable confusion. Sometimes it refers to Shunyata—the state which I have elsewhere called "Consciousness-without-an-object" and "Consciousness-without-a-subject." For the purpose of clarity, I have confined the use of the term "Nirvana" to pure subjective Consciousness.

Many philosophic thinkers have not only taken the subject-object framework as a fundamental form of all consciousness, but they have regarded desire as an ultimate determinant. Thus, for instance, the Pragmatic school of philosophy introduces desire or purpose as an essential part of their theory of knowledge. To know the High Indifference is to know that this theory possesses only partial validity. Pragmatism defines only a limited sector of consciousness. It is the very essence of

Emancipation that it transcends just this sector. On the level of the High Indifference there is no desire whatsoever, but simply unlimited potentiality. To find the Real, it is absolutely necessary to transcend desire. But it is impossible for the desire-bound consciousness to imagine the supernal value of that Consciousness which is free from desire. In the whole notion of desiring Desirelessness there is an inherent contradiction until somehow one has Realized that superior State and thus Knows directly Its superiority. The pragmatic epistemology has only pragmatic value within a relatively narrow field of consciousness and no more. As compared to Enlightenment, Pragmatism seems cheap.

In the Sutras contained in the "Buddhist Bible" frequent references are to be found referring to the "turning about in the deepest seat of consciousness." I find that this also has a two-fold meaning. In the first place, ordinary consciousness is bound to the object by a force which we may call 'gravitation.' The early struggle for Emancipation is against this force until ultimately a point is reached where it has become neutralized. This is a point of peculiar difficulty on the Path, for the old motivation has ceased to operate, and the opposite force does not yet dominate. It can easily become a place of despair. One can continue at this point only through the exercise of the will without any affective aid. But, if the individual persists, presently he finds himself within the field of another force, which we may call 'levitation.' From this point on through the next phase, the attraction of the Subject acts as spontaneously as formerly did the attraction of the object. The battle with obstacles is finished and the formerly most difficult accomplishment becomes the easiest. This is clearly a kind of 'turning about' in consciousness. But it is not the "turning about at the deepest seat of consciousness." The latter requires the turning away from the subject. The record of this second 'turning away' is given in the above discussion. My own conscious part in it was merely the renunciation of private enjoyment of Bliss. For the rest, it just happened.

I consider it a fortunate fact that prior to the cycle in 1936 I had not been a student of the profounder Buddhist teachings. For thus it gives to this cycle the value of independent verification. It shows, further, that Buddha discovered an universal Reality, and not merely something that is valid for Oriental consciousness alone. In this we are dealing with the underlying Roots of all Consciousness.

January 19, 1939